Laughton Osborn

Dramatic Works

Vol. 1

Laughton Osborn

Dramatic Works
Vol. 1

ISBN/EAN: 9783337344535

Printed in Europe, USA, Canada, Australia, Japan

Cover: Foto ©Thomas Meinert / pixelio.de

More available books at **www.hansebooks.com**

DRAMATIC WORKS

BY

LAUGHTON OSBORN

VOLUME I.

TRAGEDIES

NEW YORK
JAMES MILLER, 647 BROADWAY
M DCCC LXVIII

AGATHYNIAN PRESS.

TO TRUTH,

MY MISTRESS,

WHOSE WAGES ARE OBSCURITY AND POVERTY,
BUT WHOSE ULTIMATE REWARD

IS IMMORTALITY.

CALVARY

MDCCCLXIV

CHARACTERS

Primary

JESUS OF NAZARETH.

RAPHAEL, } *Archangels.*
MICHAEL, }

CAIAPHAS, *High-Priest.*
PONTIUS PILATUS, *Procurator of Judea.*
NICODEMUS, } *Of the Sanhedrim.*
JOSEPH OF ARIMATHEA, }
JUDAS ISCARIOT.

LUCIFER.
BEELZEBUB.

MARY, *Mother of Jesus.*
MARY MAGDALENE.
MARTHA.

CHORUS OF ANGELS. — CHORUS OF EVIL SPIRITS.

Secondary

A CENTURION.   A SCRIBE.
SIMON PETER, } *Disciples of Jesus.*   *Three* WITNESSES.
JOHN, }   *Certain of the* PEOPLE.
AN ELDER.
  A SUB-CENTURION. — MALCHUS, *Servant of the High-Priest.*

Mute Persons

JAMES, *Disciple of Jesus.*
Members of the Sanhedrim. Officers in attendance. Soldiers of the Guard. Lictors. Servants. People.

CALVARY

Scene I. Heaven.

RAPHAEL. MICHAEL. CHORUS OF ANGELS.

Raph. Deep gloom broods over Heaven; the Seraphim
    Veil their love-glowing eyes.
    Their song of praise, whose accents wont to rise
    In gratitude and joy of heart to Him,
    In hush of wo and awful reverence dies.
Mich. The ever-burning orbs that gird the Throne,
    Not now revolve with their concentric fires,
    But fix'd grow pale:
    The inmost flame, that still has changeless shone,
    Whose blaze even Seraphs durst not gaze upon,
    Nor we approach, no more the vault aspires,
    But seems to fail.
Raph. And hark! those notes of more than wail,

That breathe responsive to the plaintive tone
Struck from the golden wires.

Chorus.

Lo, the wing'd hour flits near,
Foredoom'd of Heaven
In that far time,
When through the vast inane the Earth's red sphere,
In its new prime,
From the Sun's lap of fire was rolling driven,
And round the parent planet whirl'd the year.
Then rose the acclaim, when, riven
Asunder, Morn and Even
By turns appear.

Now breathes the low-voic'd strain
Of wo, and wailing
For human crime.
What though the heart-wrung sweat, the thirst, the pain,
The cry sublime,
Of the Incarnate God, to Man bring healing,
Can we unmov'd behold the bloody rain,
In large drops downward stealing,
And the pierc'd hands revealing
Their purple stain?

O that the heavy clod
Of slumber, given
To toil-worn men,
Would on our senses press its grateful load,

Till from our ken
The horrors of the hill of death were driven,
And He whose feet as man with men's have trod,
And heart with grief been riven,
Ascending his own Heaven
Should sit with God!

Raph. But for the gloom of night,
　　The effulgence of their day-star when arisen
　　Would waken in Earth's children no delight.
　　When from the tomb's black prison
　　The Lord in his own nature mounts the skies,
　　The consciousness of that dread sacrifice
　　Will make his glory to our tearful eyes
　　And swelling hearts more bright.
Mich. But oh the interval! to see that sight,
　　When on the cross the Lord of Heaven dies.

CHORUS — *receding.*

O that the heavy clod
Of slumber, given
To toil-worn men,
Would on our senses press its grateful load,
Till from our ken
The horrors of the hill of death were driven,
And He whose feet as man with men's have trod,
And heart with grief been riven,
Ascending his own Heaven
Should sit with God!

SCENE II.

Before the Procurator's Palace, at Jerusalem.

PONTIUS. CAIAPHAS.

Pont. I see it not. Is your religion true,
    Be this man's doctrine false it mars it not,
    If right it aids it. 'Tis your bigot creed.
    We Gentiles have a faith more mild and broad:
    It persecutes not, and admits all gods.
Caia. Because your gods are creatures of the brain.
    Ours is the dread *I AM*, that was and is,
    And ever shall be, sole and sempiterne,
    As was reveal'd in thunder from the cloud,
    'Mid lightnings, when the mountain shook and smok'd,
    Where Moses stood on Sinai.
               Pont. Thou hast heard,
    Our Sabine Numa had his nymph as well,
    That taught him without thunder. 'Tis one thing,—
    Priestcraft and statecraft join'd, to bind an age
    That was not docile and had scouted Truth
    In her grand nakedness. I blame it not,
    Albeit your great law-maker should have feign'd
    The Godhead mightier than to tire so soon
    And need a Sabbath. No, the gods of Rome
    Are not vain fictions; they but shape us out
    The attributes divine, and we who kneel
    Do homage to these separate, you in mass.
    This Jesus teaches what the wise and good
    Have taught in every creed and from all time.

He would in Rome be reverenc'd if a sage,
If a mere sophist laugh'd at and let go
As harmless.

    Caia. And a breaker of the laws!

Pont. He bids the people everywhere obey them.

Caia. [*with irritation.*] He is a vile impostor, and pretends
  To work out miracles and heal by touch
  And word diseases.

     Pont. Rather say, he does.
There is a brave centurion, now within,—
Wouldst thou inquire? will tell thee on that point.
By Hercules! he paints me such a scene
That I myself might find it in my heart
To tremble and believe.

     Caia. For the belief,
Even as thou wilt; but think whereon thou stand'st,
And tremble, noble Pontius, with a fear
That were more politic and less devout.
Thou hast heard, thou hast seen indeed, and knowest
    as well,
What an unruly and seditious race
Our people are, still hankering for their kings,
And easily led by all who promise such.
Witness the robber Ezekias' son,
And Simon, who was simply the king's slave,
And the obscure Athronges and his brothers.
Did not this last achieve, and for a time
Actually wield, the power of a king,
And do great damage to the Roman troops?

Pont. But that was when nor king nor ethnarch reign'd.

And with what promptness Varus put him down!

Caia. Because it was tumultuous revolt
And had too many heads. But here is one,
Who works by moral power, and slowly moves,
But surely, onward to a greater aim
With loftier pretensions.   Need I warn thee
We are a haughty people, restive ever
Under a foreign yoke?

    Pont. By Castor, no!
But I shall make it heavier on their necks,
If the team struggle. 'T is not very long
Since the hid daggers of my faithful men
Made mute their bellow.[1]

    Caia. Please thee, hear awhile.
This is no rude pretender, no arm'd brawler,
But a most cunning man, of gentle manners
And of seducing eloquence, who claims
Descent by David from our line of kings,
And to be that Messiah under whom
We are to have our laws again and triumph
Over all our foes.

    Pont. If that be over Rome,
Your land must grow, and every Jewish captain
Be multiplied a thousand fold.

    Caia. Of yore
We counted not the number when Jehovah
Commanded to the fight.   If this false prophet
Persuade the people he is their rightful prince,
How long think'st thou they'd hesitate to strive,
God-driven, as they 'd deem it, to break down

All obstacles that bar him from the throne?
Hast thou forgot the self-call'd Alexander,
Who claim'd to be the son of Herod king?
Flock'd the Jews round him when he came to Rome,
And bore him on a litter through the streets,
Deck'd as beseems a king, there, even there,
In your imperial city.

    Pont. Where his robes
Fell from him and the litter bore no more,
And shame succeeded to the popular joy.

Caia. But after plague to Cæsar.   As a friend
To thy great master, thou should'st clear his path
From every pebble that may make it rough:
And this is one.

    Pont. To pieces break it then:
Crush it, and rid me of the dust. — But, sooth,
Deem'st thou this Jesus dangerous?

       Caia. In sooth,
I know not, care not.   This alone I know,
The people must be quiet, and one man
May well be made a sacrifice for more.

Pont. True policy, for ruler as for priest.
Do as thou wilt; but when thou hast done all ——
Whence is the victim?

     Caia. Where born, meanest thou?
He is a Galilean.

    Pont. Send him then
To Antipas for sentence; that the blood
Of his seditions subjects, shed by me,
May no more be betwixt us.[2]   So, farewell.

Scene III.

A room in the dwelling of Jesus' Mother.

Jesus. Mary.

Mary. And canst thou speak with calmness, when my heart
　Is aching for thee? Jesus, O my son!
　Think on thy mother, and avoid the storm
　That now is darkening o'er thee, and whose shadow
　Makes my blood curdle with the chill of death.
　For my sake, O my darling!
　　　　　　　　　Jesus. Shall the palm
　Say to the fruit that leaves the parent stem,
　Think on thy mother? When its time is come,
　It drops from over-ripeness, and the tree
　Knows it no more. Deem'st thou the Son of Man
　Can flee the hour appointed from all time?
　He who is busy with my Father's work
　Must not be laggard, and not heed the rain,
　Nor howling wind, nor thunder.
　　　　　　　　Mary. Still thou speakest
　As if thou aye wert toiling at the work
　Thou dost no more and hast not done for years.
　Who is thy father, who thy brethren, son?
Jesus. My Father is the Word that sent me hither,
　My brethren are the Children of the Word.—
　Let me be gone: behold, the night is deepening,
　The hour is nigh when I must watch and pray.
　Pray thou too; for the cup that I shall drink
　Will leave its dregs for thee.

                Mary. Give me it all,
Or let me share it with thee!
                   Jesus. Thou? my cup?
The ringdove pray'd the eagle, Let me soar
Unto the clouds with thee and share thy nest.
Poor timid wood-bird, yet her tender eyes
Could not endure the sun, nor her soft wings
Sustain her to his eyrie. What I am
Thou canst not be, O woman, nor canst follow
Whither I go. But watch thou here, and pray,
As I shall do where I must watch and wrestle.
And may that bosom, where I once was laid
Quiet and happy, be more calm than mine.
Mary. Stay yet a little. By that happy time
Thou hast thyself remember'd, when these breasts
That now are wither'd fed thee from my blood,
I do adjure thee! Thou hast call'd me Mother
With that sweet voice, although again the tone
That is so stern and lofty, when thou speakest
Those riddles that I dare not try to solve,
Has aw'd and check'd me, — thou hast call'd me Mother.
I am thy mother, Jesus, and my heart
Warms to thee now as when I first beheld thee
After my weary travail; see me now
Embrace thy feet, and pray thee as my god,
For my sake, for thy own!——
                  Jesus. What is it, mother?
Thy prayer is broken by sobs. So -- let me lift thee.
Thy tears are on my hands. This should not be.
Were I a soldier, and the trump of war
    1*

Summon'd to instant fight, thou wouldst not strive,
Even though thy heart were breaking, to detain me.
Why shouldst thou then when now my Father's voice
Calls me to combat demons and to wrestle
In spirit with that weakness of the flesh
Which I must share with all of women born?
To-morrow thou wilt see me once again;
But where, O mother! ——

Enter MARTHA.
                    Martha, is it thou?
What brings thee to Jerusalem?   Art thou come
To give me warning as my mother does,
And strive to shake my purpose?
                    Martha. Not so, Lord.
Who can do that?   But neither, when we pray,
Do we pretend to arrest or modify
The will of the Almighty.   Yet the sentry,
Who but obeys, and has no voice in counsel,
Gives warning of new danger to his chief.
Jesus. Thou hast spoken, Martha, loyally and well.
    But, in that faith and wisdom, seest thou not
    That I should need no warning?   Even now
    The heart that shall betray me is convuls'd
    With its distracting passions, and the hand
    Is itching for the silver that shall buy
    My body for the cross.   It is decreed.
Mary. Mean'st thou this fully?   Canst thou still so calmly
    Speak what to credit is ——   My son! my son!
    Kneel with me, Martha!   He has love for thee.

Tell him he kills me! Tell him! —— Jesus, son!
Have mercy on me! Save thyself — and me!

Jesus. Thou hearest, Father! Strengthen this weak heart!

Marth. Lord, thou hast fled before, when danger dogg'd thee.
Now, that the hounds are near to lap thy blood,
Why shouldst thou stand at bay?
       Jesus. At bay I do not.
I am no deer before the hunters, Martha,
I am the Lamb of Sacrifice. Before,
The altar was not deck'd, the hour not come.
Stay with my mother, Martha, and console her.
Stay, and pray with her. Wait what ye shall hear.
Simon and James and John are coming for me:
Their footsteps sound already nigh the door.
The blessing of my Father be upon you.
Mother, and sister before God, farewell!

ACT THE SECOND

Scene I. Hell.

LUCIFER.   BEELZEBUB.   CHORUS OF EVIL SPIRITS.

Chor. Onward strides the time,
When the Prince of Heaven,
For whose sake down-driven
From the heights sublime
Hitherward we fell,
Shall with human anguish,
Wo divine as well,
For a spell,—
Though the weight decrease **not**
Of the bootless crime
Crush'd by which we dwell
Here in Hell, —
By his sharp partaking
Lighter make the aching,
Changeless which and fell
Makes us groan and languish,
Ever though we cease not
To rebel.

Flames that circle Hell,
Lift your waves rejoicing,
With your roar loud-voicing
What we feel so well,

> We the unforgiven,
> O'er the wo of Heaven,
> From whose heights down-driven
> Here we fell.

Lucif. Near-sighted as ill-fated, why rejoice?
    Saw ye as far as I do, your parch'd throats
    Would give emission to a direr voice,
    More like the wail above than that which floats
    Now on Hell's vapor, as your sooty wings,
    Confin'd by yon sheer walls and fire-flood moats,
    Scour painfully the region not your choice.
    I cannot sympathize with those vain cries.

Beelz. Yet hope of vengeance prompts the note each sings
    In wo elate,
    Knowing the sorrow which decreed by fate,
    This hour of Earth, man's crime on Heaven brings.
    Ere twice on that small planet which we hate
    The star that gilds its meanness shall arise,
    The Immortal, who forsook his envy'd state
    To bear a mortal's forfeit, dies.

Lucif. Ay, for a race that are not worth the throes
    They cost their mothers, shall this son of God,
    Whom we refus'd to worship, bear the blows
    Of bestial human hands, the servile rod,
    And all the filth of contumely man
    Heaps in his hate, his envy, or disgust,
    On his own fellows, though not worse than he,
    Saving, as chance may will it, in degree,
    Since all are worthless as their Earth's own dust,—

For these vile reptiles he shall even die,
To give them — them! our immortality!
So be it, if it must.
But I shall thwart the planner and the plan.
Beelz. Even yet?

         Lucif. Even yet I trust.
This god, his godborn nature laid aside,
Partook the woman's from whose bowels he sprung
Into that meaner being. Hence have clung
To his dimm'd soul her weaknesses, ally'd
With something of the godhead's fire and pride,
Which flit its duller particles among
Like meteors in Earth's darkness. Thus my power
Already hath the changeling once defy'd.
But now a better hour
Approaches, and again the same temptation,
With loftier aim and surer expectation,
May make his past endurance idle pain,
And we, who for his sake bear Heaven's chain,
Shall Heaven deride.
Beelz. Hark, ominous the song of exultation,
    Borne by the blast, floats lightly to our side!
Chor. [*in the distance.*

         Flames that circle Hell,
         Lift your waves rejoicing,
         With your roar loud-voicing
         What we feel so well,
         We the unforgiven,
         O'er the wo of Heaven,
         From whose heights down-driven
         Here we fell.

Scene II.

The abode of Mary Magdalene.

Judas Iscariot. Mary Magdalene.

Judas. The night is chilly.   Hast thou not a coal
 To feed the brazier?   Not one drop of wine?
 Ugh! and the lamp looks dying.   Where is gone
 The shekel that I gave thee yesternight?
Magd. Be not displeas'd, dear Judas.   I bestow'd it
 But as the Master seem'd to say we ought:
 I cast it in the Treasury.
    Judas. Like that widow
 Whose paltry mites he made of more account
 Than all the rest, because they were her all.
 So thou must give thy all!   Of many fools
 Of Magdala, thou, Mary, art the best.
 Why not have gone at once to the perfumer's,
 Like thy Bethanian namesake, and anoint
 His yellow locks, or even smear his feet,
 As I have seen thee sweep them oftentimes
 With these long delicate hairs (I could defile them!)
 He would have thought still more of it.
    Magd. For shame!
 Thou speakest of our Lord, the Christ, our King.
Judas. I know not that: I know that I am weary
 Of waiting for his kingdom, which I thought
 Would make us rich at least, — both thee and me.
 That starv'd look worries me: and oh, the chill
 Of this unwholesome lodging!   With that shekel
 Thou might'st have bought us fire and light and food.

Magd. Vex not thy soul for me; I am content.
That bit of coin has bought us better fare
In the new kingdom, which is yet to come,
And is not earthly.

    Judas. Who says that? who thinks it?
None of us save you women. Name one else.
Not the hot-headed James, not pale-ey'd John,
Whom I left leaning on the Master's breast, —
(He favors him because of his fair face,
As he does thee, — but I despise the boy) —
None of these overzealous "sons of thunder,"
As thy Lord terms them, for a single day
Would sail from town to town and Tribe to Tribe,
Backwards and forwards, in his changing wake,
But for this promis'd kingdom. If he be
The true Messiah and our hop'd-for Prince,
Why does he not ascend his throne in glory
And make us lords and rich?

    Magd. Bethink thee, Judas,
How he reprov'd Salome. Yet who else,
If not his kinsfolk, might aspire so well
To sit beside him, if that throne and glory
Were of this earth. If then both James and John——
Judas. Accursed be he! — Look not so aghast.
I have good cause of anger. In his ear
The Master said what had respect to me;
For both look'd on me ——

    Magd. What was said? Why pause?
Why art thou discompos'd?

    Judas. It is the lamp

Deepens the shadow on my face, as thine.
It will go out.   Hast thou no oil to feed it?
Magd. None. Mind it not. The moonlight through the lattice
    Will be enough.
         Judas. No oil, no food, no fire?
And I have nothing — or dare touch no more.
What wonder I am discompos'd?
             Magd. But that
Is not the cause.   Thou wast at entering.   Judas!
What was there said against thee at the feast?
Judas. How should I know?   The Master had pronounc'd
That one of us — did evil.   All inquir'd,
But only unto John was answer given,
And that was whisper'd; and John look'd at me.
I shortly slipp'd away, and, in a word,——
Thou mayst imagine it, being put to shame
Before them all.
        Magd. Believ'st thou, Judas dear,
It was because of me He found thee evil?
Judas. No, as thou wast forgiven a greater sin,
When the chaste rabble brought thee out to stone;
And now being husbandless —— Why dost thou weep?
Thou knowest I love thee, Mary, and should love,
Hadst thou thy seven devils in thee still.
This is so small an imp, thy care for me!
Magd. It is for that I weep, not that thou mock'st me,
For there is something bitter in thy smile
That marks thee ill at ease.
        Judas. It is the cold.
It is that sinking lamp which makes me grim.

'T will leave us soon in darkness. Is it that
Makes thee so pale? When hast thou tasted food?
Magd. It is no matter; I am not ——

              Judas. Speak truly:
When hast thou eaten?

                Magd. Not since yester eve.
Judas. When thou hadst money! This must be no more.
Thou shalt have food. And there! the lamp is out!
And we are left in darkness with the devils.
It suits my purpose. I am now resolv'd.
Magd. Judas! Where art thou? Do not leave me thus!
What is thy purpose? What hast thou resolv'd?
Oh Heaven!—Thou art not gone yet. Answer me.
Judas!
Judas. Thou shalt have more than food. Farewell.

Act the Third

Scene I. *The Palace of the High-Priest.*

The Chief-Priest, Elders and Scribes in Council.

Caiaphas. Nicodemus.
Joseph of Arimathea. An Elder.

Caia. What you propound is just. The antique pomp
Of our God-taught religion; the deep awe
That fell upon the people from the Ark
And made our function heaven-like; the respect
Paid to you, Elders, and the potent voice
Of you, the wise in law; all these, the soul
And ornate body of our form of state,
Will have their power, which knows not yet senescence,
Palsy'd with premature decay, and soil'd
With popular contempt their grand adornment,
If this half-craz'd fanatic be allow'd
To gather mobs and agitate reform.
The life of our old polity at stake,
Shall we stand timidly to face a scruple
That, were the life of simple men involv'd,
Would on the instant be o'erleap'd? The law
Of nature, and the law our fathers made,
Taught by the God of Sinai, both demand
The quenching of this firebrand, which has flar'd
And threaten'd conflagration all too long.
Nicod. Before we call for water, were 't not wise

To inquire if the brand be really such,
Or if it burn not with innocuons fire,
That gives out heat, but only then destroys
When the winds rage against it?   Doth the law
Our fathers made give anywhere the right
To sentence even incendiaries unheard?

Caia. 'T is not a question of the law ; 't is not,
I dare to assert it, even one of right :
It is to inquire if we have in ourselves
The power to save ourselves ; if this great court,
Time-honor'd, and deserving in itself
Of honor, has the manhood, life yet left,
To pluck away with its own hands the thorn
From out the festering body of the State,
Or will permit the Roman intervene,
Giving his sword new scope to lop away
What little of autonomy remains.

Jos. Arim. No, were there such a danger.   But this man
Aims not to stir sedition.   I am myself
With eye and ear a witness, Jesus now
Is but what all our prophets were of old,
In days when we had prophets and they taught.
And for his teaching shall we stone him now,
As they ston'd prophets in the days of old?

Caia. Thou art thyself, as Nicodemus here,
A favorer of the Nazarene.   God grant
Ye both become not something more.

                               Nicod. What's that?
His followers?   If to love the right, to stand
By the oppress'd, though men of Galilee,

To welcome truth, good-sense and moral lore,
Although Samaria taught them, and to own
We never had more need of all than now,—
If this be following, then should I be proud
To tread in Jesus' footsteps, and as much
I think will he of Arimathea say.

Elder. What profits this dissension? And, in time,
Lo, one is here who craves to be admitted
On business of concern.

                Caia. Let him come in.

Enter JUDAS ISCARIOT, *conducted by an usher.*

Nicod. [*to Jos. Arim.*] What a vile look he wears! I have
        seen, methinks,
That face before, but surely not, as now,
Troubled and full of mischief.

              Jos. Arim. 'T is the awe
Inspired by our assemblage. On he comes,
Abject, but throwing furtive looks around,
Full of an evil meaning. Surely too
I have seen him elsewhere. 'T is — one of the twelve
That follow Jesus constantly.

              Nicod. Thus here,
And with that look, his coming bodes no good
Unto his Master.

        Jos. Arim. Hush; they have made him stop.
And now the high-priest waves his hand.

              Caia. Stand there.
Fellow, who art thou? And what brings thee here?

Judas. A matter of grave import to the State.

Caia. So we were told; else hadst thou not got in.
    Speak out.

       Judas. I am a follower, or have been,
Of Him of Galilee.

           Caia. A traitor, then.
Nicod. [*to Jos. Arim.*] No doubt.

              Judas. I am not to the Sanhedrim,
Nor yet to Rome.

        Caia. Thou art bold.

              Judas. I have need to be
Who come on such a work.

          Caia. And that?

             Judas. To give
Into your power the Master.

         Caia. Jesus?

          Judas. Him.
Caia. What are thy motives? What dost thou propose?
    Speak quickly; and be brief.

          Judas. Despair, disgust,
Resentment, want of money: there you have
My motives, if I know them. You desire
To arrest the Rabbi Jesus.

          Caia. Without noise.
Judas. I understand it so, and so propose.
    What will ye give me if within the hour
    I make you masters of his body?

             Caia. How?
Judas. By showing where he may be found alone,
    Or with his followers only.

          Caia. Thou shalt have

Thirty full shekels.

        Judas. 'T is a niggard price.

Nicod. For a vile object.

        Judas. Is the object vile,

Why then employ me?

        Caia.- Thou art not suborn'd.

Know, thou irreverent fellow, that with thee
The object may indeed be vile, and is;
For thou betrayest who trusteth thee, and makest
Thy friend's sore damage turn to thy behoof.
With us, who are the guardians of the State,
And the ordain'd custodians of its laws,
The act of using thee, whereby we save
The State from jeopardy and check i' the midst
The infraction of the law, is worthy praise.
Tak'st thou the shekels? lendest thou thy aid?
Speak. But be cautious in thy phrase.

        Judas. I had

No thought to be irreverent. Forgive me.
Why should it be accounted in me vile,
That, seeing my error, and enamour'd still
Of the fair faith our fathers taught, and tired
Of vagabondage, fearing too the ills
Which the free doctrine of the poor man's rights,
Encourag'd in his envy of the rich
And taught to deem himself preferr'd of Heaven,
Might cause in our sedition-loving race ——

Caia. Tak'st thou the thirty shekels? Ay, or no?

Judas. It is too little for so great a work.

Caia. Then we arrest thee as confederate with

The dangerous Galilean.   Take thy choice,
Betraying or betray'd.

     Judas. I have no choice :
She whom I cherish wants for common bread.

Caia. That concerns thee, not us.   Tak'st thou the price?
Judas. I do.

   Nicod. Thou abject wretch! reserve thereof
One gerah for a cord to hang thyself.

Caia. Go wait without.   But first — respond to this: —
If, as is said, this Jesus is not mark'd
By any special sign, and does not lead
But mixes with his crew, how shall the band
We send to arrest him know him in the night?

Judas. By the devotion which surrounds him still
Whate'er his place in the midst of us; so that,
As with all other leaders, there, that place,
None other, is the head and centre-point.
Besides, there is a something in his mien,
A strange look in the eyes, profound and sad,
Into whose depths though clear no eye can pierce,
As in the Sea which God loves,' and whose gaze,
When fix'd upon you, none can bear : nay, more,
There is at times a singular light that plays
Like moonshine o'er his visage ——

      Caia. Driveler, peace!
We ask not for thy fancies.   Wilt thou tell us,
So we will let thee, Moses on the Mount
Was nothing more transfigur'd?   Give some sign
That will not, like thy visage-moonlight, vanish

Before our lanterns.   Thou thyself shalt lead :
How wilt thou mark him?
                Judas. Is that needful?
                       Caia. Ay.
By what act wilt thou make thy Master known?
Judas. I rather would forego ——
                Caia. Thy money then,
And be thyself arrested?   Take thy choice.
Judas. Me miserable! —   Whom then — I salute —
On meeting, with a kiss, — that same is Jesus.
Caia. Go wait without ——
              Nicod. Thou wilt not trust this wretch?
Caia. No, I will use him.   Thou, and Joseph here,
Alone I think of the whole Sanhedrim,
As their approving nods and signs attest,
Would let the occasion by. —   Thou, wait without,
And when the guard appear, do as thou sayest.

            2

SCENE II.

The Garden of Gethsemane.

JESUS.

SIMON PETER. JOHN. JAMES.

Jesus. Tarry ye at the gate; I must apart.
My soul is very heavy, even to death.
Can ye watch here a little while?
                    Peter. Yea, Lord,
Until the morning, shouldst thou bide so long.
Jesus. Simon, be not too sure.
              Peter. Why not sure, Lord?
Even James and John will watch. Shall I then tire?
But rather let me go with thee apart:
I have a sword wherewith to brave thy foes,
Should any such affront thee, as thou badest.
Jesus. Thou didst mistake me.
              Peter. Master, thou didst say
That two would be enough.
            Jesus. And truly said;
For what would it avail though all were arm'd?
Simon, the Devil would sift thee. Take thou heed!
Peter. I am as good grain, Master, as the rest.
Let me go with thee, bear what thou shalt bear;
Though all men else desert thee, will not I.
Jesus. Sayst thou? Verily, ere the cock shall crow,
Thou, Simon Peter, wilt deny me thrice.
       He leaves them and comes forward.

Poor sons of Adam! in your own weak hearts
Never more firm than when most prone to fall.—
And my weak heart, does not its human blood
Flow with a troubled current?   In this dread hour,

[kneeling.]

When I need all my courage, O my God,
Father in Heaven, let me not grow faint.
Let the brave spirit which comes of Thee alone,
And drew no nurture from my mother's milk,
Aid me against the torture whose mere thought
Already is such anguish, and whose pangs
Seem in that forethought still more hard to bear
In that I might avoid them ; for Thou knowest,
Thou, and Thou only, that these death-cold drops
Are forc'd not from my forehead by coward fear,
Fear of a suffering which, though long, shall end,
But by the struggle between what I should do
And what my mortal nature prompts me do,
Between Thy bidding which commands me stay
And my blood's frailty which would urge me flee.
Oh it is fearful!   Help Thou, Father! God!
This cup, which is so bitter, if thou canst,
Take from me!   But Thy will, not mine be done.

After some minutes, Jesus rises.

Simon!   But he is sleeping; and the rest.
So brief a while, and yet not watch for me !
For me, for whom they were so prompt to die,
And Simon most.

LUCIFER *appears.*

Lucif. Who will be first to abjure thee.
Thou hast thyself thus told him.
               Jesus. Who art thou?
I need not question. In the glowing eyes,
The godlike port, and the strange light that floats,
Visible spite the moonshine, on thy shoulders,
I read thee all, without that mocking voice
Which brings to mind the mountain where I bade thee,
As I do now, Get thee hence, Satan!
               Lucif. No,
Not then as now. I offer'd power and glory,
And set a price upon them. Then thy gaze
Was made to cover at a single glance
All of Earth's kingdoms. Now I bid thee see
And hear but with man's senses. Look around.
The moon is o'er the hill-top, and her light
Floods the hush'd city and the mighty wall
Which stood the Assyrian fire when all the rest,
Temple and tower, went down, and David's throne
With its weak kings, six hundred years ago.
How peaceful! and how still! Thou mayst distinguish
Sole of all sounds the bubbling of yon brook.
But in a little while how all will change!
Even now I hear, as thou mayst wilt thou use
The ears that are not earth-made, martial steps;
I see the gleam of torches, useless sure
In the broad moonshine, and the uncertain gleam

Of many spear-heads.   'T is the armed band
That come to catch thee.   Wilt thou wait them here?
Jesus. I will.

  Lucif. Hast thou bethought thee, God-born, then,
Of what the end is?

    Jesus. Satan, I have said,
Go from before me.   Thou didst fail with Job.
Shall I do less than he?

    Lucif. He was not tried
As thou wilt be : I might not touch his life.
Think'st thou the Roman will refuse to yield?
He will approve thee, but thou wilt be given
To quench the blood-thirst of a frantic mob,
That will outwatch the stars to see thee die,
And grumble, if thou should be spar'd one pang.
Jesus. Simon! Awake!   Beloved John! ——

    Lucif. The cold
Hath numb'd them.   And these wretched men as well,
Who follow thee, thou know'st, for what they hope
Will be their gain on Earth, nor wait for Heaven,—
Their nets, thou didst assure them, should catch men —
Jesus. Peace, Devil! and avaunt!

    Lucif. The Christ will pardon.—
These to-be-sainted fishermen, as well,
Will watch thy crucifixion, not indeed
With the brute satisfaction of the mob,
Nor in the hungry curiousness alone
To mark how thou canst suffer and wilt die,
Though haply some such craving, being men,

Will mingle with their heart-ache; but can they,
Or can thy mother's anguish, wept she blood,
Keep thy raw wounds from smarting, or assuage
The thirst that burns like fire thy throat and lips?

Jesus. Father! this cup! —— Let not the serpent's gall
Add to its bitterness!

     Lucif. Yet 't is honey-sweet
Compar'd with that thou presently shalt drink.
Hear'st thou not yet the footsteps? In brief time,
Their measur'd tramp will sound without the gate.
One of thy zealots leads them. Son of God!
What though incarnate, wilt thou be arraign'd
Like a vile robber and abide the law?
I hear thee sentenc'd. 'Mid a rabble rout,
Who rain on thee dire curses and foul words,
Who buffet thee and void their filthy rheum
On thy resistless visage, thou 'rt push'd and dragg'd
To the high place, where nail'd on either side
A cut-throat suffers with thee. Thou art stripp'd.
I see thy body bound to the cross'd planks.
And now large spikes are driven through thy hands,
And through thy feet. Thick in the wintry air
The blood flows slowly o'er thy pallid limbs
And stiffens there. O weary, weary time!
When death, though still before thee, fails to strike
Though pray'd for, and the fever in the veins
Brings not unconsciousness. See, that head,
Into whose bloody front the plaited thorns
Press their sharp points, droops lower on the chest

And spots it with the mingled sweat of death
And tears of gore. And yet thou canst not die.
Will not the sun go down? Thy parch'd lips ope,
And while thine eyes turn languidly to Heaven,
Yet full of agony that is reproach, thy voice
Calls feebly unto God who lets thee die.

Jesus. Father! have mercy!

    Lucif. Ask it not of Him.
Of me thou wilt obtain it.

      Jesus. Fiend! Of thee?

Lucif. Son of the maiden Mary and of God,
 Ere thou wast man I did defy thy power,
 And scorn'd to worship thee. Since here on Earth,
 I promis'd all the kingdoms of the Earth,
 So thou wouldst worship me. If thou wilt flee
 And leave these ingrate fools, who know thee not,
 To their own ruin, I, I will kneel to thee,
 Here on this spot, avow thee as my lord,
 And ever more do reverence.

    Jesus. If thou wilt,
Father, I would this cup might pass from me!
Yet not my will, but Thine be done.

     Lucif. So be it.
Die in thy pride and folly; and may the thought
Heighten thy pangs, that, though thou bleed'st for man,
Thou sav'st him not. He is my vassal still.
Part we. I could admire, but that my wrongs
Breed everlasting hate and keep us foes.

    Lucifer *disappears.*

Jesus. The agony is over.— Angels' hands?
Their fingers wipe my brow, their broad wings fan me,
Their soft breath soothes me, and their silver tones
With whisper'd words of solace and of love
Renew my courage.   Am I then approv'd?
O God! my Father! since it is Thy will,
Let me drink boldly, though the draft is death.

            He moves toward the sleepers.

Simon, awake.   The time is gone for rest.
The hour approaches when the Son of Man
Is given unto his foes; and lo, at hand
He that betrays me.   [*The disciples gather round him.*

                Enter

        A band of SOLDIERS, MALCHUS
        and others, JUDAS *in advance, who presses
        hurriedly forward and kisses* JESUS.

                Is it with a kiss
Thou mak'st betrayal of the Son of Man?
Whom seek ye?   [*to the Band.*
        Malch. Him of Nazareth.
                        Jesus. 'T is I.
Why fall ye back in doubt?   Again I ask:
Whom seek ye?
        Malch. We have said, — the Nazarene.
Jesus. I told ye, I am he.   If I alone
Be he ye come for, let these go their way.
Malch. Seize him.
        Peter. Thou villain! [*wounds Malchus.*

Jesus. Simon, put thy sword
Back to his place: all they that take the sword
Shall perish by the sword. If I had need,
Think'st thou that angels would not guard me now?
The cup my Father giveth shall I not drink? —
Suffer thus far. [*to Malchus, touching his wound.*

        Have ye come out to me
As to a robber, with your swords and staves?
When I was daily with you in the temple,
Ye stretch'd not out your hands to me; but this
Is now your hour, and darkness hath dominion.

   They bind JESUS, *and lead him forth,*
   the DISCIPLES *fleeing, all but* PETER, *who*
      follows at a distance.
   2*

Aᴄᴛ ᴛʜᴇ Fᴏᴜʀᴛʜ

Scene I.—As in Act II., Sc. 2.

Jᴜᴅᴀs Iꜱᴄᴀʀɪᴏᴛ.   Mᴀʀʏ Mᴀɢᴅᴀʟᴇɴᴇ.

Judas. Here take the flint.   I cannot force a spark:
My hands are numb.
                    Magd. Thy fingers are like death!
Yet thy brow drips with sweat!   Is that from cold?
Judas. Yes; hasten.
                    Magd. How thy voice shakes!
                                        Judas. Mind it not.
The light; quick, quick! the fire.   It is so dark —
Is the door barr'd? — and cold!   I had such toil
To get these things at this late hour — Ah, so!
The faggots now.   Canst thou put in the oil? —
And that is why my brow drips and I tremble;
I had to run so fast from shop to shop,
Finding all closed but one.
                    Magd. Yet thou art cold.
Thy running should have warm'd thee.
                                        Judas. And it would.
But then the thought of thee ——
                    Madg. Why look'st thou round?
Judas. Heard'st thou then nothing?
                    Magd. Nothing.   This is fear.
How pale thou look'st!

Judas. It is the flickering flame.
The brands will soon cease smoking, and my face
Will not look haggard.   'T is the thought of thee,
Thy hunger that distress'd me, made me cold.
Break the bread, Mary.
           Magd. I did not say *haggard.*
Yet haggard 't is and pale.   'T is not the fire
That flickers, for the lamp is burning clear.
What is it ails thee?
           Judas. Give me of the wine.
And drink thyself, and eat.   Eat, Mary dear.
Now I am warmer.
           Magd. Whence hadst thou these things?
Judas. What matters it?   Thou art starving.   Eat, I say;
And here, drink off that wine.
                   Magd. I will not drink,
Nor eat, till thou hast told me whence this comes.
Thou hast not —— God of Heaven! on thy hand
Is blood!
       Judas. A spot.   A splinter in the wood.
Seest thou? there is the scratch.
                   Magd. Thou couldst not——
                       Judas. What?
Dost thou suspect me?
           Magd. Thou hast done no murder?
Judas. Oh no!   Oh no, no, no! not yet.
                   Magd. Not yet?
And said so gloomily.   Thou hast not robb'd?
Judas. I would I had!

Magd. Thou wouldst thou had ?   And tears ?

> [*removing one of his hands, with both
> which he has covered his face.*

Judas, where gott'st thou money ?   Till thou tell'st me,
I will not eat that bread, nor drink that wine.

Judas. The bread and wine are what remained to day
  After the feast.   The master of the house
  Bestow'd them on me.

   Magd. Did he give thee too
  The oil and faggots ?   Thou didst let me think
  Thou gott'st them at a shop, the sole one open.
  Where didst thou get the money ?

    Judas. Fill my cup.
  And drink thou too, and eat.

    Magd. I will not eat
  Till thou hast told me if the bread be honest.
  Fill thou, thyself; I cannot pour that wine.
  Nor shouldst thou drink it, if I could prevail.
  Thou tremblest, and thy eyes are dropping tears.

Judas. It is the smoke.   I tremble with a fear ——
  Why dost thou doubt me, Mary ? — with a fear
  Some evil is betiding.   Heard'st thou aught
  While I was absent ?   Sawest thou no sign ?

Magd. What dost thou mean ?   What sign, what sound ?   To
  whom
  Should evil be betiding ?   Is 't to John ?

Judas. To all of us.   How know I ?   It will happen
  When least we think it.

   Magd. As the Master said :

Offences needs must come ; but wo to him
Through whom ——

    Judas. More wine!

        Magd. Thou shalt not drink again :
Thou art already wild.

    Judas. Ah, wo indeed!

Magd. Oh what a sigh was that! Hast thou done aught? ——
Judas! thou know'st I love thee. On my knees
I do adjure thee, by that sinful love
For which I live in daily terror and grief
That make all joy forgotten, tell me, tell,
What is it weighs upon thy soul this night?
What hast thou done? Where didst thou get the means,
For me unhappy, for my most wretched sake,
To buy this oil, and wine, and bread, and wood?

Judas. Eat, let me see thee eat. Heard'st thou not aught?
Saw'st thou not aught this night? Eat, do but eat!
Or thou wilt drive me desperate. 'T was for that,
To ease thy hunger —— Saw'st thou naught to night?
Naught from thy lattice, Mary? It o'erlooks ——

Magd. Why dost thou pause? O'erlooks ——

    Judas. Eat, do but eat!

Magd. [*springing to her feet.*

    Ah! I remember now. It cannot be —
Thou canst not be so wicked — Oh my God!
Let me not hear him say it, let me die
Not knowing of such treason!

    Judas. Treason? What?
What should I do with treason? And to whom?

Magd. Look in my eyes. Thou spak'st this very night

Bitterly of the Master, and a purpose ——
What money hast thou?

       Judas. Here are seven pieces.

But take them not to the Women's Court again.
Magd. Where didst thou get them?

       Judas. Say I borrow'd, begg'd:

What matters it? Eat, drink. Was that a noise?
Magd. I heard none. 'T is the moaning wind perhaps.
Judas. It sounded like a sigh.

       Magd. It was thy own.

Twice hast thou heav'd one, from thy inmost breast.
Something weighs heavy there and would have vent.
It makes thee restless, gloomy, fearful, wild.
Am I a child, that I should see all this
And not conjecture? have I grown so old
As to forget already what, not hunger,
Made thy stay long to me? Whence came that coin?
I will not touch it till I know fully whence.
What didst thou mean by signs and sounds? What ill
Is there betiding?

       Judas. There was in the street
A rumor, that — the Master —— Heard'st thou naught?
I thought that, being so near the wall —

       Magd. Why pause?

'T is not to stir the brands. Thou hid'st thy face.
The Master? And that whisper'd word to John?
What hast thou done? Thou hast not —— There were
      shouts,
Lights through the trees, and armed men I thought,
In the vale from the Mount of Olives. Judas! man!

Thou didst not lead them? Thou didst not betray ——
Speak, if thou wouldst not kill me. Only sobs?
And for this money?

        Judas. Woman, it was thou —
Thy suffering drove me.

        Magd. Thou hast done it, then?
Oh, I had hopes —— But say not 't was for me!
My hunger could not make thee wicked — wicked?
Oh, wicked unspeakably! A wretch like thee
Never yet liv'd, and is not fit to live.

Judas. Sayst thou? This my guerdon? Thou art right;
I am not fit to live. I go. But thou,
For whose sake I have sinn'd thus, take this coin —
All but one piece. Eat, live, be happy. There:
It is my life's worth.

        Magd. 'T is the price of blood.
I will not touch it; nor the bread, nor wine.
This fire shall not burn here, this lamp shall out.
There. In a moment, when these embers die,
I shall again be in the dark, and cold,
But with a pang that will not let me feel
Hunger or thirst. I would, ere thou hadst come,
I had been colder, in a darker place,
Where is no hunger.

        Judas. Would I now were there!
Mary, I go. Give me that wine once more.

Magd. Thou shalt not taste one drop. It is the blood
Of thy good Master. Thou hast over-drunk,
Even were it honest wine. Where dost thou go to?

Judas. Farewell — forever!

Magd. Judas! Stay. Thy face
I see but dimly ; but thy voice, thy step ——
There is something makes me shudder. Let me hold
    thee ;
Be not so violent. Whither dost thou go ?

Judas. To atone my guilt, to make redress, if 't may be.

Magd. And save our Lord ? Oh ! do but that, but that —
Do but that, dost thou hear me ? and come back,
I'll love thee as I never lov'd before.
But take the money with thee, what is left.
Promise the rest to-morrow, — as thou mayst ;
We'll find it somewhere. Why so mute ? Wrench not
Thy arm so rudely from me. Thou 'rt not wroth ?

Judas. O no, no, no ! not wroth.

                Magd. Thou hast no cause.
Hasten ! But, if thou fail to amend thy fault,
Come never more again !

                Judas. Ay, never more !

Scene II.

As in Act III., Sc. 1.

The Sanhedrim assembled.

Jesus *before them.*

Caiaphas.   Nicodemus.   Joseph of Arimathea.

On one side, three Witnesses.   On the other, Malchus.

Soldiers of the Guard, Officers of the Court, &c.

Caia. Answer to what we ask thee.   What art thou ?
 Whence is thy mission ?   Is it true what men
 Allege of thee ?
    Nicod. With deference be it said,
 We have no right to make him plead, himself,
 To show what he is not, or what he is.
 If he be chargeable with grave offence,
 As I dare doubt, let the man stand arraign'd
 Until we prove it.
    Caia. Thou dost strain the law
 In his behoof.   Unwisely ; for our course
 Gives him in mercy privilege to plead
 From his own consciousness, advancing all
 May best avail him and withholding aught
 That cunning would conceal. — Art thou still mute ?
Jesus. Say I should answer you, will ye believe ?
 Or should I question, will ye make reply ?
 What I have said was said unto the world.

In synagogue and temple, there, where Jews
From all parts gather, was my doctrine taught,
At all times, openly, in secret not.
Why ask ye then of me? Ask them who heard me.
Lo, they will know to tell you what I taught.
Malch. [*striking him.*

   What! to the High-Priest mak'st thou answer thus?
Jesus. Have I spoke evil, witness to that evil.
   If I said what was well, why smit'st thou me?
Nicod. Is this an outrage to be tamely borne?
   Are we a court? or shall the Sanhedrim
   Allow the robe of justice to be soil'd
   By ruffian servitors? The culprit's tone
   Was nothing bolder than becomes a man,
   A man so question'd; if to be reprov'd,
   Censure should come of us, not in the form
   Of scoundrel violence.
             Caia. Malchus, leave the hall.
   Thy superserviceable zeal, albeit
   Rightly inspir'd, revolts the prophet's friends.
   Bring the first witness. What hast thou to urge?
1st Witn. This fellow call'd himself the Son of God.
Nicod. Passing thy insolent levity, unto us
   Much more dishonoring than to him, the arraign'd,
   Heard'st thou this said thyself? And when? And
      where?
   But we assume the fact. The Sanhedrim
   Need not be told it is written, "I have said
   Ye are gods, and children of the Highest, all."

Could this apply to many, surely one
Who doth, or claims to do, the righteous works
Enjoin'd by Him who is Father of all men,
May speak as is reported, nor blaspheme.

Jos. Arim. I am a witness as to the intent
And meaning of those words.   'T was in the porch
Of Solomon, when the people took up stones
To slay him for the imputed crime here urg'd,
That he disprov'd it, citing the same phrase
Which Nicodemus hath.

                Caia. But was this all?
What hast thou else to charge?

                        1st Witn. We took up stones
Because he claimed that he and God are one.

Jos. Arim. Further misapprehension.   Heard I not
How he said elsewhere, when one call'd him *good*,
" There is none good but one, and that is God?"
My testimony weighs at least as much
As this coarse fellow's.

                Caia. But may be more bias'd.

Nicod. Ever, I trust, toward truth and common right.

Caia. That is a matter of opinion now,
But will be soon of judgment.   Honest man,
Hast thou more evidence?

                  1st Witn. This Jesus said,
Once in Capernaum, that his flesh was bread,
That he would give us of this bread to eat,
And that it came from Heaven.   Whereat, not few
Of his own followers left him.

                Nicod. What is that,

Even if 't be true ? Most palpably the sense
Is moral. Taken at the letter's worth,
It were a madman's utterance, and could claim
Nowise consideration on our part.

Caia. Save to corroborate the facts adduc'd.
Call the next witness. What hast thou to state,
Of thy own knowledge ?

        2d Witn. That this Jesus claim'd
To have been before our father Abraham was.
For which we would have ston'd him, but he fled.
And, at another time again, declar'd :
"Destroy the Temple, and in three days' time
I will rebuild the same."

        Nicod. Assertions both
Whose quality rests on the mode of speech
Habitual with the assertor, known to all
To talk in figures. Give a literal sense,
He is a god, or lunatic and fool.
We cannot touch him, if he be a god ;
If mad, or void of sense, we have no right.

Jos. Arim. Justly remark'd. The temple meant his body.
This I have heard his near disciple say.
He inculcates, it is known, a future life.

Caia. You as his friends, if not his followers, both,
Should help the god exemplify his lesson
In his own flesh, — as soon may be. For lo,
A witness more unanswerable. Speak !

3d Witn. The accus'd, with his disciples, gather'd corn
Upon the Sabbath-day, and, censur'd, said,
David had more profan'd it, and the priests

That serve the Temple do it without blame;
Adding, "Here is a greater than the Temple,"
Meaning himself, — "for he, the Son of Man
Is master even of the Sabbath-day."
Elder. Horrid impiety!
    Scribe. Pretention blasphemous!
Nicod. That is as it was said; the tone is all.
For what was said is borne out by the law
And record.
  Caia. By the law? Wilt thou maintain
The law has made him master of the law?
Or find'st thou, thou, this ape of prophets gone
A greater than the Temple?
     Nicod. I find nought
Before me, in that unresisting form,
But a good man most shamefully betray'd,
Whose zeal may be excessive, but whose claims
To greatness, as imputed, are belied
By his own conduct.
    Caia. Dost thou know it all?
Lurks there no craft beneath an artless mein?
Is meekness never made the facile mask
To an ambitious spirit? Speak once more,
And tell the Council, man, what thou hast seen,
What know of this aspirant— such he is,
Humble though he stands here — to David's throne.
Nicod. The question guides and prompts to a reply.
Caia. Mind not the Elder. Speak; thou shalt be heard.
3d Witn. One day he rode in triumph, and the crowd,
Like madmen, spread their garments in his path,

And shouted ——

Nicod. Where was this?

    3d Witn. Upon the way
From Bethphage to the city.

    Nicod. Thou wast there?

3d Witn. I was. They shouted: "Blessed be the king
That cometh in the Lord's name! Peace on earth
And glory in the highest." When rebuk'd, —
As some there bade him chide them —1 was one, —
This Jesus answer'd: "Should these hold their peace,
The very stones beneath us would cry out."

Elder. 'T is a clear case.

    Scribe. So think we all.

    Nicod. Why then,
When, at another time, the rabble strove
To make him king by force — this can be prov'd, —
Why did he flee? 'T was nigh Tiberias,
Over the Sea. He fled, and hid himself.

Caia. The people then *did* seek to make him king?
So much is prov'd.

    Nicod. But not that 't was his fault.

Caia. Proceed. [*to Witn.*

    3d Witn. He assur'd the Twelve that make his train,
That, when he came to glory, they should sit,
Themselves, upon twelve thrones and judge the Tribes.

Caia. What more is needed?

    Elder. Let him be condemn'd.

Nicod. Upon this evidence? The very words
Us'd by the witness mark the innocent sense
Of the accus'd, supposing he thus spake.

His glory is not of this world; the thrones
Are seats in Heaven.
　　　　　Jos. Arim. Else, let the witness say,
Who has learn'd so much, why, as is known to all
The twelve he calls the train, the Nazarene
Refus'd the sons of Zebedee their choice,
When, in their ignorance of this mystic sense
Which Nicodemus hath so well divin'd,
Their mother pray'd him that the two might sit
On either hand of him in that new realm.
What was his answer? 'T was not his to give,
But theirs for whom his Father had prepar'd it.
Caia. Atrocious blasphemy!
　　　　　Nicod. Be it, if thou please.
But, if not so design'd ——
　　　　　Caia. Ye Scribes and Elders,
Priests who with me look on the law of God
As violated in the lightest act
Of all ascrib'd to this mad Nazarene,
Why need we sit here longer? Is 't your will,
As mine, to pluck this irritating thorn
Instantly from the body of the State,
That it may rest, and we put off the dread
Of being endanger'd with our conquerors worse,
Ye will not give to Nicodemus here
And Joseph, who is, like him, sway'd at least
By predilection for the dangerous ways
Of this smooth-tongued and subtlest instigator
Of the bad passions of our mutinous race,

Ye will not give them time to argue more
In such a cause.

   Elder. No, we have heard too much.

Nicod. Ay, from this Jesus, who has rous'd your hate
By openly denouncing, at all times,
Your white-wash'd irreligion, the false pomp
Of a knee-homage, and your empty vaunts
Of charity where lives but self-conceit
And pitiless avarice and revengeful pride.
Had he but left your vices unreprov'd ——

Caia. Let him say no word more.

   Elder. Ay, and take heed.

Nicod. Of what? from whom?

   Jos. Arim. [*apart to Nicod.*] Be cautious; 't is in vain.

Nicod. [*to Jos., but aloud.*

  Art thou so lukewarm? Were I not to speak
Against this violence done to sense and right
And decency, in this innocent person's words,
" The very stones beneath me would cry out."

Caia. Enough. The prisoner's friends have pleaded long:
Why is he mute himself? By that dread name
Thou dost profess to reverence with ourselves,
I charge thee, tell us, art thou then the Christ?

Jesus. Thou sayst it.

   Caia. That our ears should hear these words!

Elder. Take him to death.

    Scribe. On to the Judgment, on!

  JESUS *is borne out, amid the scoffs and mockery of the
crowd,—the* SENATE *rising after,—when,*

Enter JUDAS ISCARIOT,
forcing his way through the Servants of the Court.

Judas. Stop me not! 'T is on life and death. Way! way!
    I must to the Senate.
                  Caia. Fellow, what is 't now?
Judas. Take back your silver; what is wanting there
    Will be made good to-morrow. I have lied.
    I have betray'd the innocent blood. Set free
    The Rabbi Jesus, and take me instead.
Caia. If thou hast lied, that is thy own affair.
    Take up thy hire, and with it get thee hence.
    'T is nothing to us now, no more than thou.
Judas. Let it lie there then. — I have kept one piece,
    As thou didst counsel. [*to Nicod. as, on going out,*
        Judas passes him.
             Nicod. No, not now; not now.
    Go home, unhappy wretch, and make atonement
    By a new life.
          Judas. I have promis'd — "Never more."

3

Scene III.

The porch without the palace of the High-Priest.

Peter, *weeping.*

Enter hurriedly, John.

John. I have come to seek thee.   Why dost thou weep here?
    They have dragg'd Him to the Judgment-Hall.   Come,
      come!
Peter. I am weeping not for Him.   Didst thou not hear
    How he foretold I should deny him thrice?
    I felt ill-treated then.   But, wo is me!
    I am weaker than I thought.
                John. What hast thou done?
Peter. I stood below in the Hall where thou didst leave me,
    And when they said that I was of his men,
    In fear denied it.   Then the cock crew loud;
    And the Lord, turning round to where I stood,
    Look'd for a moment at me.   But that look!
John. Well mayst thou weep.   We all are weak.   But one,
    One only has been devilish; and that one
    Repented, and hath made atonement.   Come!
Peter. What, what atonement?   Judas?
              John. Hasten.   Yes,
    Judas has taken his own life.   On the way,
    I will tell thee what I have heard.   Come, Simon, come!

Scene IV.

The Gabbatha or Pavement.

In the background, Pontius *on the Judgment-seat, attended by his officers and lictors. At his right hand waiting, a little apart, a Servant of his household. The chief members of the Sanhedrim — among them, but aloof and moving reluctantly,* Nicodemus *and* Joseph of Arimathea *— are approaching the Pavement, to arrange themselves on either side, the People following, to place themselves in front.*

Pontius. [*his face half-turned to the Servant.*

  Tell her, her dreams accord with my day-thoughts
I will do what I can; but the High-Priest
Is bent on his destruction. Lo, they come,
And wait me on the Pavement. Mark thou that!
These bigot Jews will not approach my house,
Lest they contract pollution from a Gentile,
But meet me when without! Go tell her that,
And bid her hope for nothing from such fools.

Jesus,

*guarded, is led up through the crowd, and made
to stand in the centre of the Pavement,
before the Judgment-seat.*

Caia. Behold the Nazarene. The tetrarch Herod
Remands him unto thee.

Pont. Because, like me,
He finds no fault in him.   Must I again
Go over the same grounds with like result?
He does not merit death : I will chastise him,
Then set him free.
        Jesus. Take heed to what thou dost;
For with what measure thou shalt mete to me,
It shall be meted unto thee again.
Pont. Threat'nest thou me?
        Jesus. I have no will to threaten,
· But I have power given me to forewarn.
Thou art a man who art not idly cruel,
But, where thou think'st there is need, thou dost not
        stop
Were 't for ten thousand lives.   Beware thou then,
Nor lend thyself to cruelty that pleads
No pretext like thy own ; for God decrees,
In retribution, violent ends to those
Who practise violence.[4]
        Pont. If I set thee free,
Wilt thou go home unto thy mother now,
And brethren, and, thy own good seeking only,
Keep from all business that is not thy own?
Jesus. My business is my Father's.   He who doth
His will Who is in Heaven, the same to me
My mother is, my sister and my brother.
Caia. Thou seest; he will not own himself the son
Of the dead carpenter, though all the world
About him know it and have seen him work

At his mean trade.   What sayst thou, fellow ? who
Art thou in fact?

     Jesus. The faithful shepherd, come
To lay his life down freely for his flock.

Caia. That will be seen.   Most noble Pontius, end
 This mockery.   This person breaks, has broken
 For years our laws, he makes himself to be
 The son of the Most High, profanes our Sabbath,
 Derides the priesthood.   For these crimes alone
 His life were justly forfeit : but he is
 The cause if not the inciter of sedition,
 Proclaim'd by the idle, ignorant throng, that gather
 About him everywhere, to be their king,
 The prince of the House of David, whom the prophet
 Foretold should come to build us up again
 Our ruin'd kingdom, and the sceptre wresting
 From conquering Rome restore it unto Judah.
 Already in the Wilderness they sought
 Compulsively to make him king. ——

     Jesus. Why need
Compulsion, were my kingdom of this world ?

Caia. Break'st thou my speech? — Because, in his own
  words,
 His time was not yet come.

    Pont. [*to Jesus.*] And is that true?
Hast thou this wild ambition to be king ?

Jesus. Ask'st thou this of thyself?   Or speak'st thou thus
 As they who accuse me ?

     Pont. Am I then a Jew ?

They, who have brought thee hither thus arraign'd,
Are thy own people. Is their censure just?
Jesus. Let my acts answer. He, who for himself
Speaketh and acteth, seeketh his own glory;
But seeketh he to glorify alone
Him who has sent him, he is wholly true
And doth uprightly.
     Nicod. Noble Pontius, hear.
The charges that are made against this man
Have not one been sustain'd. Nor thou, nor Herod
Find ought in him to punish. That the rabble
Should seek to make him king — if that be so,
May at the time give trouble and vex the State;
But is the fault in him? and should we ever
Make innocence suffer?
     Pont. I have, as thou must see,
No wish to punish, as I find no cause.
But your own rulers find one, and insist.
Caia. Art thou a friend to Cæsar, thou must condemn.
This man is hostile to the rule of Cæsar.
Nicod. He paid the tribute-money at Capernaum.
Jos. Arim. And with this phrase, which in itself alone
Defines his purpose and shows the realm he claims
To be unearthly : " Render unto Cæsar
That which is his, to God what is of God."
Caia. I have said before, he but abides his time.
Are we to wait until the serpent's egg
Is hatch'd ? A known contemner of the law,
Blasphemous, sacrilegious, full of guile,
Seditious, a corrupter of the people,

We find he merits death, and call on thee,
Where only is the power, to pronounce it.
Pont. People, — it is your custom on this day
    To free a prisoner. Two await your choice.
    One is Barabbas, a determin'd villain,
    Who rous'd you to revolt, and in the act
    Caus'd or committed murder. He is chain'd.
    The other, now before you, is a man
    Whom I esteem a teacher wise and good,
    Such as ye need, and such as in your faith
    Has in all time been common. By mischance,
    Or malice of his foes, or through a zeal
    Too warm perhaps and headstrong, brought in fault,
    He is led to this tribunal to be doom'd.
    Bid me release him to you; for to me
    He is in no wise guilty.
                    Scribe. But he is
Before our law. Release to us Barabbas.
Elder. And crucify this Jesus, would-be king.
One of the People. Ay, crucify him!
                    Another. And release Barabbas.
Pont. What! crucify him whom you would make king?
Priest. They have no king but Cæsar.
                    People. To the cross!
Others. Away with him!
                    Others. And give us up Barabbas.
Pont. The man of crime? and slay this harmless one?
    Look on him well. What evil hath he done?
Elder. He made himself the Christ. Away with him!
People. Away with the blasphemer! To the cross!

Pont. Bring water. — Thus, before you, with your rite,
 I wash my hands of the blood you bid me shed.
Elder. Be it on our heads.
     People. And on our children's heads.
Nicod. Even so, ye madmen.
     People. Crucify! Away!
Pont. [*to the lictors.*] Take him. And see they set above
  the cross,
  " King of the Jews."
     Scribe. Not so, but "self-call'd King."
Pont. What I have said is said. Away.
     People. Away!
Others. To the cross!
    Others. To Golgotha!
     Another. Put on the crown.

A wreath of thorns is set on Jesus' head.

Scribe. Give him a sceptre in his royal hands.
Soldier. [*putting a reed in Jesus' hand, and bending the
      knee before him.*
  Hail, King of the Jews!
     People. Away with him! away!

JESUS *is led off hurriedly,
amid the shouts and derision of the People.*

ACT THE FIFTH

Scene I.—A highway near and leading to Calvary.

NICODEMUS *and* JOSEPH OF ARIMATHEA.

Approaching them in face,

A CENTURION.

Jos. Arim. The darkness still continues, the thick clouds,
   Black as in summer-showers when thunder rolls,
   Have yet no motion, and the wind is still.
Nicod. Nor is there dampness. 'T seems as if the sky
   Were not spread with a level mass of cloud,
   But metal-plated, solid to the sun,
   Which hides as God forbade it to give light
   To this foul crime.
                  Jos. Arim. What if he were the Christ?
Nicod. Think'st thou? He was a prophet at the least,
   And Heaven by this unnatural blackness notes
   Its anger or its sorrow. Who comes yon?
Jos. Arim. 'T is he whose servant Jesus render'd whole,
   The good Centurion.
                  Nicod. Doubtless from the Mount.
   His brows are knitted and his lips compress'd,
   His head cast down. —— Hail! com'st thou from the
      scene?
Centur. Of unjust death and torture? Ay. You Jews
   Are a malignant and a stiff-neck'd race;
      3*

You know not your own fortune.   Not at Rome
Had we so slain our teachers. ·

          Nicod. Athens did,
And lo! Rome's procurator, Pontius, now!
He had the power to stay the insensate mob,
But in one breath acquitted and made over
To shame and death the man his soul approv'd,
Then wash'd his hands, — as if the innocent blood
Could not bespot a conscience turn'd to steel
By selfish fear and tyrannous disregard
Of human rights.

          Centur. 'T is boldly said, but well.
I love thee. — Let us pass that. — Go ye now
To see the end?

          Nicod. We do. How bears he up?
Centur. Like a true soldier — hero, — like a god!
But 't is a horrid sight. I have seen men slain
And mangled often, — felt, yet fought through all;
But this I could not bear. Go not, ye.

          Nicod. Nay,
'T is all, the last, that is left us now to do.
Jos. Arim. Wast thou there from the first?   Tell, tell us all.
Centur. On his way to the place of death, a rabble throng,
As usual in such scenes, preceded, follow'd,
Accompanied on both sides, — some overjoy'd,
Some simply curious, — laughing, hooting, eager.
But some there were more decent, and with these
Were women weeping, unrestrain'd, though low.
Looking on these, the Rabbi, who through all

Mov'd undisturb'd, though sadly serious, said :
" Weep not for me, ye daughters of Jerusalem ;
Weep for yourselves and children.   For, behold,
The time approaches when they shall call blessed
The barren, and the womb that has not born,
The paps that give no suck.   Then shall they cry :
Fall on us, O ye mountains ! and ye cliffs,
Conceal us !   For, if in the yet moist wood
They do these things, what shall be in the dry ?"
Nicod. Sad prophecy !

      Jos. Arim. And true.

           Nicod. But doom'd, not less,
Only to be regarded when found true.
Centur. Arriv'd at the fatal hill, they strip him bare,
Disputing for his garments, which they part.
The bitter drink is offer'd, and refus'd :
Hero or god, but truly sacrifice,
He will not deaden pain.   His hands and feet
Are nail'd to the cross, which then is set erect,
Amid the shouts of the rabble, and the sobs
Of some of the women, but without a groan
From the poor sufferer, who but op'd his lips
In prayer for his torturers :   "Father," — thus he
    cried, —
"Forgive them ; for they know not what they do."
Nicod. O more than human !

      Jos. Arim. Like an angel !

           Centur. Say,
'T was as a man made god, a son of Jove,

Alone might speak.   But once he rais'd his eyes
Slowly to Heaven ; and oh, with such a look,
Of sorrow and pain and resignation mix'd,
Awful yet beautiful, my own eyes swam,
Which have not been so mov'd since, at ten years,
I saw my mother die.

    Nicod. We wonder not.

Centur. Just at that moment, over all the sky
There came this darkness, and the shouts were hush'd,
And even the hideous gaiety and jeers —
While the awe lasted.

     Jos. Arim. Staid'st thou there till now ?

Centur. Only at intervals.   Still around the cross
The women sit or kneel, some bath'd in tears,
Some sobbing softly, some, their faces hid
In their spread palms, their bodies rocking slowly
With a continuous motion to and fro,
While, further off, the men in various groups,
And busied variously to while the time,
Unwearied watch to see a brave man die.

Nicod. Is it near the end ?

    Centur. He is sinking even now.
One of the robbers is already dead.   Before
Ye leave me, tell me, ye who know him well,
What think ye is this being for whose last hour
Jove wraps his throne in darkness ?

     Nicod. If not man,
Haply he is that Christ our prophets told
Should come to bless us.

Jos. Arim. But we have misred
Their prophecies, and slay where we should worship.
Centur. I will go back with you, and see the end.
There have been men, the earth-born sons of gods,
Whom Heaven's high King has chosen to dwell with
    him,
As Hercules and Æsculapius.   This
May be of the kind.   I will behold the end.

SCENE II.

Golgotha or Calvary.

JESUS, *on the cross.*

At its foot, at one side, MARY *his mother,* MARY MAGDALENE, MARTHA, *and other women. Behind them,* JOHN. PETER *and* JAMES, *a little more removed. — A little later, behind these latter,* NICODEMUS, JOS. OF ARIMATHEA *and the* CENTURION, — *who, throughout, speak in suppressed tones. On the other side, a guard of Roman soldiers, with their* SUBCENTURIO *or Lieutenant, and two of the Procurator's Lictors.*

The PEOPLE *are variously dispersed on every side. Here and there, a few of better condition ; among whom, and near the cross, the* SCRIBE *and* ELDER, *interlocutors in previous scenes.*

One of the People. Thou who destroyest the Temple and
      again
In three days buildest it, come down.
                         Another. Not yet.
The Christ sav'd others, or profess'd to save.
Himself he cannot.
              Another. If the Son of God,
Come down, and we will worship thee.
                     Scribe. Dost hear ?
King of the Jews, descend from thy high throne,
That we may look on thee and kiss thy feet.
Elder. Those feet are bloody, and those gory hands

Look not like godhood.   Yet we will believe,
If thou wilt loose thyself and come to us.
Centur. Noble, unmov'd, he will not deign reply.
There is more godhead in those speechless lips
Than any human blood can wash away.
Nicod. But lo, his mother speaks.

     Mary. My son! my son!
What shall I do when thou art gone from me!
John. He heeds thee not; his mind is far away.
Magd. No, he looks on ye both.   Alas, alas!
Those dying eyes!   O God!

     Jesus. Behold,
Woman, thy son.   And thou, behold thy mother.
John. She shall indeed be unto me a mother,
And I from this day, Lord, will be her son.
Martha. Be comforted.

     Mary. Talk not to me of comfort.
Look on those lips,—is any comfort there?
Those pallid cheeks blood-spotted, and those eyes
That call in vain on Heaven.   O my son!
Would I had never born thee for this day;
Or would that I had died ere it was come!
O Jesus!   O my son! my son!

     Centur. Look now!
The end approaches.   'T is the dying thirst
That tortures.

     Nicod. Yet the immortal soul yields not.
His head droops lower.   Was not that a sigh?
Mary. Speak to me once again.   Dost thou not hear me?

Dost thou yet suffer greatly, O my son?

Nicod. He hears her not.   He is past human sound.
Still lower sinks the head.

                    Jos. Arim. He lifts it now.

Centur. There is again that look I told ye of.

Jesus. My God! my God! Why, why hast Thou forsook me?

People. Hear to him there; he calls upon his god.
Why comes he not to aid him?

                 Sub-centurion. Peace, thou Jew!

He bears him in a way to teach you all.
This to release him.   [*Takes a spear from a soldier and
                            pierces the side of Jesus.*

            People. Hark! he speaks again.

Jesus. My God! my God! into thy hands — I yield —
My spirit. —   It is finish'd.

                Mary. Jesus!   Son!

Scene III.

As in Act I., Sc. 1.

Raphael.   Michael.

Chorus of Angels.

Chorus.

" 'T is finish'd."   In the wintry air
The blood congealing
Is not renew'd.
That pale head, with its thorn-encircled hair
Matted and glu'd
With gore-drops from the spine-pierc'd forehead
    stealing,
Presses and crimson-spots his shoulder bare,
Like the stark limbs revealing
That human sense and feeling
No more are there.

Silent, their cruel mood
No longer keeping,
The murderers stare
On the dead Lamb with eyes that no more rude
With malice glare.

The pall has left the sky; the breeze comes sweeping
Over the Mount; all other sounds subdu'd
As if the slain were sleeping, —
Save from the women weeping
Around the rood.

O for the wo we bear!
The Lord of Heaven
By angels view'd
Between two sinful men stretch'd bleeding there,
Mangled and nude.
O for the wo! lo, they to whom 't is given
The Incarnate God for sepulture prepare.
The Mother sits heart-riven,
Weeps the frail Mary driven
Nigh to despair.

Triumph now Hell's grim brood,
In harsh song yelling
Their blitheness rare.
They see but shame and torture in the rood,
Wo and despair.
But other sounds will shake their flame-girt dwelling,
When from the vault the Lord, with power indu'd,
Returns to Heaven, dispelling
The grief our hearts now swelling,
With happier mood.

Raph. Hell's joy is futile as our wo in Heaven,
    And more unmeet.
    It is our triumph now and their defeat.
    The heart of Mary may with grief be riven ;
    But in that pallid, blood-stain'd human shape,
    The Almighty Father sees His Chosen One,
    The Lamb through whose atoning blood escape
    Eve's forfeit race, even those by whom is done
    This deed of shame, and owns with joy the Son,
    Whose fight with mortal trials, well begun,
    Is now complete.
Mich. Wait not until the Sepulchre shall ope :
    Now, now rejoice.
    Those livid limbs need not the hue of hope
    To color them with beauty like the rose,
    And the red wounds, through which no longer flows
    The Virgin's blood,
    Have each for fallen man a voice,
    Would he but listen, loud as Ocean's flood.
Raph. Deep in the listening skies
    The accents penetrate : Rejoice! it cries.
    Ascends to grateful Heaven the tone,
    The death-cry of the slaughter'd one,
    The Lamb of Sacrifice.
Mich. And lo, the awe-hush'd Seraphim
    Lift up the clos'd lids of their glowing eyes.
    And soon their rapture-breathing song shall rise
    In ecstacy of grateful love to Him,
    The Light from its own brightness dim,

The Source Unseen where, bubbling to the brim,
The Fount of Being lies.
Raph. And see, the eternal lights divine
That circle round the aye-hidden Throne,
Orb within orb of fire,
Begin with wonted blaze to shine.
The flame within, whose awful glare alone
No Seraph's eyes dare gaze upon,
Will upward soon aspire.
Mich. And hark, again the ecstatic tone
Struck from each golden lyre!

CHORUS.

Joy in the Highest!   Ere
Earth's star has risen
Three times, the tomb shall tear
Open its prison.

Then shall the Lord appear
In his soul's whiteness,
No crown his brow shall wear,
Only its brightness.

Not while the World shall last
Men shall more view him,
Not till the trumpet's blast
Summons them to him.

Then shall the gates of Hell
Open more never,
Then shall the righteous dwell
With him forever.

Oh come, thou welcome time,
When the Lord, risen,
Leaves the World's wo and crime
With the tomb's prison!

SCENE IV.

As in Act II., Sc. 1.

LUCIFER. BEELZEBUB. CHORUS OF EVIL SPIRITS.

Chorus.

Flames that circle Hell,
Lift your waves rejoicing,
With your roar loud-voicing
What we feel so well,
We the unforgiven,
O'er the wo of Heaven,

From whose heights down-driven
Here we fell.

For the deed is done.
In the Earth's chill air,
Naked, nail'd, and bleeding,
Stretch'd upon the tree,
Suffering pains exceeding
Those we hourly bear,
Pains the Christ might shun,
Will'd he to be free,
See stretch'd bleeding there,
On the midmost tree,
'Twixt a robber pair,
God's anointed Son.
On his pain-drawn brow
Beads of sweat are lying,
With the blood-drops vying
Oozing large and slow
Through his thorn-crown'd hair.

See that head droop low ;
See the red stream falling
Down his side, and now
Hear his pale lips calling,
Calling Heaven to spare,
In a prayer,
Where if human weakness,

Conquering his meekness,
Forces not a groan,
Yet is all the tone
Of despair.

Ah, the head droops lower,
Ah, the blood drops slower,
Listless is his air.
Look, ye sons of Heaven !
We, the unforgiven,
Do we triumph there?
Wounds that we are feeling
Find therein their healing,
Though that blood be sealing
Our despair.

Let the tomb close o'er him,
Let his Saints deplore him,
Hosts in Heaven adore him ;
Ours is not the loss.
Weary though we languish,
Though with heart's pain aching,
Yet our woes find slaking
In the sweat and anguish
Of the Cross.

Lucif. Peace, thoughtless that ye are !   'T is true I said
The Incarnate God was dying, true, is dead.
But this is not our triumph ; and your song,
So ill elate,

Should rather wail the dead, whose human fate
Sets free mankind and makes your chains more strong.

Beelz. How should that be? The disappointed Jews,
Who look for their Messiah in a king,
Even common faith refuse
To all the man-god's works, and lend no ear
To what their prophets sung, and, should he rise
Before them all, would close their bigot eyes,
And to their disbelief more closely cling,
Though they should angels hear.

Lucif. 'T is not the risen Christ, the dead I fear.
Those wounds, that sweat, that dying cry to God,
These are the traits which in all time to come
Shall make him lov'd wherever man has trod,
And keep the skeptic dumb.
The soul that had its sorrows like their own,
The Virgin Mother that bewail'd her son,
The tortur'd flesh, the heart-wrung prayer, the groan,
By these will faith be won.
Man keeps for man alone his sympathies,
And truly follows only what he sees.
Before the God unseen, the Christ ensky'd,
The knee may worship, but the thoughts run wide:
But paint the blood-stain'd rood, or, scene more mild,
The earth-born Mother with her sleeping Child,
The heart then bends, self-love, enlarged, refin'd,
Lends its warm color to the colder mind;
Each woman smiles as Mary's self has smil'd,
And nobler man his steadfast spirit's pride
And suffering frame, where torment is beguil'd

By sense of wrong inflicted and defy'd,
Sees in Christ crucify'd.

Beelz. Fades then our hope in air?   Not such of late
Spok'st thou this god.   Now stoop'st thou to admire?

Lucif. Ay, without stint, though all the while I hate.
Shall I be blind where mope-ey'd mortals see?
Were I not what I am, I would be He.
And yet, I fling defiance unto fate,
Here, in this realm of fire,
Where even though thou, and all, of wo should tire
And bend in penitence the adoring knee,
I am what I have been, and dare be free
Despite both Son and Sire.
No, all is as before.   Though Christ has bled,
Yet Man shall not yet bruise the Serpent's head.
He who has once beguil'd can still deceive,
And Adam's heirs are yet the sons of Eve.
Some will be better'd, but, while tongues adore,
Man's carnal heart beats stubborn as before.
The common work none perfect, all begin,
And what the Christian worship, yet to be,
Shall bid men flee from as the Devil and Sin,
Shall tempt, delight, and torture, o'er and o'er,
And, like their Mother, make them slaves to me,
Till the last Conflagration sets them free,
And time, and Earth, and Hell shall be no more.

Beelz. Then raise again your joy-song as before,
Ye Spirits who float upon this sulphurous air,
And pierce the Heaven, which was your home of yore,
With notes of exultation and of scorn;

For grief shall find an echo even there,
While Adam's sons of Adam's flesh are born
And Eve's frail kind shall suckle those they bear.

CHORUS — *in the distance.*

Flames that circle Hell,
Lift your waves rejoicing,
With your roar loud-voicing
What we feel so well,
We the unforgiven,
O'er the wo of Heaven,
From whose heights down-driven
Here we fell

NOTES

NOTES TO CALVARY

1.—P. 6. *Since the hid daggers of my faithful men,* &c.] Ὑδάτων δε επαγωγην εις τα Ἱεροσολυμα, κ. τ. λ. In brief, thus: Pilate introduced water into Jerusalem at the expense of the sacred treasure. The Jews took this in dudgeon, and in great crowds—which the historian has exaggerated into myriads (πολλαι ... μυριαδες) endeavored to force him by their tumult to desist, using even personal abuse. The Procurator thereupon had some of his soldiers dressed in the Jewish garb, who carried cudgels under their habits (σκυταλαs ὑπο ταις στολαις); *

---

* Σκυταλαs is translated by Hudson (*Oxon.* in fol. 1720. t. ii. p. 798) " *sicas,*" and by Whiston with the corresponding, " daggers." But the word cannot signify, in this place, anything but either *scourges* (leathern: Th. σκυτος, *corium*) or *cudgels;* and I see Gelenius gives it this latter sense: " clam armatos *fustibus*" (*Antiq.* fol. Lugd., 1566): the correctness of which is confirmed by another account of the same affair in the *History,* where Josephus uses the word ξυλοις, which indicates the very material, *wood* (sticks), though that the use of the dagger, or of the short Roman sword, is implied, might be supposed from what the historian subsequently says, when recording the result: ὡστε αοπλοι ληφθεντες ὑπ' ανδρων εκ παρασκευης επιφερομενων, πολλοι μεν αυτων ταυτῃ και απεθνησκον, ὁι δε και τραυματιαι ανεχωρησαν. But unfortu-

and when the assemblage refused to disperse, these men, at a precon-
certed signal, began to lay about them indiscriminately, and with a
severity that transcended their orders. The Jews with their national
obstinacy persisting, the soldiers, it would seem, for it is not directly
asserted, used their ordinary weapons against the unarmed multitude,
so that many perished and others departed wounded. Jos. *Antiq.*, lib.
xviii. c. 3. *ex ed.* RICHTER, in 12mo. *Lips.* 1826. t. iv. p. 131, *sq.*

2.—P. 7. *To Antipas for sentence.*] Two of the other readings may
serve to elucidate the text.

> ———————— Send him then
> To Antipas. I would have peace restor'd
> 'Twixt him and me ; and this man, thus remanded,

nately for this supposition, Josephus has, in his usual way, with some varia-
tions and contradictions, repeated, as I have said, the story in his *Wars*, and
there we have not only a renewed evidence of Pilate's moderation, who positively forbid the use of the sword (ξιφει μεν χρησασθαι κωλυσας), but the result
is made to arise solely from the cudgeling and from the precipitation of the
crowd who trod down one another in their flight : Τυπτομενοι δε οι Ιουδαιοι,
πολλοι μεν υπο των πληγων, πολλοι δε υπο σφων αυτων εν τη φυγη καταπατηθεν-
τες απολωντο. *Bell. Jud.* Lib. II. c. ix. §4. p. 219. t. vi. ed. supra cit. As there
is a doubt however,—for here too the soldiers are described as *armed*,—I have
chosen that phrase which suits best my occasion.

I may add that Eusebius, who quotes this passage from the History entire,
(*Hist. Eccles.* II. c. vi. p. 154, sq. t. xx. *Patrologiæ Græc. ed.* MIGNE. *Par.* 8o.
1857,) speaks of this disastrous tumult as if it were a punishment for the crucifixion of the Saviour. Was it then *after* that event ? But he has committed an
error, as the commentator shows (*ib.*), directly before it, in ascribing alike to the
divine vengeance the tumult occasioned by the introduction of the Roman
ensigns with their images, (*Bell. Jud.* xx. ix. 2 & 3,.) whereas we are told that
that happened in the beginning of the administration of Pilate, which was
in the 12th year of Tiberius, three years before Christ's baptism.

Will show the Tetrarch, when the rebel blood
Of Galileans stain'd my soldiers' swords,
I thought not of his rights, and meant no scorn.

Otherwise:

Will show the Tetrarch, 'twas not in my thought
To invade his jurisdiction, when the blood
Of Galileans stain'd my soldiers' swords.

See *Luke* xiii. 1. and xxiii. 6, 7. and a note in Whiston at the preceding passage of Josephus.

3.—P. 24. ... *the sea which God loves.*] The Sea of Galilee. A
proverbial expression with the ancient Jews.

4.—P. 52. *Beware thou then ... for God decrees In retribution violent ends to those Who practice violence.*] According to Eusebius, who
gives a little chapter of his History especially to the event, Pilate was
reported to have fallen, in the reign of Caius, into such calamities, that
in sheer desperation * he became his own destroyer and self-punisher,
vindicating thus the divine justice: της θειας, ως εοικε, δικης ουκ εις
μακρον αυτον μετελθουσης. *Hist. Eccl.* II. 7. *ex recens.* Burton; *Oxon.*
in 8°. 1845; p. 40. The same still more briefly in *Chronicor. Lib.* II.
(*ap.* Migne, *ubi cit.* xix. p. 557-8). But here he advances as authority

---

* In a note on the phrase, εξ αναγκης, the commentator in Migne (*Patrolog.
Græc.* t. xx. p. 155) cites King Agrippa (*cp. Philon. in Legat. ad Caium*), who,
having been an eye-witness of the doings of Pilate, describes his character.
Apart from the man's natural disposition, which is said to have been unyield-
ing, arrogant and harsh, his corruptibility, rapacity, and acts of oppression, and
of violence even to homicide, were not peculiar to him as a Roman governor
in the times of the Empire.

certain unnamed writers of Roman story—ὡς φασιν οἱ τα 'Ρωμαιων συγγραψαμενοι—as before he had ascribed the tale to certain Greek chroniclers.†

---

† What degree of credit may be assigned to Eusebius as a narrator of events may be judged by what Scaliger says : "Eusebius, quo nullus ecclesiasticorum veterum plura ad historiam Christianismi contulit ; nullus plura errata in scriptis suis reliquit, &c.—(in *Elencho Trihær.* c. 27. *Veter. Testim.* c. *Euseb.* in *Patrol. Græc.* t. xix. p. 98.) The same (*ib. cit.*), assigns him much reading, but little judgment.

VIRGINIA

MDCCCXLVII

CHARACTERS

Primary

LUCIUS ICILIUS, *plebeian of tribunitial rank.*

APPIUS CLAUDIUS, *chief decemvir.*

LUCIUS VALERIUS POTITUS, ⎱ *senators of consular rank,*
MARCUS HORATIUS BARBATUS, ⎰ *hostile to the Decemvirs and friendly to the rights of the people.*

SPURIUS OPPIUS, *colleague of Appius in the city.*

LUCIUS VIRGINIUS, *father of Virginia.*

MARCUS CLAUDIUS, *client of Appius.*

AULUS LUCRETIUS, ⎱ *senators,*
TITUS QUINCTIUS, ⎰ *friends of Horatius and Valerius.*

PUBLIUS NUMITORIUS, *maternal uncle of Virginia.*

VIRGINIA.

ICILIA, *sister of Icilius.*

LIVIA, *a creature of M. Claudius.*

Of secondary importance

2D CITIZEN.

1ST CITIZEN.

A MATRON (termed in the final scene 1*st Matron.*)

Other persons — *of no distinctive character*

CAIUS NUMITORIUS, *son of Publius, and Virginia's cousin.*

QUINTUS ICILIUS, *brother of Lucius.*

A LETTER-CARRIER (*Tabellarius*) *of Appius.*

LUCILLA, *Virginia's nurse.*

Citizens; Matrons; Nobles, partisans of Appius; Lictors; Soldiers; a Messenger in waiting; a Herald or Crier.

———

SCENE. *Various places in Rome — chiefly at the Forum.*
In Act III., Sc. 3, in a diversorium (or inn) near Rome.

TIME. *That occupied by the representation.*

COSTUMES. *Those of the early republic.*

VIRGINIA

Scene I. A room in the house of Appius Claudius.

APPIUS; SPURIUS OPPIUS;
with certain young NOBLES, *partisans
of* APPIUS. — *At a little distance,* MARCUS CLAUDIUS.

Spur. Yet, have a care!   Stretch thou the cord too much,
　　It snaps i' the midst, and the recoil offends thee.
App. Tush! Know I not the strength of every strand?
　　'T will bear the strain.   I'll force the dull mass down,
　　Set my foot on it, and so keep it there,
　　Till ye have drawn the string.   'T is not a hydra;
　　And if it were, we nobles in our strength
　　Wield the huge club should crush its thousand heads.
　　If not, so be it!   retire; and I alone,
　　As my great-grandsire, the first Appius, swore,
　　Alone will do it!

Spur. And alone will fail.
Thou speak'st as if the people were one mass!
With all its heads, the snake had but one body;
This has more bodies, though it has fewer heads.
App. I speak of it as it is; one mass, one head,
    Flock, if thou wilt, of many thousand sheep.
    A single man may pin them in one fold.
A Noble. And sheer, and slaughter them.
                    Spur. But then, observe,
He feeds them too.   'T is what the unfolded flock,
Our people, bleat for : *Give us lands,* they cry.
Noble. And free us of our collars.
                 App. And what else ?
Let the brutes earn their freedom first.   For lands —
When they have paid for what they browze on, why ——
It is not many years since Caius Marcius
Drove, all but single-handed, troop on troop
Of Volscians back into Corioli,
And fired it in their faces.   Know ye why ?
They were the rabblement, your bleating sheep.
He knew and scorn'd them.   And they bent their backs,
Because their hearts were craven and they felt
He knew and scorn'd them.   Had he back'd one step —
On his Mars-visage had they read one doubt —
They had turn'd, as curs do ; and his after-name
Caius had lack'd.
            Spur. What did it profit him?
He show'd the same mien to the people here —
Flouted their tribunes — and, with all his valor,
He died in exile.

App. Ay — because he flinch'd.
Thou mayst look, Spurius; 't is the naked fact.
Did not all Rome lie prostrate at his feet,
Bleeding, exhausted? grovel in the dust,
Admit his wrongs, and pray to be forgiven?
He might have made conditions, as I would,
And bound the rabble in their chains for ever.
But in his heart, right royal though it was ——
Why look ye frighten'd? all your hearts, I trust,
Are royal — that is, made for kingly rule,
As fits a noble, though he be of Rome.
And Caius' heart was royal, though not strong,
Not wholly so; it hid one tender spot.
His wife and mother kneel'd to him; and the face
That scar'd a thousand foes wept woman's tears.

Spur. Wouldst thou have trod upon the womb that bore
thee?

App. Why, no; I see no need of that: I had bid
The woman mind her spinning, and stepp'd over.
By Hercules! methinks that with my twelve
Poor lictors, I alone could awe this mob!
But while our colleagues, and you, noble friends,
Stand by our side, against our serried force
What shall make head? The Fabii all alone,
Six and three-hundred only, but all born
Patrician as are we, against a host
Stood up and battled ——

        Spur. And fell down, and died,
All to a man.

      App. Thou bird of evil omen!

The shadow of thy wings, three times this hour,[1]
Hath gloom'd my sunniest prospect.   I had thought
Thou, Spurius, wast my right hand.

Spur. And I am.
The wings thou givest me flap before thine eyes,
Not to deter, but check.   The gloom they cast
Is transient, partial, chills not, and is needed.
Thy ardent temper spreads a light too broad,
Too vivid on thy outward path.   All shines,
One blaze of sunlight ; crags look smooth, and chasms
Show no disruption — where thou 'lt find, too soon,
Rocks Atlas-high, and fissures deep as Hell.

App. Does the way fright thee?

Spur. Scarcely more than thee.
And 't were too late.   If thou go down, my head,
Be sure, rests not unmuffled.

App. Now, no more. —
Are we resolv'd?   The senate, all our order,
Will not erase one letter of their rights ;
And the decemvirate shall not expire,
To give place to the people's tribunes?

All nobles. No!

Spur. Valerius and Horatius would say, Ay.

App. Lucius Valerius!   Have not all his name
Cring'd to the rabble, since the consul's day,
Who bow'd his valiant knee to this mud idol,
And gain'd —— what for it? The people laid him out![2]
He had not left an ounce to pay for torches,
This good Publicola!   Odious after-name!

Spur. Thou need'st not fear; no Claudius will deserve it.

App. No Appius has.   The people, did they hate
  My grandsire, as his sire, fear'd him more.
  They honor'd too his obsequies, for all
  Their tribunes' clamor.   Let them honor mine,
  I reck not; but I will be fear'd as he.
  I set not, I, the goddess of the sewers
  Above high Jove! —   For young Horatius' voice,
  'T is not so potent as a tribune's veto.

Spur. Yet has a clear loud tone that makes it heard.
  Witness that day, so recent, when our right
  To call the senate for the instant war
  Met question.   Thou might'st thank Cornelius then,
  When Lucius from the senate-porch made cry
  Unto the people, his arms about thee cast
  Sav'd thee from violence, and us both from ruin.[3]
  The Fathers all, but that they hate the commons,
  Would join these madmen, and the temple's walls,
  Sacred in vain, once more reverberate
  The tribunes' thunder — haply from the throne
  Of thy sworn enemy, Icilius.

                    App. Ah ! ——
  Thou dost remind me. —   Noble friends ! to-night
  Meet we again in secret, and our plans,
  Already ripening, make mature.   The sun
  Warns me we nigh to mid-day, when I sit
  For justice.   Kæso, bring thy brother over.
  Thy uncle, Op'iter, shall have all he asks.
  Mutius, thou wilt not fail me ?   All, farewell.

                    [*Exeunt Nobles.*

Spur. 'T was time.

         App. Most true. Thy evil genius, Spurius,
Had got dominion of thee. Was it well,
To cross my arguments, and fright those boys?

Spur. Who need no Pan. Didst thou not note, thyself,
How pale they grew? thou didst but hint at kings.
Thou art too fiery.

         App. And thou waxest cold.

Spur. I have had a dream.

         App. A dream!

               Spur. 'T was at mid-day.
I saw the tender spot, which Marcius had,
Spread over thy whole heart, and Rome again
Lost to her conqueror for a woman's tear.

App. Thou hast no mercy.

         Spur. Will the people have?
Was there in Rome no other girl but this?
Virginius' daughter, and the plighted spouse
Of dread Icilius! If the father's merit
Wake not the mob, that will the lover's tongue.
Were she hedg'd in with fire, 't were peril less
To come at her. — Thou heed'st me not. I see,
The madness which no hellebore can heal
Will have its course. I leave thee to thy client.

                             [Exit.

App. Come hither, Marcus. Is this thing of thine ——
How didst thou name her?

            Mar. Livia, noble patron.

App. Is she prepar'd? Will she go through the part?

Mar. Through, and with spirit, such as gives revenge.
    The wrong she fancies that Virginius did her, —
    Some such a wrong as one might do a fig,
    Who found it rotten, throwing it away, —
    This rankles in her heart — and that, a woman's.
    I'll answer for her.
             App. Do my lictors wait?
Mar. They guard the vestibule, most noble Appius.
App. While thou shalt help me to dispose my mantle,[4]
    I'll question further. — This way. — But, remember!
    I'll have no stumbling. If she trips, her life
    Shall pay for it.
             Mar. My own upon her faith!

SCENE II.

The Atrium, or quadrangular Hall, in the house of Icilius.

VIRGINIA, *with spindle and distaff, spinning wool.*
ICILIA, *weaving at a small loom (before which she stands,*
as in the antique fashion, working upwards).
A little distance removed, but seated, Virginia's nurse,
winding the thread for Virginia.

Ica. Our fears, I have heard my brother say, Virginia,
 Make omens for us, and our heart's own hue
 Gives accidental color to these things
 Which in themselves are nothing.   Not but Jove,
 In matters which concern the general weal,
 May give us warnings, which his augurs gather,
 From the dread thunder, or from birds and beasts:
 But that each atom of the mighty mass
 Should for its pettiest movements need, or needing,
 Receive celestial guidance, staggers sense,
 And blasphemously littles the great gods above us.
Va. How well thou talkest!
     Ica. It is Lucius, all. —
That sweet lip's sadness, let my kiss dispel it.
The thrill of thy heart's longing makes thee tremble: —
Two little days, and thou and Lucius one!
It seems a dream: thou fearest to awaken.
This must be all.   The vile decemvir's passion
Cannot affright thee now.   Thy valiant father
Ere sunset will have come: the pressing message,

Borne by thy cousin and my brother Quintus,
Leaves him no choice.

            Va. Ah, did he know the cause!
· That Rome, to guard whose honor, though already
Defended by a thousand hearts as brave
As his, his pious breast is bar'd in Algidum,
Cannot from insult shield the motherless girl
His absence orphans! —

            Ica. Better as it is.
His wrath, already, for the people's sake,
Kindled against the usurping Ten, might there,
There where alone their power can reach his life,
Burst into flame.   Enough, and all too soon,
When he shall come.   For Lucius——

            Va. Never,
O never, may he know it!

            Ica. ⁵ Not at least
Till Hymen's torch is lighted, and the couch
Here spread i' the hall bids mystery henceforth cease
Twixt him and thee; when the flame-color'd veil
Deepens thy blushes, and the fring'd robe is on thee
Whose purple border I am weaving now,
And, girded with the woolen belt whose knot
My brother's hand alone shall loose, thou standest
Trembling beneath the garland-cover'd porch,
And greet'st him with the soft yet solemn form,
Where thou art Caius, I am Caia; when,
In fine, thou art plainly as in heart my sister,
Virginia Icilii.   See, Lucilla, see!

Her sadness has all vanish'd ; and her cheek —
Love's own is not more rubious !   Happy brother !—
Tell me, my sister, tell me now, for what
Lov'st thou our Lucius most?   Is 't for his form ?
His stately step ? or for his manly brow ?
Or that he is good ? or for his eloquent tongue,
Or valiant heart ? or ——

                    Va. Why not say for all?
For all he is dear to me, as he is to thee ;
But most for what endears him to the people :
For his upright soul, for that he dares be just,
Scorning all falsehood, and more proud to be
One of the down-trod commons, from whose limbs
With his own breast he wards the crushing heel,
Than head of the cruel Claudii, whose proud lords,
From Attus down, have kept their iron foot
Ever upon the people's neck, nor lift it
But just so much as may give room to breathe.
For this my father loves him, and for this
He bade me, pointing to the people's hearths,
Where everywhere Icilius' image stands,
Invisible but distinct, nor dreads their smoke,
Sole tutelar-god, he bade me, if I could,
To make him too my house-god, by the hearth
Of my yet virgin feelings shrin'd for ever ;
And — and [*throwing herself on Icilia's breast.*
        —I did.

    Ica. [*soothing her.*] Nor art asham'd, I hope,

To have done it.   Weeping? — Silly child! —— Who
comes?

Enter, from the door of the hall, LIVIA, *meanly dressed.*
Her cloak, drawn over her head, hides her features.

Liv. Asks that the sister of the good Icilius?
Protector of the poor, here in his house
The word for the poor is " Welcome," not " Who comes?"
Ica. Welcome then, mother.
                                   Liv. I am not so old
To be thy mother ; neither am I fit
To sit before ye [*as the nurse, at Ica.'s beck, places before*
her a stool.] — though this slave may do it.
Ica. Fie, woman! If thou know'st Icilius, know
His house permits no slight on those it covers,
As his true heart reproaches no condition.
What wouldst thou?
                                   Liv. Charity.
                                   Ica. That thou shalt have.
What is thy need?
                                   Liv. I rent a wretched shed
Of Marcus Claudius, the decemvir's client,
And pander to his pleasures. Dost thou shrink, [*to Va.,*
                                   who draws up to Icilia.
My pretty maiden? 'T is a bold, bad man.
Ica. Spare mention of him, and proceed.
                                   Liv. The rent,
Full five denarii, has consum'd my all.[6]
Ica. Thou shalt have money. [*Exit.*

Liv. [*to the nurse.*] 'T is a mettled maid,
Most like her brother.   But this timid child
Savors not of him.   She is scarce so near?
Nurse. Yet will be nearer soon, as dearer now.
Va. Hush, my Lucilla!   To a stranger, this ——
Liv. May yet have interest.   Thou art, well I see,
The brave Virginius' daughter, and for him,
As for Icilius, guardians of our rights,
Foes to our wrongers, may this breast beat kindly,
Though rude my speech — as oft with the unhappy.
On these auspicious nuptials, Juno Pro'nuba,
Shower down thy joys, and bless united Rome!
Shall our Icilius — he belongs to all —
Be happy soon?
                    Nurse. In two brief days from now.

Enter ICILIA.

Ica. Take these few sextants for thy present need.
Icilius, when he comes, shall give thee more. —
Behold him!

Enter ICILIUS.

Icilius. My Virginia! —— Sister! —— What!
A stranger?
Liv. [*to Ica.*] Jove the Hospitable quite you!
                                        [*hurrying out.*
Icil. Stay.   Why this haste?   My coming should not frighten
Whom my house renders grateful.   Art thou poor?
I am Icilius, and Icilius' heart

Yearns for the needy, as his weaker brethren
Whom Heaven is pleas'd to humble, but whom men
Must pity and love, or they most foully sin.
Let me look on thee.   Thou art of the people.
Why shouldst thou shroud thy face ?   Icilius' blood
Boasts not that noble taint which puffs the heart
Spite of the sepulchre ; nor has hoarded brass
Made him wealth-swollen.   So.   What! do I dream?
Thou art—— Know'st thou Virginius? Art thou dumb,
Yet tremblest?   Woman, I like not thy looks.
Yet I will not condemn thee.   Go in peace.
Icilius' house is open to the poor,
But for the vicious has no room, till empty.

Liv. Thou art Icilius.   In thy inmost heart
Rankles the pride thou spurnest in the noble.
Plume thy false feathers.   In a little while,
They will be ruffled, never more to smooth.
I see the beak that 's whetted for thy gore,
And for Virginius'! —   Take thy niggard brass,
Thou scornful maiden. [*flinging the money towards
                          Ica.*] May its scanty ounces
Weigh like a thousand pounds upon thy spirit.
To the infernal gods this house I consecrate ! [*Exit.*

Icil. Weep not, Virginia ; turn not pale, my sister.
Think ye the curses of an impious heart
Can sway high Jove, or speed the shears of fate?

Va. ⁷Alas, I weep not therefore, though my heart
Shrunk in me, quailing under her fierce eyes,
Whose gaze made cold my blood.   Icilia too,
Forgetful of her gentle spirit, spoke brief.

Ica. She pleas'd me not; and I am Lucius' sister:
  I cannot make my tongue belie my heart.
Icil. Heaven plants in us these instincts for our good.
  The dullest hound the man that likes him not
  Knows by the look; and in its nurse's arms
  The child makes like distinction, though around it
  All seem to smile and fondle it alike.
  The dog, being dumb, his vigilance retains;
  The man, no longer mute, neglects the gift;
  And oft the small voice of a passing doubt,
  Unlisten'd as irrational, recurs,
  Alas too late when echoed by regret.
  What troubles thee, Virginia?
                              Va. To this stranger
  Thou nam'dst my father, Lucius.
                              Icil. 'T was my thought
  I saw a Volscian woman thy sire knew,
  And knowing scorn'd.   What was her plea for alms?
Ica. She talk'd of hardship — beggary by her rent
  Paid Claudius, Appius' client.
                              Icil. A strange tale,
  To have so strange an ending!   Claudius! tool
  Of the deprav'd decemvir! —   What means this?
  Why look ye one to the other so confus'd?
  What should two innocent girls know of this man?
Ica. Virginia, I must speak.
                              Va. No, no! not yet!
  I do beseech thee, my Icilia, not!
Icil. Virginia, is that right?   When on thy finger
  I put this iron ring, plain like my truth,

And solid like to it, I deem'd our hearts
Were as its circle, that nor mine nor thine
Show'd where the one began, the other ended.
Why this reserve? ·

     Va. For thy sake, not for mine,
Believe me, Lucius!

     Icil. Is not Lucius fit
To be entrusted with his own protection?

Va. Ask me no more — not now. It does not rest,
Should not with me, an ignorant girl, to judge
If I may speak. Before the sun be down,
My father, sent for ——

     Icil. Sent for? Who did that?

Ica. I did, my brother. 'T was not rashly done.

Icil. Yet two days hence, Virginius would be here!
Now is it strange, that I, Virginius' friend,
Chosen by Virginius for Virginius' son,
Should have no voice to speak in an affair
Seeming so urgent for Virginius' sake!

Va. Oh! no, thou wilt not say so, when thou knowest!
Icilia, speak for me. As Lucius' spouse,
Could I do otherwise, not self-condemn'd?

Ica. Had Lucius' sister else encourag'd thee?

Icil. Forgive me. Jealous though my mind, its trust
Is boundless in your loves and matchless faith.
I will have patience. Does Virginius know?

Va. Nothing; and for like reason. I had pray'd
Thou might'st be spar'd this grievance. Now, alas!
Thou must know all; and from my father's lips
Thou shalt. O Lucius! ——

 5

Icil. Why that mournful look?
Why do those eyes so sadly fix on mine,
And swim in tears?

    Va. I know not; but my soul
Is sore disquieted; a ceaseless dread
Of ill impending, shadowy-vague, yet vast,
Weighs down my spirit. Even as I gaze,
'T seems as a mist rose like a veil between us
And shut thee from my sight, which strives in vain
To catch thy fading features. Do not leave me!
Stay by me, Lucius! [*throwing herself on his breast*
       and sobbing.

   Icil. Will I not forever?
My arms encircle thee : what shouldst thou fear?
This is some sickness that distracts the brain.
Thou hast look'd pale of late, and thy blue orbs
Are purpled underneath with heavy watching.
Why dost thou shake thy head? That untold tale!
Thou fill'st me with disquiet, and my man's-heart,
Though now thy pillow, trembles with a fear
Would mate thy own. Alas! and 't is a moment
Icilius needs his courage, for Rome's sake!

Ica. This must not be. Cheer up, Virginia, sister!
Art thou Virginius' daughter, and of Rome?

Va. I am Virginius' daughter, and a Roman :
I try, for Lucius' sake, to look less sad ;
But the weak heart will not be school'd. Bear with me ;
I shall be better soon. Thou wilt not leave me?
Not till my father comes?

    Icil. Unhappy chance!

I had —— No matter : 't is the only time
Icilius has broke faith. I will not leave thee.
No custom'd cause would move thee thus. The gods
Perhaps give warning ——
                            Va. Never, to break faith.
If thou art promis'd elsewhere, go. My love
Lives in thine honor only : to love less
Were not to love Icilius.
                            Icil. Peerless maid !
Thou leading and sustaining, virtue's height
Is no-way hard to climb. — But should he leave thee,
What heart, Virginia, could Icilius have ?
What power of judgment? Thy distress, his fears,
Doubt, and conjecture, would pursue him still,
And Rome's best interests suffer. Let me stay !
Va. Before I knew thee, Rome had all my love.
When, happy in thy suit, my indulgent sire
Would have me listen it, he bade me note,
First of thy virtues, love of Rome and freedom.
For my love's sake were 't well, Icilius, then,
To wrong that virtue which first won my love ?
Forget my passing weakness. Ere the night,
Rome's liberty shall be, even for my sake,
And for thy own, a thousand-fold more dear.
Icil. Strange riddle ! which I dare not try to read. —
Thou wilt await my coming back ?
                            Va. No, no :
Thy duties might be slighted ; and for me,
My tarrying long might make me found too slack
To meet my father.

      Icil. Now, the all-conscious gods,
Thou dear Virginia, mark thy worth and bless thee!
Thou mak'st my passion reason, that before
Was happy impulse. — On the homeward way,
Passing the Forum, I shall look to join thee:
But at thy uncle's, surely. [*Exit.*

       Ica. Why, Virginia!
Had the gate clos'd upon Icilius dead,
Thou could'st not look more blank.

        Va. 'T is all the same.
There is a weight here [*pressing her heart.*] crushes out
  my life;
And the gloom'd spirit whispers, as 't were Fate,
No torch shall light me — save unto the tomb.
Ica. Virginia! Are my brother's words so vain?
The statutes of the most high gods shall stand,
Nor hopes nor fears can alter them one jot.
Va. I know it, I feel it, and I am resign'd.
Yet, not the less, I shudder.

       Ica. And thou dost!
This must be sickness.

      Va. Oh yes, of the heart.
I would the night were, and my father come!
    ICILIA *presses her soothingly to her bosom, whereon*
     VIRGINIA *has laid her head; and, slowly,*
       the Scene changes.

Scene III.

The Via Sacra — with the Forum, having the Capitoline Hill on the left, seen in the distance, — the street winding obliquely to the right into the Forum. — The houses, on either side of the street, are scattered, low of structure, and of humble appearance, as in the earlier days of the republic.

Valerius *and* Horatius.

Val. Thou doubt'st then, Marcus, Quinctius will make one?

Hor. I know not. If thou art Valerius, I
A true Horatius, Titus has no less
The blood should love the people. Would he stand
To Appius now, as opposite as his sire
Fronted his bloody colleague of that name,
'T were much. Not every heat gives fire. Few men
Burn like Icilius. Quinctius may yield smoke.

Val. Well! so it sting our enemy's eyes, not ours.
But see! Icilius! with his wonted stride.
By Hercules! but that his field 's the Forum,
Not the trench'd camp, he frowns ⁸ a second Marcius!

Hor. Not of the senate. Coriolanus' hate
Was not so strong as is Icilius' love,
To the down-trodden commons.
                                    Val. It may be
With like extreme.
                        Hor. I think not. Yet if 't were,
Better, a thousand times, the unsparing hurricane

Of popular tumult, than the stifling calm
Of absolute power!   That, its violence spent,
May leave the air of the commonweal more pure ;
But from the dead stagnation of the other
What shall purge off its pestilent miasms,
And make it vital ?

     Val. Why, another hurricane.
And lo ! the Æolus shall loose the winds.

    Enter ICILIUS.

Thy brow is overcast.
     Icil. A passing cloud
Brought from the sky of home.   The public sun
Shall leave no speck to o'ershadow you or me.
What of the senate, friends ?
      Val. A blank account,
Or unity the total.
    Hor. Scarcely that.
We have but the half of a man, his soul being parted
'Twixt would and would not.
     Icil. That is ? ——
      Val. Titus Quinctius.
Icil. His sire was lov'd of the soldiers.
      Hor. But the son
Will never be lov'd of any — save his heir.
He comes ! and —— How is this ?   Who is that
  beside him ?
Val. Aulus Lucretius.
     Hor. Is he mad ? or dares

The hound betray us, thinking we are so?

Icil. Neither, or either.   Either is all one.

We are no dark conspirators, though sworn
For the public good.   What do we, that we do
In the light of day, as now: else were Icilius
None of your league.

Enter

TITUS QUINCTIUS *with* AULUS LUCRETIUS.

        Be welcome, Titus Quinctius.
Thou knowest why we are met, and com'st resolv'd
To aid us, head and hand.   But this, thy friend,
Aulus Lucretius? ——

            Lucr. Is alike resolv'd.

Icil. I am Icilius, and I hold the people
The sole legitimate source of sovereign rule,
For that they are the many, and their thews
Strain to heave up, to prop and keep sustain'd,
The edifice whose chambers ye but fill.
Were Appius not your master as our tyrant,
My hate to your cruel order were not less,
And, the decemvirate overthrown, Icilius
Steps on its carcase, to do battle still
For freedom and the people's rights.   Thou hearest: —
These are my motives.   What are thine?

                Lucr. I am

Lucretius, and the common folk of Rome
I have in hatred less than in disdain.
But is there eye so blear'd that sees not Appius

Striding to sovereign rule across our necks?
He cring'd to the people, and they set him o'er them.
He trod them down. He cringes now to us.
And Rome beholds the guardians of her state
Become mere servitors to the usurping Ten,
Whose plural tyranny even now is merging
Into the singular rule of this bold man.
I love my order, and will let no Tarquin
Level its pillars to rear himself a throne.
These are my motives.

    Icil. And they please me little;
As does thy purpled tunic, which they suit.
But thou dost much; for thou 'rt a man; thy tongue
Fears not to utter what thy soul dares think.
Aulus, there is my hand.

     Hor. And mine.

      Val. And mine.

Icil. Thou seëst, Quinctius: not alone the commons,
But thine own order smarts beneath the yoke.
Hast thou not heard of Tarquin, nam'd the Proud?
What did he to the Fathers? Slept the axes
Then in the fasces? Let your house-gods tell.
War, peace, state-treaties, then no more were made
By council and allowance of the senate:
The State was Tarquin. Now, there reign ten Tarquins,
Girt with their twenty and a hundred axes,
Which soon will pale but one, and ported bare: [9]
Meet emblem of a spirit as haught and bloody
As that his prototype's, whose chariot-wheels
Crash'd through the butcher'd trunk of his wife's sire,

And made the street *Accursed* to this day! [10]
Quinc. Why speak so loud?

     Icil. Because I would be heard.
Why ask not too why stand we here i' the street,
When a house-wall would shield us from the air,
And treason? Fear'st thou Appius?

     Quinc. No; I fear
The unripeness of this complot. Should the people
Gather around us ——

     Icil. They would spare me trouble:
I go to gather them. Should the tyrants come ——
Quinc. Lo, Oppius now!

     Icil. Well: let him pass. What hinders?

   Enter SPURIUS OPPIUS,

*preceded by his twelve lictors, marching in file, one by one,
  with the fasces shouldered.*
As they pass before the five, going up the street, QUINCTIUS *gives
way, and seems about to go, while* ICILIUS *and the rest maintain their ground,* ICILIUS *talking as they pass.*

Aulus Lucretius, seest thou these fellows?
Now is it not a shame, that thou and I,
Valerius and Horatius, and all true men,
Whose blood boils at such insolent parade,
Should stand by quiet, when a private man,
Of no more right than ourselves, dares ape the king
Even in our faces?

   Spur. Thou talkest big, Icilius.
 Icil. Not bigger, Oppius, than I feel, or look,
 5*

Or mean to approve myself in act, some time.

Spur. That we shall see — some time.   Move, lictors, on !

               [*Exit, the procession, up the scene.*

Hor. Thou hast scar'd the heart out, of our Quinctius,
    Lucius.

Quinc. Perhaps not, Marcus: but, I thank Minerva,
    'T is not so choleric as to choke my wit.

Hor. Thy wit having never life, that were not easy.

Quinc. And let me ask Icilius, is it wise
    To taunt the enemy ere our battle 's order'd ?

Icil. Our forces need not, nor would suffer order :
    'T is here the people, and abroad the soldiers.
    We leaders give the signal, and set on,
    And the mass follow as their passions dictate.
    Ours is no plot: was ever such with thousands?
    Nor would such suit me : but the Ten have theirs,
    Secret and sworn.

            Quinc. A plot?

                Lucr. With what intent ?

Val. To make their power perpetual, set aside
    The holding of elections, and destroy,
    At least in part, the senate.

               Lucr. Know'st thou this?

By honor's god ! there 're some that sit i' the House,
Will not be tamely butcher'd.   Who assist them?

Val. Some of the younger nobles, vicious friends,
    Or followers more, of Appius.

         [*Here* QUINCTIUS, *looking down the street, steals
             off in the direction of the Forum.*

Hor. Come with us:
This is no street-talk, and thou shalt hear that
Will make thee certain, while Icilius goes
To fire the people.

       Lucr. Where is Quinctius?

               Val. Look!

           [pointing down the street.

Hor. What, Appius coming! I forgive him then.

Lucr. Still, thou mayst trust him.

          Hor. True — for passive aid.

       Enter,

in the same order as Oppius, APPIUS CLAUDIUS, — *the 1st Lictor holding, besides his fasces, a rod to clear the way.*

At a little distance from the decemvir, and aside, MARCUS CLAUDIUS, *his client.*

ICILIUS, *as before, keeps his place unmoved.*

1st Lict. Way! way, for the great decemvir! — Stand aside!

        [offering to touch Icil. with the rod.

Icil. Aside! thou insolent slave! Aside! To whom?
Is it to thee, [*striding deliberately up to Appius, who,
in turn, moves a step towards him.*
usurper of a charge
By law expired? Icilius bows to law,
Not to law-breakers, and gives place to no man,
Save whom the sovereign people set above him.

Enter
two or more CITIZENS, *in their tunics.*[11]

1st Cit. Worthy Icilius!
      2d Cit. Out upon the tyrant!
App. Hot-headed fool! Must I bid strip the rods,
To scourge thee hence?
    Icil. [*rushing on him.*] Now, by! ——

VALERIUS, HORATIUS, *and* LUCRETIUS *spring between the two,*
and at the same time keep off the lictors.

            Val. Quirites! freemen! ⎫
Help your Icilius!   ⎪
    Hor. Break the fasces!   ⎬ *Speaking together.*
       Lucr. Appius,   ⎪
Go on your way, or! ——   ⎭
      App. Lictors, do your duty.
Beat back the rabble. Seize, bind, the ——
       Marc. El. Noble patron!
This word. [*whispers a moment.*
    App. O brave! — Forbear we once. Peace, all.
Icilius, I shall take a fitter time
To punish thy presumption: the tribunal
Waits now my sitting. Aulus, as for thee,
Thou knowest me now thy foe.
       Lucr. And such, defy thee.
App. Move on! [*to the lictors.*] I yield — to triumph.
      [*giving way to Icil. and smiling on him as he*
          passes, — Icil. standing still.

Exit, the procession, up the scene.

MARCUS, *loitering behind, stops in the background at a signal
from* LIVIA, *who, in the disguise of Scene II., enters as*
ICILIUS *turns to the Citizens.* LIVIA *goes up
to* MARCUS, *and they whisper.*

        Icil. Citizens,
Put on your mantles, gather your friends, the friends
Of law and liberty. On to the Forum. There
Wait me, but peaceful.
     2d Cit. Peaceful! No; but quiet.
           [*Exeunt Citiz.*
Icil. [*to Valer.*, etc.
  Brave friends! true senators! [*Sees Livia walking off
with Marcus, and looking back at Icil. significantly,
as they confer in whispers.*] Ah! — What means
that?
Val. The cloud again, Icilius?
       Icil. Ay, I fear
Its shadow this time threatens rain. Dost know
That woman?
    Val. No; but he that whispers her
Is Appius' filthy pander. We may guess.
Icil. [*to himself.*] No — no — no — no. O let me not
think that!
Val. [*softly.*] Let us away.
     Hor. [*same.*] 'T is strange! What can it
        mean?

Lucr. [*same.*] Is he so often?

      Val. Never so before.

He met us sadly. But the gloom was brief.

Icil. [*to himself.*] Horrid suggestion!

        Lucr. 'T is not fit we stay.

    [*Exeunt, quietly, the three senators.*

Icil. Was this thy dark foreboding, poor Virginia? —

But the dread arrow shall have other mark!

Help, ye avenging Furies! [*moving rapidly up the*

    scene.] — I am mad. [*coming back*

       slowly.

On mere suspicion! — Appius would not dare,

So plac'd, so hated : daring, what his means?

No, no! 't is but a fancy, — yet a fancy

So horrid-torturing, my tough heart cracks,

And my brain seems unsettled. — My Virginia!

    The drop falls.

Act the Second

Scene I.   The Forum.

*In front, at the upper part of the scene, the tribunal, with the
curule chair.   On the right [left of spectators], a row of
seven shops under a portico, and, between the shops and the
tribunal, the statue of Venus Cloacina.*[a]*—   On the left,
Citizens move about, or converse in groups. —   Lictors
ranged on either side of the tribunal.*

Appius *and* Marcus.

App.   Two days, sayst thou?   It must not, shall not be,
　　Even if I touch his life!   But that were rash.
　　Marcus, thy plan.   Give 't instant execution.
　　Is the hag ready?
　　　　　　　Marc. Always.   And the time
　　Seems opportune.   Her sire at the camp, Virginia
　　Dwells with her uncle, and her way now home
　　Crosses the Forum.   But she may not come.
App.   Why dost thou dash my hopes?
　　　　　　　　　Marc. Because, dread patron,
　　Livia's detection must alarm the maid,
　　May keep her hous'd.
　　　　　　　App. Besiege the door.
　　　　　　　　　Marc. A violence
　　So bold might startle even thy subject Rome.
　　This would I say : in case the girl come not,

Virginius must be stay'd, to give us time.

App. Or if she come. Well thought! Till I have tam'd
This bird to her perch, and taught her know my call.
Thy tablets — quick! and style. [*Marcus takes them
from the lap of his mantle, and Appius
writes rapidly one or two lines.*
See that my messenger,
My speediest, carries this in all haste to Algidum.
Thou 'lt see to whom. And bid him shun Virginius.

Marc. Were 't not best, first transcribe it on a leaf?

App. No, waste no time. Thou think'st they be alarm'd.
They might then get before us. Haste thou back.
Revenge has given new edge to my desire.
[*Exit* MARCUS.
But what will come of it? Have I thought that well?
To achieve this loathing maid, what do I hazard?
The crown I 'd clutch, whose visionary round
Burns on my temples nightly. What if more?
The father's virtues, and the popular name
Of the affianc'd lover, may rouse this Rome
Which I have drugg'd to so deep slumber; and then! ——
I see — O horror! 't is the new Lucretia,
Dead in her father's arms! the bloody knife,
Smoking and dripping, lifted! Brutus calls,
With arms spread out, upon the gods of Hell!
Was that crash thunder? 'T is the o'erthrown tri-
bunal —
Lictors and fasces trampled down together!
The rabble like a pack of wolves rush on me!
How their throats yell! I hear their panting! nearer —

Nearer! Their hot breath scorches! Help! oh, help!
> [*aloud, and running.*

'T is nothing, men: I did but clear my throat.
> [*The lictors, who had advanced to him at*
> *his cry, resume their station.*

A horrid dream! But this, the Forum [*looking around*
> *him with a shudder.*] — sunlight:

I am awake, and still decemvir, still
Decemvir paramount! — and will be — more.
Yet, oh! — Virginia! [*with a degree of softness.*
> —— Oppius spoke too true:

Marcius' soft spot spreads over all my heart.
Why did I make that law ? what is plebeian,
That flesh patrician may not mate therewith ?[1][2]
Sprung from Lavinia's self, in line direct,
This maid were not more precious. — I will do it!
Will break the law! will wed her! But will she ——
Icilius —— Death and Hell! —— Off, lying visions!
Though Heaven should rain down blood, I will not yield!
> [*Turns up the Scene,*
> *which shifts suddenly.*

SCENE II.

Another part of the Forum.

ICILIUS *and* NUMITORIUS *meeting.*

Icil. Publius Numitorius! — Thou art well met!
What brings thee to the Forum?

                    Num. Natural care.
I seek my sister's child. — But thou look'st ruffled!

Icil. And thou o'er-sad. 'T is like we have one cause.
For I too seek Virginia. Why shouldst thou,
With so unusual care, her nurse being with her,
Forsake thy house — Virginius too expected?

Num. Thou know'st that then! Canst thou say why
      expected?

Icil. Would that I could! And yet the bare conjecture
Makes my blood curdle. Why are Rome's free streets
No longer safe for virgins? Asking that,
Do I show why Virginius might be look'd for?
Why I am ruffled, and thou over-sad?
Does thy heart, Publius, freeze and boil at once,
As mine does, at the sound of one man's name
Coupled with pure Virginia's?

                   Num. And that name?
'T is? ——

  Icil. Appius. Speak!

              Num. It does. What dost thou know?

Icil. Nothing. Thou? what dost thou? Protecting gods!
Who from your favor'd Capitol look down

On prostrate Rome, Pena'tes of her state!
Jove the all-great, all-good! thou sovereign Juno!
Armipotent Minerva! if once more
Your shrines shall beam on freemen new-create,
Exact not like atonement!   Let not blood
Bedrop this time the white fleece of the lamb!
Num. Thou mak'st me shudder.

           Icil. 'T is my own heart's echo.
Seest not I shiver?

       Num. Yet thou knowest nought:
Nor I.   Be calmer.

         Icil. Thou didst ask the name.
Said I not — Appius?   Wherefore art thou here?
Why should we both fear outrage for Virginia?
Num. Yet neither may have ground.   What thou hast heard,
What seen, I know not.   When thy brother, Quintus,
Came for my son to journey to the camp ——
Icil. They told me not of that!   Say on!   Say on!
Num. The boy could nothing tell.   But from his haste, —
The sudden need, — from strange, mysterious looks
And hints of the nurse, — from —— What is that?

      Nurse. [*within, from the side.*] Help! Romans!
'T is Virginius' daughter!

          Num. [*hurrying after Icilius, who,
at the first sound, has sprung forward in the direction of it.*]   Gods! we are too late.[13]

            [*Scene shifts suddenly to
Scene 3.*

Scene III.

Same as Scene I. of the Act. — Appius *is seated on the tribunal, girt by his lictors. Near the shops,* Virginia *and her* Nurse, *struggling with* Marcus Claudius. *The People, who are now mixed with one or two Women, making towards them.*

Nurse. Romans, 't is false! She is the promis'd spouse
   Of your Icilius.

                    1*st Cit.* Cneius, hear'st thou that? [*to 2d Cit.*
Unhand the girl. [*to Marcus.*] Thou art known.

                              2*d Cit.* For Appius' pimp.
   Tread down the dog!

                    Marc. She is my slave — Come on —
                              [*dragging Virginia.*
   Born of my slave.

                    Enter Icilius *and* Numitorius.

A shout from the crowd. Icilius!

                    2*d Cit.* [*as Icilius, still without
   speaking, hurls Marcus across the scene.*

                              That is it!
   Brave Roman!

                    Va. Lucius, must it all come true?

Icil. Think better of the gods, Virginia. Cheer thee.
   None can molest thee, now. Come home. Behold!
   Here is thine uncle, and thy husband's arm

Is folded round thee.

    A Matron. Husband!   Hear, Drusilla!
Shame on the coward!

      Icil. [*moving with Va. through the*
    throng.] Thanks, kind friends.

         Marc. Icilius,
What means this violence?   Open, if thou wilt,
Thine eyes still wider, and bite through thy lips;
Thou canst not stare me from my rights, nor frighten.
Num. Thy rights?

    Icil. Let him speak on.

       Marc. My rights: the right
Of every Roman citizen to his own goods.
The girl's my house-ware. [*extending his arm to take Va.*

     Icil. Liar and slave! [*striking him*
    — *his left arm still around Virginia.*

        Take that!
Tool of a tyrant's lust! stretch thou one finger
To touch this virgin, I tread thee into clay,
And hurl the carrion on thy master's throne
To make his footstool!— Come, Virginia, come.
Marc. Not yet. Nor words, nor blows, make null my rights.

     [*making a sign to Appius, who*
       sends forward two lictors.

I appeal to the tribunal.   Come.

     Icil. Go then,
Virginia, with thy uncle.   I must stay,
And front the tyrant.

     Marc. No! the girl goes not.
Lictors!

1st Lic. Back, citizens! — What means this clamor?
Who breaks the public peace?

       Marc. I claim my slave. ——

Icil. Thou foul-mouth'd villain! — Romans! freemen!
  brothers!
Ye know me; I have never spoken false.
This is Virginius' daughter; on her finger
This ring I gave her speaks Icilius' spouse.
She has no mother, now; for you, her sire
Offers his bosom to your enemies' knives.
Ye will not suffer that a maid so lone,
So unprotected, one whose boast it is
She is made of clay like yours, plebeian mould [14] ——

       [The people murmur.

Marc. Lictors, your office! Let him not speak treason.
2d Cit. Treason, to be of the people! Hear him out.
 Finish, Icilius.

     Icil. You are not so abject,
As let this maid, whose cradle was as yours,
Your daughter, and your sister, orphan'd too,
Because her sire defends your household-gods
And her poor mother wanders with the bless'd,
Happy to know not this! you will not suffer
Icilius' promised spouse, Virginius' child,
Blood of your blood, and freeborn as are you,
You will not suffer her to be torn from 'midst you,
To serve the lust of a patrician!

      2d Cit. No!

Down with the lictors!

     Marc. Citizens, are you mad?

I ask but for a hearing. If my claim
Be baseless, let him take the girl.
          1st Cit. 'T is just.
Let him have hearing.
          Icil. Just! O fickle hearts!
Is 't just the claimant should himself be judge?
Know ye not ——
      Num. Lucius, thou wilt ruin all.
Hope in Virginius' coming, hope not now.
See [*glancing round on the people.*], and believe
   resistance is in vain.
Icil. Lead on. And yet — I did put trust in you.
             [*addressing the throng.*
I thought —— No matter. [*They move up to the tri-
          bunal followed by the crowd.*
      1st Cit. What could he expect?
The Matron. Were I a man, thou shouldst not want reply.
Marc. Mighty decemvir! this young ——
          Icil. Have a care!
If thou dare touch her, though it be the form,[15]
Even in thy master's face I keep my word.
App. Now by the manès[16] of my sires, thou vile! ——
          [*springing up in his seat.*
Marc. Hear, gracious ruler! let me wave the form.
I would not have the whiteness of my claim
Spotted by violence. —
      App. Then for thy sake, be't,
Not his.
    Icil. For thine own sake, thou! ——
          Va. Lucius! pity!

For me! for me!   Wouldst thou destroy me?

                Num. Appius,

I am the uncle of this maid: 't is mine

To answer.   Let the Assertor now proceed.

Marc. This maiden, as the Roman law prescribes,

    I say is mine, and the possession in her

    Demand to be assign'd to me.

                Num. And I,

By the same law assert her to be free,

And as her guardian, in the father's room,

Demand the right to lead her where I will.[17]

App. Let the assertor unto servitude

    Make out his claim.

           Marc. Virginius Lucius, sire

Suppos'd of this young maid, being in the wars,

A child was born to him in Rome, which died

Soon as it snuff'd the air.   The selfsame day,

A Volscian girl, my household-slave, gave birth

To a female child, which promis'd well.   Her sister,

Midwife to both the women, mov'd to see

The mother weep her young thus born to chains,

Herself too sorrowing, plac'd the living babe

On the free pillow, and took away the dead.

Behold the false Virginia! for the true

Is dust.

    Icil. Is there a Heaven above us?

                Num. Lucius! ——

Leave me to answer.— See! Virginia faints!

App. The case is plain.   What hast thou to reply?

Num. Did the false mother come, in after time,

To know of this strange fraud?

          Marc. Not till the child,
Grown up in worth and beauty, had won her heart.

Num. Nor told Virginius?

          Marc. Why disturb his peace?
He had come to love the darling as his own.
'T is thought, however, in her dying hour
The truth came out. This we shall ascertain.

Num. And by the midwife and the mother-slave
Thou hop'st to prove this?

          Marc. And Virginius' self.

Num. O monstrous fraud! effrontery unmatch'd!
Hear, Appius; hear, ye citizens! I am
Twin-brother of Virginius' wife, had ever
Her most full confidence; yet see! her heart
Kept this huge fact from me!

          App. And is that all?

Num. Much to make wise men doubt. Hear, Romans, hear!
This man would cite the midwife, therefore living,
A Volscian, and the sister of a slave.
Known is it to me, to many — and there stands
Virginia's nurse who knows — the midwife was
A Roman, and is dead!

          App. And is that all?

Icil. What wouldst thou more? [*resigning Va. to Numit.*

          App. No evidence of thine. —
Let the pretended sire appear.

          Marc. Till then
Possession in the girl remains with me.

6

App. That is but just.   Assertor, take thy slave.
                                [*General murmur of indignation.*

Icil. Thou dar'st not! by thine own law, dar'st not, tyrant,
   Decree this wrong!   Decision must be made,
   In such a suit, on the side of freedom.
                                   1*st Cit.* Right!
   It is the law.
           2*d Cit.* He made it: let him keep it!

App. What know ye of the law, ye clamorous curs?
   That Appius made it, proves that Appius leans
   To liberty and mercy.   But this case
   Was not provided for.   The general act
   Supposes equal litigants.   Where such,
   Who stands for actual owner matters little;
   But here it being the father of the girl,
   So call'd, the Assertor yields to only him.
   Pledg'd to produce her when he shall appear,
   'T is fit he keep her now. — It is decreed.
   Lictor, disperse the assembly.
               Va. [*running to Icil.*] Save me! save!
   Or kill me, Lucius!
               Matron. Cowards! do you hear her?

Num. [*thrusting back Marcus, while Icilius, clasping Vir-
       ginia with his left arm, covered with his mantle
       (toga), confronts Appius, and waves back with his
       right the lictors.*

Virginius' daughter! who is now abroad,
Fighting your battles! [*to the people.*
               1*st Cit.* The decemvir knows it.

Lictors. [*opposing their fasces.*
          Decreed!
                    Matron. Where are your daughters? [*again to
                              the people.*] *2d Cit.* Are we slaves?
Down with the lictors!
                    Lict. Back!
                    Matron. O shame!
                              Lict. Bear back!
"It is decreed!" [*The people yield, though sullenly,
                    leaving Icilius, etc., exposed.*
          Icil. I knew it. When the judge
And claimant are one, what else? Do ye see that wretch?
'T is Marcus, Appius' client; what besides,
I shame, before this innocent maid, to speak.
Ye murmur. Well ye may, knowing what I mean.
Is 't fit she should be trusted to such hands,
Were Appius even guiltless? I had thought
That honor was more dear to Roman women
Than life ——
          Matron. It is! but Roman men are cowards.
Icil. — That reverence for Lucretia could not die.
                    [*Movement in the crowd.*
Lucretia! 'T is a name ——
                    Matron. Blush, Romans!
                    [*Movement becomes more tumultuous.*
                              App. Lictors! ——
2d Cit. No! he shall finish; we will hear him out.
          [*The crowd press on the lictors and force them back.*
Icil. [*turning to the tribunal.*] Lucretia! At that name,
          thou vile decemvir,

Dost thou not tremble? Usurper like to Tarquin,
Recall his fate! But Collatinus paid
A price I will not; nor shall Rome's proud annals
Tell of a second sorrow like to his,
Though they record like vengeance. Speak, Lucilla!

         [to the nurse.

This is no time for secrets. What thou knowest,
Give 't to the people.

    Matron. Speak!

       2d Cit. We will protect thee.

App. [*thundering to the lictors.*] Ye dogs! what are ye
  kept for! Strip the fasces!
Scourge back the rabble!

       2d Cit. Death to the lictors! death!

  The crowd struggle for the possession of the fasces.
Numitorius, *threatening* M. Claudius, *stands before* Virginia,
 while the Nurse *supports her behind —* Icilius *still*
    sustaining her.

App. Arrest the rebel! Seize, bind, slay Icilius! [18]
Marcus, secure the slave!

    Icil. On, Romans, on!

  He dashes back Marc. Claudius *violently, consigns*
  Virginia *to* Numitor., *and, putting aside the*
    lictors, makes directly for the tribunal.

Strike for your freedom! Twelve, against you all?
Trample them under you! Leave to me the tyrant.

App. To the tribunal, lictors! guard the office. [*The lictors*
 retreat and form between the tribunal and Icilius.

Citizens! Appius wars not upon you! [*The citizens re-*
main motionless, and Icil. stands once more exposed.
                                        Why, so!
Have ye forgot your reason? Know ye not
The ambition of Icilius? Not for her,
Ill-fated girl! this tumult. 'T is sedition,
Veil'd with the pretext of Virginius' cause.
He would be tribune, and to found his power
Make odious the decemvirate. But the people
Shall judge between us. To Virginius absent,
To liberty, to the paternal name,
Yields Appius what your violence nor his
Should wrest, entreats the Assertor wave his right,
And, the decree revok'd, prorogues the trial.
                        [*Murmur of applause.*
Silence! Icilius needs your tongues, not I. —
Once more to-day will Appius sit in justice,
But, the sun down, Virginius not appearing,
He gives the law its course, nor will he need
To enforce it more than these. [*pointing to the lictors.*
                1st Cit. So soon;
Virginius cannot come!
                2d Cit. He knows that well.
Icil. He thinks it, friends; but let the tyrant learn,
To his confusion, Virginius even now
Is on his way. [*A movement of great joy.*
        Num. My son, that was not wise.
See where the pander and his lord change looks!
Marc. Be 't, great decemvir; Claudius asks but justice.
But who are surety that the girl appear? ' ⁹

Enter

VALERIUS *and* HORATIUS.

Val. Lucius Valerius.   { *from behind the people, who*
      Hor. And Horatius, I!   { *make way for them, with*
                                { *demonstrations of joy.*

People. And I!

[*holding up their*   And I!

right hands simultaneously.]   And all of us!

      VALERIUS *and* HORATIUS, *going up the scene, confront*
            the decemvir a moment, then turn to
                  ICILIUS, *and his party.*

                              Val. [*to Icil.*] We have heard

Thy sad misfortune.   But [*in undertone and signifi-*
                              cantly] we came too late.

Hor. [*like manner.*] Hope.

      Icil. [*to the people.*] Thanks! but now, we shall not
      need you, friends.

Impute to nothing mean these passionate tears:

'T is your love moves me — mingled with despair —

Despair for liberty, when one man's power

Can make a thousand offer me but love.

Go to your homes.   Wo, wo, for fetter'd Rome!

For Brutus's Rome! wo! wo! [*Exit* (*muffling his*
                  head) *with Virginia, Numit. and Nurse —*
                        the Matrons following them.

The remaining Citizens move forward, and form a close group,
      which VALER. *and* HORAT., *after seeing Icilius' party off*
            the Scene, join — while MARC. CLAUD., *ascending*
                  behind the tribunal, is seen receiving in his
                        ear some secret instructions from APPIUS.

> 2d *Cit.* It is a shame!

We are bound to assist him.

> 1st *Cit.* But what can we do?

Val. [*in a low, impressive tone.*] Meet here again as many
    as you can,
Before the trial. Icilius will harangue you.
Then shall you learn what for yourselves to do,
As well as him. Nor shall you want, to back you,
Friends such as we.

> *Hor.* [*same manner.*] And should you chance to bring
Arms hid about you, 't will not be amiss.
Hush! not a word! Away, at once!

> *Val.* Remember!

'T is the last chance for liberty and Rome.

> [*Exeunt the people.*

VAL. *and* HORAT., *looking at the decemvir and* MARCUS *a
moment, pass slowly up the scene, and Exeunt.—*
MARCUS *descends, and comes forward.*

Marc. [*in low tone.*] Murder already! Yet the knife may
    glance,
And hit its owner. Wo then unto me!
Who dare not flinch, yet tremble to obey. [*Exit.*

App. Waits no one more for justice? Lictors, move.

> [*Rises, and, as he turns to descend, the*

Drop falls. [20]

Act the Third

Scene I. *A mean apartment in the house of Livia.*

Marcus Claudius.   Livia.

[*Marcus just entering.*]

Liv. What has detain'd thee?
                  Marc. Has revenge grown cool?
Liv. Cool! If the damn'd feel half the pangs, that here,
                    [*pressing her heart.*
And here [*her head.*], consume me, since the sun arose
To light my day of vengeance, then the gods
Indeed are cruel. Think'st thou there be Furies?
Marc. 'T were best not ask me.[21] [*carelessly.*
              Liv. Oh! there must be such!
There must! I feel it. My temples are on fire,
Sear'd with their torches, and around my heart
Their cold snakes coiling sting me to the core.
'T was my long agony ask'd, What detain'd thee.
Marc. As thy pains balance, head for heart, thou need'st
No comfort. What I have to tell, may cool
Perhaps thy head, or salve thy heart, or be,
For aught I know, the scourge, that was forgotten
In thy sweet list of ecstacies. My Livia,
Thou 'rt very cunning; but the virgin dup'd thee,
With her two days. Her sire is coming now.

Liv. Thou dost not think it! thou sayst it but to plague
me!

Coming! Then fall the sure threads of my warp!

Marc. Of Appius', say; for he alone is weaver.

Thine! thou dost little more than hand the wool.

But hast thou lost thy question, What detain'd me?

Liv. I care not now. What 's thy delay to me?

Marc. Much, if 't was made to gather up those threads
That now were dropp'd.

     Liv. By what means?

    Marc. [*in her ear, but loudly.*] Murder.

        Liv. Murder!

Oh, no! — [*Recovering; and eagerly.*
  But of Icilius?

    Marc. Would it were!

My qualms were few then; for my bones are sore.

Liv. Not — not Virginius? Do not nod! speak! speak!

Marc. Whom else? Why, how thou look'st! Virginius
spurn'd thee,
As if thou wert a toad.

    Liv. He did! he did!

May his heart rot for it, inch by inch! But — but —
I would not have him dead —— No, no! no murder!
Not that I love him —— But he shall not die!
I am not yet so bad —— No, no! no murder!
Oh! no, no, Marcus! no!

    Marc. Thou art very strange!

Thou 'dst have his heart rot, yet he shall not die!
He must have wondrous insides.

    Liv. Do not mock me!

6*

Is it not I that am the cause of all?
I made thee note the daughter's beauty; [22] coming
The girl was from her school; and at my hint
Thou spak'st to Appius, set his blood on fire,
And now —— Virginius shall not die! His life:
Or the plot withers: — I'll reveal it all!

Marc. And have thy carcase flung from the Tarpeian.
Thou foolish woman! hear. By Appius' order,
I have hired three villains to assault this man,
On his way home. 'T is but a chance they meet him,
A chance that they prevail ——

     . *Liv.* But if they do,
I will denounce thy patron to the people.
By all the gods in Heaven and Hell, I'll do it!

Marc. Wilt thou! I will not die alone. The people,
Taught what thou art, shall tear thee limb from limb. —
What demon loos'd my tongue? and to a woman!
But who had dream'd, that love? ——

     Liv. Love! canst thou mean
Love for Virginius? Love? More deadly hate
Never felt woman. I would kill his pride,
Torture him piecemeal where he tortur'd me,
. But not kill *him.* Canst thou not see a difference?

Marc. A vast one. Thou wouldst murder inch by inch,
A little every day; with one blow, Appius
Takes all of his enjoyment all at once. ——
Wilt thou appear when call'd, and do thy part?

Liv. I will appear when call'd, and do my part —
As lives or dies Virginius. Thou shalt see. [*Going.*

Marc. See that we tools, that carve the master's pleasure,

Shall break our edges, and be thrown away. —

[*Exit Livia.*

Torture his pride! and piecemeal! This is conscience!
Make him supremely wretched — but no blood!
Furies? There may be, or may not; but this
Is sure; who made them female, knew what hands
Might be entrusted with the whips of Hell.[23]

[*Exit — but at opposite side.*

Scene II.

Room in the house of Numitorius.

Icilius *and* Virginia.

Virginia *is seen leaning on* Icilius' *shoulder, her face hidden,
in an attitude of distress.*

Icil. Gods, is this equity? Must your thunder singe
Alike the delicate shrub and branching tree?
I may not, and I have no thought nor will
To impeach your justice; in this mortal heart,
Frail and infirm of purpose, if ye have planted

Immutable love of truth, your deathless essence,
Temptation-proof and unassail'd by fear,
Cannot see right and wrong with equal eye:
Yet spare this innocent child! she is too young
To bide those trials, which o'er maturer hearts,
Grown callous with the storms of many years,
Sweep without ruin, and but make them strong.
O, it is hard!

Va. [*looking up with surprise.*] Dear Lucius! Do not
    weep!

Icil. Twice in one day these eyes! — I thought them stone
To any private grief: but now their dew
Drips over, spite of manhood.

                        Va. Is there, then,
No hope? none?

               Icil. Hope? It was Horatius' word.
Oh! that there were ten men in all the people
Like him and like Valerius, worthy both
Of their immortal names! Rome yet might breathe
And shake this nightmare from her. Death! to think
Men should have heads and hands, yet fear to use them!
Be born erect, yet crouch like cattle! Are there
No Romans left?

             Va. Virginius is, my father.

Icil. Yes, yes, they are all at camp. The air
Of Rome is pestilence to Roman virtue.
But we will not despair; no, my Virginia!
'T were sin to doubt high Heaven.

                Va. Yet — if my heart —

Have boded true — and no help is in man —
Lucius — wilt — wilt thou —— Promise me — O
        swear it!
Thou wilt not let Virginia fall alive
Into those wicked hands!   O swear it, Lucius!
Swear that thy own dear hand shall send me pure
Unto my mother!   Why art thou so still?
Thou dost not doubt my firmness?

                    Icil. Doubt it? No!
No; I was mute with adoration; faltering,
Because — because —— How can I else but falter?
I cannot think — 't would drive me to despair!
Thy bodements true.   We have done nothing, thou
In thy most innocent heart couldst not conceive
The thought of any thing, should bring down on us,
On thee this horrible fate.

                    Va. Thou must not murmur.
To the high gods man's individual wo   •
Counts nothing, weigh'd with the common good of all.
When we were children, thou knowest, the parent's
        rule
Seem'd often tyranny, and our transient pains
Cruel, because we saw not, and seeing could not .
Rightly discern, the aim of their infliction.
Are we not, Lucius, to the omniscient gods
As little children, and our moans and murmuring
Proofs that we are well car'd for?   Thou wast born
Not of the kind to whom life brings but pleasure,
And thy great soul, thus crucified to joy,

May from its agony gain gigantic strength
For Rome's deliverance.

    Icil. Speak on! speak ever!
Not for my glory, but for thine: speak on!
Va. Nay, I am feeble, Lucius, and unapt;
 But I am Roman; and in my woman's-breast
 A voice from Heaven cries, Murmur not, — thy blood
 Shall fertilize the soil of Roman freedom,
 And seed there sown shall yield perennial fruit,
 Justice and wisdom, honor, single truth,
 Temperance and valor, and other goodly growth
 Of the tree whose smallest leaves send up to Heaven
 Ambrosial odors.

    Icil. And couldst thou, Virginia,
 Offer thy life new-garlanded with love,
 And wreath'd with fillets of all human joys
 That wait on innocent youth, thou good, thou fair,
 Dear to thy widow'd father, and — for me —
 O how to speak thee! Couldst thou — die, Virginia,
 Slaughter'd to free a most unthankful people,
 Whose hearts, ere yet the sacrificial fire
 Has dried thy —— Speak! for I can not.

    Va. Whose hearts
. Will lose all trace of me? — Is duty measur'd
 By what it earns of gratitude? Believe me,
 Dear as my life is, dearer now than ever
 For thy dear sake, I will not struggle once,
 If Rome demand the victim, and thy hand ——
 Swear thou wilt do it, Lucius!

    Icil. I do swear.

As I would shed my own, my mother's blood,
So she were living, and the good of Rome
Call'd for the sacrifice.   Icilius' word
Should need no oath ; yet thou, beloved, I see it,
Mistrusts him for his love's sake.   Yet to him
What wouldst thou be, wert thou no more Virginia?
No! thou true daughter of the olden Rome,
Not of the Rome of now ! if thou must die,
Thus, in the yet shut flower of thy youth,
I ——· (I have less strength than thou!) — if thou
      must die,
For Rome, thy mother, thou shalt die, I swear it,
Worthy of her!

        Va. 'T is to die thy spouse,
To die unstain'd, and fearless — and die happy,
So my last breath be gather'd by thy lips.

Icil. Thou shalt not die! Rome is not grown so heartless!
Fathers and husbands are not so insensate !
Their arms must strike for me and for Virginius !
Our cause is one.   Then, have we not our friends,
Valerius and Horatius, and their friends
Who are foes to Appius?   Is the tyrant proof
To what kills other men?   Oh! we are mad !
We libel our fellows and asperse the gods,
Desponding thus.   Thou shalt not die, Virginia !
Blood shall be shed, and for the good of Rome,
But on the altars of the god of Hell,
And the black gore drip downwards!   Come, Virginia,
Seek we the hall.   There by thy uncle's hearth,
Whose tutelar-gods thy mother's childhood know,[24]

Await with him thy sire, while, now in hope,
I speed to rouse the ashes of dead Rome.
Let the black shadow from my heart now passing
Be better augury, and thy own grim omens
Vanish like dreams.

               Va. Dreams!   But thy vow remember.
                              [*Exeunt.*

Scene III.

A room in a diversorium, *or road-side inn, near Rome.*

Virginius, Quintus Icilius, Caius Numitorius.

Virg. Enough of rest.   Let us make onward, boys.
                   [*draws his hood* [25] *over his head.*
Yet my heart trembles, as I near the town.
My daughter! my Virginia! —   Who is that?
C. Num. Uncle, a slave of Appius the decemvir's,
    His messenger.   How hot the fellow looks!
  Q. Icil. Some pressing matter.
                     Virg. With some wicked view.

C. Num. He sees and shuns us.
> *Virg.* 'T is a wonder, that.
His master's slave should not have modest scruples.
Call him in, Caius.
> *C. Num.* Tabellarius! friend!

Enter MESSENGER.

Mess. Save you, my masters.
> *Virg.* Com'st thou from the town?
Mess. In all haste from the great decemvir. I seek
The camp at Algidum — scarce pause to breathe.
Virg. The camp! What is there toward? Not peace,
I trust.
Mess. I know not. I 've no verbal charge but these:
To see myself the general, Marcus Sergius,
And shun there one Virginius, a centurion.

VIRGINIUS *draws the hood closer over his face.* QUINTUS
and CAIUS *exchange looks and turn hastily to
Virgin. — which the slave observes.*

You know Virginius, then? [*to the youths.*
> *Virg.* They do. But I
Know him far better.
Mess. [*uneasily and moving to go.*] A friend, perhaps?
> *Virg.* Why, scarce.
From my birth up, he whom thou call'st Virginius
Has been my fatalest enemy. Good friend,

We are just from camp: wouldst thou declare thy
    message
'T would please us greatly — this for thy refreshment —
                              [*handing him money.*
And none can teach thee how to shun Virginius,
So well as I.
          Mess. Did I but know thee, master ——
Yet —— 'Tis but this. [*showing the tablets.*
          Virg. On tablets! O rare haste!
Now would I give the world to know thy news.
Trust me, my friend. Thy master, were he here,
Would own the Fates themselves had sent these letters
Into my hands. Come, let me see them. Boys,
            [*giving C. and Q. money.*
Take this good man within, and let the victualer
Give of his best.
   •   *Mess.* Thou art so generous, master ——
         [*suffering Virg. to take the tablets.*
And yet —— No, no.
        C. Num. Come; thou hast little time.
Mess. And that is true.
        Virg. Why, man, thou need'st not fear.
Would I dare trifle with thy great decemvir?
  Is he not Appius? Go. [*Exeunt the youths and Mess.*
          My fears compel me.
            [*opening the tablets.*
Reading.] "Appius Claudius to his colleague, Marcus
Sergius, Health. — Keep, any way, at camp
Lucius Virginius, till the third day after

The messenger's return." O too just fears!
My child! my child! — But 't is no time to grieve.

> [*Takes from its case his style, and rubbing over,*
> *with the broad end, the wax of the tablets*
> *in two places, writes over the*
> *places with the point.*

Now it reads better: *Keep the messenger ;*
And the " return" goes with *Virginius'* name.
The third day after that, is long enough ! [26]

Re-enter hastily

The MESSENGER, *followed by* CAIUS *and* QUINTUS.

Mess. Give it me back ; I cannot eat for fear.
Why — how! Thou hast chang'd the writing!

> *Virg.* Slave! dost dare?

Mess. Pardon me. — Oh! this place has been rubb'd over! —
Nor look the words the same!

> *Virg.* How shouldst thou know?

'T is as it should be. I disturb'd the wax,
And then re-wrote it. There is not one word
But what stood there at first. Knows Rome not
Appius?
Is my life nothing? Go. Thou losest time.

> [*Exit Messenger.*

And we too, sons; our steeds are not the wind.
My daughter!

> *C. Num.* What has chanc'd? Thou art so pale!

Virg. I'll tell thee on our way. — O Rome! O Rome! —

My child! — Accursed tyrant! —— Boys,
Ye have heard Virginius lie like any slave.

C. Num. Lie, uncle?

         Virg. Yes: what is it to deceive?
The words are nothing; 't is the intent alone
Makes them or true or false. That beaten slave
Had been but politic; but I, a freeman,
A Roman, and a soldier, cannot use
Ulysses' craft without both sin and shame.
Learn that of me; and be this cheek your monitor. —
Yet oh, my daughter! 't was alone for thee! —
Tyrant, I'll have thy life! — Come, boys. — My
   child!

                    [*Exeunt.*

ACT THE FOURTH

Scene I.   A part of the Forum.

ICILIUS *and* PEOPLE.

Icil. Children of Romulus! — But I would rather,
    So ye will suffer it, call you Brutus' children;
    For Brutus was your better sire; to him
    Ye owe it, that you stand not simply now
    Where the first plac'd you, subjects of a king,
    But your own sovereigns — when you dare be such —
    Which is not always. —
                2d Cit. That is over plain.
Icil. When was truth otherwise, to those whose conscience
    Fears her reproaches? If ye dare to rule,
    Why serve ye? I will tell you. As the steed,
    Broke to the bit, forgets the natural power
    Which, us'd, would fling his rider headlong, so
    Your mouths are bitted ——
                2d Cit. Fy! we are not brutes.
Icil. The horse is valiant, generous, faithful : why
    Shame ye to be his parallel? In the fight,
    Shrinks he with terror? When the trumpet sounds,
    His eye darts fire, and his spread nostrils snort.
    Yet lo! astride him are the master's limbs.
    Ye fight too — for your leaders — whipp'd and curb'd.
    'T is habit with you both, which makes this mastery

Seem like a part of you.   But let volition
Swell your big muscles to their natural force,
'T is lord and steed no longer.
                                 2d Cit. And no longer
Shall be so!   We are Romans— Brutus' children.
   Icil. I hope so.   But be still.   Icilius loves
  . Your voices, as the tyrant said; but now
He wants your hearts.   Time was, when public rights,
Invaded, spoil'd, extinguish'd, were alone
Icilius' only sorrow:[27] the bitter stream
Flow'd pure, as from one source.   Now, private grief
Mixes its current with the popular flood,
Made tenfold bitterer, but no longer pure.
   1st Cit. Why so, Icilius? there are husbands here.
   2d Cit. None the worse patriots, that they love their wives.[28]
   Icil. True, 't is the aggregate of personal griefs
Makes general sorrow, and the love of country
Is but a loftier love of self: yet 't was
Icilius' pride (man has no right to pride,
And the gods punish it), no selfish care
Peer'd through his zeal for freedom.   You all have heard
[29] I seek to restore the tribunes: Appius said it:
And I avow it.   Avow it?   I proclaim it.
[30] Alas for me!   their power suspended trials.
O fatal day!   big with Rome's servitude,
And death to me!   when, to secure you laws,
Ye gave up all for which the laws were made,
Setting these Ten above you, without appeal!
Down went the Tribunes; and rose up, more thick
Than ever your host of wrongs.   What were you, what

You are, I have said : strong steeds that bear a rider,
Fighters of battles, whose cost is all your own,
Whose glory the patricians'; yet more safe
Amid your enemies' darts, than here, where bonds
And outrage make the horrors of the field
Sweet as a bride-bed. Is the day so old,
When the brave soldier from his prison burst,
Haggard with famine, bleeding with fresh stripes,
Made bare his mangled back, where the sharp spine
Stood out uncover'd — for the creditor's lash
Had stripp'd the fell starvation spar'd, — and shriek'd
For vengeance?

   2d Cit. And our fathers heard him.

          Icil. Ay.

Mad with their wrongs, they nigh had crush'd the
   senate,
But — mark! they did not. And the consuls promis'd,
(The Volscian war was imminent;) and the people,
Believing — is there aught ye 'll not believe,
Ye credulous fools! rush'd hither in vast crowds,
To take the oath, and get reprieve from bondage
Fear'd worse than death. They fought; and when
   they had conquer'd,
Volscians, Auruncians, both, then Appius Claudius,
Meet grandsire of the man who now would violate
The citizen's dearest rights, nor those alone,
But even of Nature's self — this Appius, scorning
His colleague's promise, drew again the gyves
On the starv'd debtor, and once more the lash
And workhouse were the recompense of valor

And balm of wounds. — Nay, save your groans. —
    What follow'd ?
Why did the legions cross the Anio ; there,
With ditch and rampart fortify the Mount,
And leave Rome to her terrors?   Was it not,
Again they had been deluded, though again
They had fought and conquer'd ? when, for very shame,
The incens'd dictator (he was a Valerius,
Not a Claudius) threw his office up.
But glorious secession! which taught the proud
The uses of the humble, and obtain'd
For the state's task-worn drudges their own magistrates,
The sacrosanctity of whose office yielded
Resort against oppression!   Yet again
The thunder of the Veto shall be heard !
I hear its distant rumble in the clouds
Which black the sky of freedom ! and its bolts
May more than purge the air.

                2d Cit. Be 't !   Let them strike!
1st Cit. We will secede again.
            Icil. Secede ?
               2d Cit. Ay, now.
We want our tribunes.
            Icil. Surely, ye are mad.
Talk of secession ?   Then ye have forgot
What your Sicinius paid to speak that word?
1st Cit. No, no; we have not !
            Icil. And to whom ?
               2d Cit. Nor that.
Murder'd by the decemvirs.

Icil. Say, by Appius.
The Ten are but the fingers of one pair
Of active hands; and that one pair is Appius.
Murder'd by Appius; but for whose strong will
The fingers never could have clutch'd his life.
Let me recall the atrocious deed. 'T is true,
Not many moons have wan'd since, and the fact
Mainly is unforgot; yet Time keeps wearing,
Wearing ever the sharp impression down,
Whose lines must be retouch'd to con it fair.
What was Sicinius' crime? He spoke as I,
As you are doing. Must the tongue wear fetters?
Is thought, which has no substance for the chain,
The only natural right the free have left,
The free, so call'd, of Rome? The man was one
Worthy the name of man; and all true men
Are fear'd of tyrants. So, at Appius' nod,
The generals sent him –– with a show of honor ––––
1st Cit. Traitors! we know it.

Icil. Ay; but hear. They sent him
To explore the enemy's ground, and choose a camp-site.
At a fit place for their design, the train,
A century full 't is said, fell on the hero.
1st Cit. He was a hero!

Icil. Of a hundred fights;
The winner of a score of civic crowns,
Besides as many others; and his breast,
Broad as the sea-god's, was one scar with wounds,
Receiv'd for you, for liberty, for Rome.

7

1st Cit. We will avenge him!

     2d Cit. Life for life! [*amid a tumult*
    of voices, and the crowd swaying, as with
     one impulse of the same emotion.
      Icil. 'T is just.
But hear me out. — He was a hero. Heroes
Submit not tamely to be butcher'd. More,
He was a freeman; and his hundred foes,
Though Romans too, were voluntary slaves,
Traitors and tools of tyrants. With his back
Against a rock, the freeman and the man

   Enter VALERIUS *and* HORATIUS.

Bore up against the whole of Appius' slaves.
1st Cit. He was a Cocles!
   2d Cit. An Horatius-Cocles!
Hor. Go on, Icilius: and you [*to Citzs.*], mark the issue.
Icil. Fifteen he slew, and on their bodies heap'd
 A score of wounded, if the count be true;
 For as I told you, though they were all Romans,
 He was a Roman freeman, and they slaves,
 The slaves of your Decemvir. So they clomb
 The steep behind him, and upon his head
 Rolling unseen huge fragments of the crag,
 Finish'd their work. [*The crowd again sways to and fro,*
      with a deep murmur.
    Val. And sent the heroic soul
To wander on the spirit-shore, complaining

He still is unaveng'd.

    2d Cit. But shall be so
No longer!

1st Cit.
and others } *simultaneously.*] No! no longer!

      *[They raise their right hands with a
       vehement and threatening gesture,
        and are moving up the scene.*

         Hor. Say you so?
Come on!

  2d Cit. On with Horatius!

       Icil. Stay!

         2d Cit. No, on!

Liberty and Icilius!   Death to the tyrant.

      [The crowd take up this last cry.

Icil. Friends, are you mad? — Horatius!   Is this wise?
Hear me a moment.

     Hor. And so give them time
To cool and tremble. *[The crowd pause, and begin to
         form again about Icilius.*

    Val. Quite as well as burn
In their own fire.

     Hor. What matters, so their foe
Burn with them?

     Val. They 'd not think so; and their foe
Is little likely.   Would not all our order
Take part with Appius? — But Icilius speaks.

Icil. Romans, 't is not I doubt you; but the blow
Must be both sure and sudden.   Appius now
Would be prepar'd, and in a moment girt
With all his friends; but here, alone amidst ye,

An easy prey.   Here then, where flesh'd in crime
The assassin tyrant would enact the ravisher,
The Tarquin of man-murder stand proclaim'd,
By his own mouth, the Tarquin for whose lust
We who have wives and daughters must find food,
Here, for our wives and daughters, let us strike,
And by one blow free them, ourselves, and Rome.

1st and }
2d Cit. }   We will, we will!

     Icil. Think on Sicinius butcher'd ;
And when the assassin, in the face of Jove,
Fronting his Capitol, dooms to greater wo
The good Virginius, and his child, and me,
Think on your own Virginias, and remembering
That ye are Junius Brutus' children, strike!

2d Cit. Remembering we are Brutus' children, strike!

And the crowd moves slowly up the scene, chiming in with
  2D CIT., *at the word* "Strike!" — *Halting, they*
   watch from the background the conference
    between HOR., VALER., *and* ICILIUS.

  Hor. 'T is spoken well, Icilius.   But how long
Will those flat ears retain the eloquent sound ?
Thou shouldst have let them, when the arm was up,
Strike.
  Icil. If the blow had swerv'd, what then ?   Their chains
Were riveted for ever.   Give the mass
The deep self-interest which impels the man,
You make them constant ; but, till this be done,
The impulsive power never has that force
Which crushes obstacles.   The foes of Appius,

In bulk, might bury under them his friends:
Why do they not then do it?

     Val. Justly said.
'T is only here, i' the Forum, where the wrong
Done to Virginius shall new-point their rage
For their own daily wrongs, and Appius' measure
Of insolence and crime, already brimming,
Flow over, the popular courage will make head
Against habitual terrors.

     Hor. We shall see.
When cool'd the metal, vain the workman's art
To shape it to his wish.

     Icil. Wilt thou, Horatius,
With thine own fire, maintain what heat is now,
Keeping the iron ductile? I must go
To seek Virginius.

     Hor. What my breath may do,
Depend on: but trust more the scanty time,
And Appius' own imprudence. [*Goes up the scene, and
  beckons to the crowd, who gather round him eagerly,
    while he appears to harangue them.*

     Val. Which shall have
Full sweep. Be it mine to keep back Spurius Oppius
With his twelve fasces. — Courage! for this day
Rome will be free.

     Icil. I feel it; yet, would Heaven,
I were assur'd 't would cost me merely life! [31]
        [*Exit.* ——

VALERIUS, *looking thoughtfully after him a moment, Exit at
opposite side; and the Scene changes — the dumb-show
in the background still continuing.*

SCENE II.

The Atrium of the house of Numitorius.

VIRGINIA *and* VIRGINIUS, *meeting.*
At a little distance, following Virginia, NUMITORIUS.

Virg. My child! my child! —. But thou as yet art safe,
    As yet my virgin daughter! Jove himself
    Inspir'd thy timely summons. 'T was for Rome,
    As well as thee.
             Va. Heaven's providence. I knew not
    The oppressor's cruel purpose; but, each day
    His insolent importunities increasing,
    I could no more keep silence; and I fear'd
    To — [*turning her head in the direction of the door, as*
     listening] to invoke —— It is his step!
                     Virg. Icilius'?
    Thine ears are wondrous quick. Nay! 'tis a love
    Thou hast no right to blush for; and the eve,
    (Be it to-morrow,) that shall make thee his,
    Renders thy sire the proudest in all Rome.[32]
Va. Alas!

Enter ICILIUS.

    Icil. Virginius! father: happily come!
Virg. Lucius, my son! — Is Rome dead to all honor?
    Icil. They that are dead to freedom have no honor.
    The people stood around, and saw thy daughter,

Icilius' promis'd spouse, pronounc'd a slave;
And the foul mouth that dar'd the insult breathes.
Honor? where rule ten tyrants?

      Virg. Patience, son.
Icil. Look on this maid. Though Chastity had fled
 All other shrines, were not her temple here? [33]
 Feel that this innocent being is thy child
 Past any doubt; then hear that Appius' pander
 Laid his polluting finger on her body,
 Asserting servitude, and ask of me,
 Whom thou hast honor'd with this precious gift,
 Patience.

   Virg. To nerve thy arm for surer vengeance.
 Passion defeats its motive, and the blood,
 It forces to the vision, clouds its aim.
 He, who with fury would avenge a wrong,
 Flings off his buckler, and with naked breast
 Assaults a foe who carries sword and shield.
 But see, thy sister, with my nephew, comes.

      Enter

   Icilia, *with* C. Numitorius.

Virtuous Icilia! my dear daughter's pride!
How much I owe thy counsel!

      Ica. This alone:
That it has follow'd where her heaven-wrought impulse,
Wiser than simple reason, led the way.
But thou art come, her sire, belov'd of Rome

And honor'd; and that sadden'd brow shall clear.
Justice no more shall lend her snow-white pall[34]
To hood Oppression, or the hand of Truth
Shall strip it off the borrower. But, poor child!
       [observing Virginia, who stands in an attitude of
                sad submission, showing the resignation
                      of a pious but dejected mind.
Her heart is terror-shaken, and the voice
Of Hope is answered by no joyous beat.

Virg. Cheer thee, my daughter! when my proofs are heard,
Even lust and tyranny will shame to answer,
And the rous'd Forum thunder with our triumph.

Icil. Or if that tyrants know not, as I deem,
The sense of shame, its temple-walls shall shake
With thunder that is more than sound.

                    Virg. Thou mean'st? ——
                        [eagerly.

Icil. The people are at last awaké. The voice,
That dooms to slavery the free of Rome,
Has struck on their drugg'd senses; and the sun
Now going down will pour his level ray,
Not on a cringing crowd, and in their midst,
Bound to the altar of a tyrant's lust,
This innocent victim, but the o'erthrown tribunal,
And Rome's last tyrant making with his blood
Atonement for her violated laws.

Virg. Thy brows are knitted, and thy bearded lip
Gather'd within its fellow, and thine eyes
Burn with a fire too steady for mere rage;

And Publius' own are fulgent with new hope.[35]
It must be so.   O joy!   The people then? ——
Icil. Champ on the bit, and hardly were rein'd in.
Horatius would have driven them on at once,
And ply'd the lash.   But 't was too dread a risk.
'T is on the trial, when the blow is sure,
Their rage shall work.
     Virg. Be welcome then the trial!
Rome was my mother, ere thou wast my child,
Virginia.
    Va. And what mother has thy child
But Rome?
    Virg. Do ye hear this, eternal gods?
Your thrones are bas'd on everlasting right:
Ye will not suffer virtues like your own
To be the sport of vice.
Va. [*to Icilius, where they stand apart.*] Alas, my father!
He sees not, were my virtues truly such,
They have no place on earth!
     Icil. For pity, hush!
Num. 'T is not to be the sport of vice, when vice,
Outraging virtue, proves but Heaven's touchstone
To assay its gold; nor will affliction, brother,
Which is the fire to purify that gold,
Be suffered to confound it with the dross.
Va. Except to achieve some mighty good, whose weight
Makes the pure ore rise flimsy as the dross.
What is Virginia, that Virginia's wo,
If instrumental to the general joy,

7*

Should move Heaven's pity ; when even to herself
Its bitterness would be welcome ?

                   Virg. O my child!
Thou griev'st and gladd'st me equally.   The gods
Will not desert thee !

            Icil. Nor shall man.   The fire,
Thy wrongs have stirr'd, Horatius' eager breath
Will not permit to gather-o'er its ashes. —

Virg. And I have what shall fan it to a blaze.
Caius, thou hast been long o'erlook'd.   Thy friend,
The brave young Quintus, how appears he now ?

             [*Icil., Virginia, and Numitorius, but
                 especially the former, show earnest
                       attention and surprise.*

C. Numit. The wound proves but a slight one, as thou saidst,
Good uncle.—

          Ica. And the foolish boy so proud
To have gain'd it, and in such a cause, I doubt
Its speedy scarring will much please him.

                 Icil. Wound ?
And Quintus?   What is this?

               Virg. A fan, of two,
Kept for the fire we speak of.   Wait their blast.
To hear it now, thy rage would know no bounds.
Gentle Icilia, and thou, boy, be close :
Even prudent Numitorius must awhile
Content him with like ignorance. — My son,
The awful moment — whatsoe'er our fate —
Must be at hand.   'T is fit we part.   Go thou,

Mix with the people, and their wavering mood
Make steady with thine eloquence: their ire
Must take from thy strong passion keener edge.
Most kind Icilia, who art come, I feel,
To be beside thy friend, go thou with her,
And let Lucilla robe her in the garb
In which she mourn'd her mother. I myself
Will borrow of thee, Publius, some mean mantle,
Whose sordid folds accord with my distress.
Come, we must soon be summon'd.

            Va. Father ! [*looking*
      from him, and stretching her arms to Icilius.
                Virg. Yes ;
Embrace, my children. Thou all-seeing Jove,
      [*spreading his hands over them, as Icil.*
        clasps Virginia to his breast.
Whose awful eyes look down with love and pity
On this most innocent pair, O let their woes
Here end forever, and this last embrace
Be but as parting on a gloomy eve
To meet a cloudless morrow !

*A single and loud clap of thunder rolls over the scene, and
shakes the walls.*

VIRGINIA *and* ICILIUS *part instantly — all present listening
with horror as the sound dies away.*

C. Num. [*clasping his hands in terror.*] Merciful Heaven !
   'T was on the right !

Va. [*to Icil.*] Thy promise!

Icil. It is vow'd.

VIRGINIA *and* ICILIA *Exeunt at one side, while, in the opposite
direction,* ICILIUS, *muffling his head in his mantle,
Exit hurriedly.*

VIRGINIUS, *burying his face in his hands, remains in his position, supported by* NUMITORIUS, *while* CAIUS *seems to
cower with fear, his face still upraised to the
roof, and his hands locked together.*

The Drop falls.

ACT THE FIFTH

Scene I. A part of the Forum.

M. CLAUDIUS, *going up to* LIVIA, *who enters.*

Marc. Thou art here.
     Liv. But is Virginius? — Palter not!
If he appear not —— Thou hast heard me.
        Marc. True,
And need no echo. Till the girl appear,
How can I answer thee? Come on.
       Liv. No, here
I wait my summons. Is thy patron come?
Marc. Behold! [*pointing off the scene.*
    Liv. Even now ascending; with an air
As if earth would not suffer him to fall.
Yet he may down.
    Marc. Perchance. But, being up,
'T were well to think that he may see us here
From his high place, and bid me drag thee thither.
Liv. That thou may'st do; but canst thou make me speak?
Nor thou, nor thy decemvir. Here I stay.
When the sad father passes with his child,
I follow. If he fail, thou want'st me not.

MARCUS, *regarding her steadily a moment, Exit — when* LIVIA,
*who has returned his look, draws her mantle over her head,
and the Scene changes.*

Scene II.

Another part of the Forum.

A. Lucretius; T. Quinctius; L. Valerius.

Val. Titus, behold! our Jove is on his throne!
    See where his subject mortals group around —
    With looks that would affright more vulgar gods.
Lucr. Not without cause. Why, Lucius, look again!
Val. By Hercules, thou art right! The lictors' rods
    Are chang'd for spears! their heads are helm'd; and, see!
    What glitters on their breasts in the sun's rays?
    Does simple wool shine thus? What say'st thou now,
    Thou lukewarm Titus? Aims yon sceptred hand
    To grasp the kingly diadem, or no?
    Aims; for he shall not reach it! no! his arm,
    Or mine, shall first drop nerveless.
                      Quinc. All my hopes
    Thou knowest are with thee. Yet I still must doubt.
    His friends are legion; and his foes ——
                        Val. A host.
Quinc. Of —— [*pointing disdainfully off the scene.*
       Val. Men, good as his foes: at least, as strong;
    For I see Aulus little likes the praise.
Lucr. My tastes are in abeyance till the issue.
    I doubt your commons will not be too sage
    After their victory, and foresee the day
    Their tribunes will usurp a power, might make
    Even Appius blush. But, for the nonce, your mob

Shall have their way — unless those dozen spears
Cool their intent.   My friends are posted: Appius
Will cry in vain for succor.

      Val. Part we then.

Keep Quinctius. [*in undertone.*]   Liberty ! [*going off.*

       Lucr. The senate's rights!

       [*Exit with Quinc. in*

     opposite direction, and Scene changes to

Scene III and Last.

The Forum, as in Act II, Scenes 1 and 3.

Appius, *on the tribunal, holding his sceptre of office, and sur-*
rounded by his Lictors armed.   Behind the tribunal are
seen other soldiers; and near him, but a little behind, a
Messenger attending. — Marcus Claudius. — *A Her-*
ald or Crier. — P. Numitorius; C. Numitorius; Q. Icilius — *his arm in a sling.* — *Citizens.*

Enter

Virginius, *in an old and soiled toga, leading* Virginia, *in a*
mourning-cloak, [b] *her head muffled with the same.   Be-*
side Va. walks Icilius, *and behind her* Icilia *and the*
Nurse; a train of Matrons, weeping, follow immediately,
and, at a little distance, comes also Livia.

App. [*starting.*] Virginius! — Traitor! [*to Marcus, in an*
undertone.

           Virg. And to thy dismay.

Hear, Romans! hear what ——

       Num. Patience, yet awhile.

[*Marcus, at this moment, gives a signal to Appius,*
by looking quickly and significantly at Livia.

Lose not what little chance thou mayst have left
For a fair trial.

       App. Trial thou shalt have —
Though the tribunal might be spar'd it, sure
Beforehand the defence is futile all,
Or mere imposture. [*Murmur in the People — while Nu-*
mitorius is seen restraining Icilius.

      Silence there, ye frogs!
If ye 'ld not have me fling a stone among ye,
Or drain your filthy pool, since undisturb'd
Ye croak thus! Herald, rise. And let the Assertor
Bring on his proofs.

Num. [*indicating to Icil. and Virg., while the Herald steps*
out, the evident and deep resentment of the people.

      The pool heaves like a sea.
More of this insolence, and we are safe.

Herald. Silence! [*Marcus leads up Livia.*

      Marc. Behold the mother of the slave.

Icil. Let her unhood. And thou, Virginius, mark!

Virg. Livia! — Slave? the mother free? [*to the people,*
with an expression of scorn and indignation.

           App. Be still!
Else here are those shall make thee. And, observe —

When 't is thy time to speak, to us, thy judge,
Turn that bold visage. Woman, now proceed.

Enter HORATIUS,
behind the crowd, and, mixing with the people,
is seen earnestly exhorting them.

Liv. A plain tale, great decemvir. I was slave
To Claudius, when Virginius, here in presence,
Had knowledge of me. Witness that, his child,
Born of our commerce, on his dame impos'd
For her dead babe, to save his blood from thraldom.
This let Virginius, if he dare, gainsay.
His love for me is known.
                    Virg. And they who know it
Know that I freed this woman, for that love.
She was my captive, brought from taken Antium.
I lov'd her honestly ; ('t was ere I had met
Thy sister, Publius.) But, being taught in time
Her falsehood with yon Claudius, plaintiff here,
I flung her off, as I would fling a viper, [*Livia draws her*
                        mantle again over her face.
Never having known her in the way she says.[36]
I swear it by yon Heaven, which now let down
Its thunder on my sacrilegious head,
If I swear falsely !
                    App. Yonder heaven is clear.
The cloud is spent, whose solitary clap
Late shook the Capitol, nor has Jove bolts
To waste on such as thou. Vouch more profanely.
Nor canst thou be a witness for thyself.

Icil. [*advancing.*] But I can, for him. [*Horatius comes forward.*

      Virg. And Virginius' honor,
  Like that of all true Romans, is most fit
  To swear by, since thou settest nought by Jove.
 App. Thine honor, and his evidence, [*indicating, by a con-*
    temptuous and slight toss of the head, Icil.] alike
  Weigh nothing here, where each has puissant cause
  To falsify.
Numit. [*adjuring Icil. and Virg. and putting himself in their*
    way.] Yet, for Virginia's sake!
 Hor. [*restraining Icil. and Virg. by motion of the hand.*

        But I
  Have none. I, for Virginius' honor, pledge
  My own; and what Icilius may not vouch,
  That shall Horatius. [*Murmurs of satisfaction in the*
    crowd.] Yonder wretched woman
  Is either slave or free. A slave, she has
  No right to give her testimony, save
  By torture; free, she is perjur'd, and the suit
  Falls to the ground, and her vile life is forfeit.

       [*Murmurs increase.*
  But even if not, and could it be the child
  Of a free woman should be born a slave,
  Still is the witness worthless, for that I,
  Marcus Horatius, know her lewd of life.
  This vouch I by mine honor, and in face
  Of the high gods! [*Burst of applause.*

    App. What! dare ye clamor, curs?
  Who is Horatius, that his simple word
  Should make ye yelp thus, more than his, or hers?

Hor. Thine equal, Appius! in all points but one,
    And in that one thy better; nor dar'st thou,
    Spite the high place thou holdest over long,
    Make me the mate of such things.   I have given
    My evidence.   Impeach it, if thou canst;
    If thou lik'st, swear me.

                    2d Cit. Ay, and let *them* swear!
    He has not sworn, nor she.

                                Hor. Nor has the judge.
    'T is proper on all sides.

                    1st Cit. But make them swear.
    Give them a stone.

                            Liv. I am ready.   [*As she takes the stone
                                offered by Marcus, Appius whispers
                                the Messenger, who disappears.*]
                                            *If, from guile
    I bear false witness, may the day's dread sire,
    Even as this stone I cast away, so me* ——
Icil. [*to the people.*] Let her not proceed!   Had she the right,
    As she has none, being woman, slave, and vile,
    Let her not swear!   Who could not do as much?
    They who dare lie in Heaven's face, what risk they,
    Calling high Jove to witness to their truth?
    Nor swear that valiant Roman and true man,
    Horatius.   Such need no attest.   Time was,
    That honor was to Roman freeman what
    Hell's awful flood is to the gods, of oaths
    The dreadest, and their sworn or simple word
    Was better than the bonds of other men,

But now [*facing App.*], since tyranny has set its yoke
On our curv'd necks like cattle ——

         App. Hast thou done?

Icil. Thou hear'st. — We crouch like them, and tremble;
More bestial still than cattle, that we have tongues
Which fawn, and cringe, and skulk; and, honor now
But little known, man trusts man's word no more,[37]
But calls the Unseen, whose vengeance is remote.
Thus they, who outrage Heaven by daily crime,
Swear sooner than good men, having less to lose.
Witness yon tool of your decemvir. Him,
Give *him* the Jove-stone? Cast-away of Jove,
What recks he of a second hurling, so
His carcass 'scape the throw decreed them here
Who mock thus gods and men; for 'scape it will ——

         People. No!

Icil. Yes; for who made the laws sits there, and breaks
    them
Openly in your faces. I have done. [*to Appius.*

    Enter LUCRETIUS — *slowly,*
      (*keeping apart.*)

App. Insolent rebel! It is such as thou,
Who mock both gods and men, affecting justice,
And making even religion but a stool
To mount to station; it is such as thou,
Who turn yon rabblement to coward cattle,
Making them crouch and lick the treacherous hand
That smooths their coarse necks but to yoke them.
    Tremble?

Was it an Appius in the Volscian war
That made them tremble, when the villains fled,
Leaving my valiant sire? whose soul, thank Heaven,
I bear as well as name!

[*The people are seen in violent commotion,* HORATIUS *among
them gesticulating in an animated manner, yet
as if secretly.*

LUCRETIUS, *a little removed, looks on.*

     Icil. Even so. — Quiritès!
Children of Romulus! Ye have not forgotten
'T was Appius, this man's sire, whose soul he boasts,
That scourg'd and gave to the axe your bravest soldiers,
Pick'd men, and the centurions, bastinading
So cruelly every tenth man of the rest,
That hundreds died, whence, after, the rous'd troops
Refus'd to fight, so that their enemies jeer'd them;
Whereas with Quinctius, Appius' kindly colleague,
So ready were they then, these recreant legions,
The Æqui durst not even march by the camp!
      [*The commotion has increased,
      and now, with one voice.*
      People. 'T is true!
Icil. Why do ye stand then? Come! [*moving towards
the tribunal, while the people rush forward, led by
Horatius — Lucretius taking no part. Appius
makes a sign to the lictors, and they advance
with ported spears, when the people halt.*
      App. Because I bid them.

Assertor —— Thee [*to Icil.*], and thy true Roman there,
        [*indicating Horat. with like significance.*
Presently. — Assertor, take thy slave.
Va. [*while the people, still led by Horat. rush boldly between*
    her and the Lictors, — Lucretius now moving, but
      slowly, with them.   The Matrons press still
        closer to Virginia, and hem her round.
                  Now, Lucius!
Icil. All is not hopeless yet.   See! [*indicating the people.*
Lucr. [*advancing before the people.*] Appius, stay !
  Albeit cattle, the drove is over strong,
  Even for thy spears.
      App. [*furiously.*] Make way there!   Dastards!
                    [*to Lictors.*
                    Hor. On !
On !
App. Do your duty! [*Lictors attempt to charge.*
        Lucr. Halt there!   we have horns.
    [*pointing quietly to the crowd, several of whom*
        have put their hands to their tunics.
  Appius, be wiser.   Credit me, even now
  The shears close on thy life's thread.
                App. Rather thine,
  Thou recreant noble.   People! men of Rome !
  I thirst not for your blood ——
         2*d Cit.* Why then those spears?
App. Because of treason, plots against the State,
  Whose head am I — plots of Icilius.   Wherefore
  Wear ye else hidden arms? [38]
          Icil. Because of treason,

Treason against the State, whose head thou art not,
Except by usurpation.   Such the law
Of great Valerius makes deserving death.[39]
[*Turning rapidly to the people.*] Brothers! children of
    Brutus ! what·avails it
Our fathers drove out kings?   And for what crime?
There sits your Tarquin ——
             App. But thou stand'st not Brutus.[40]
Lictors!   Seize, slay Icilius !
             Va. Me! rather me !
Save him, Romans!
       Lucr. [*stepping between Icil. and the Lictors,*
            while Virg. holds back his daughter,
                 pressing her to his breast.
Appius, art thou mad?
'T is the last time I move to shield thee.
               App. Thou !
Stand from the way : I would not shed thy blood.
People of Rome! resistance is in vain.
The majesty of justice shall not bow,
Save o'er my fallen body.   Look behind me,
       [*The people, already not over ardent,*
          are seen to falter, despite the
              efforts of Horatius.
Where stand twelve armed men to back these twelve ;
And Oppius hears my summons for twenty more.
Hor. Thou wilt not get them.
App. [*looking around in alarm.*] How now !
               Lucr. It is sure.
Thou art beset on all sides, or cut off

From other aid than these.   Give justice way,
Thou'rt safe — at least from violence.

      App. Who but ye
Are her impediments?   The sire was heard —
Prov'd nothing; sentence was decreed.   If still
Respondent have aught left to urge, we hear him.
But, the next outrage! —   Speak.

       Virg. And all give ear.
I have two arrows left.   Though the first miss,
The next shall hit the mark.   And thou, beware!

          [to App.
App. Bend thy bow quickly, or I break the shaft.
Virg. [*turning Va. to face the people, uncovers her features.*
   Daughter, unveil. [*Pauses.* —   *A   general   burst
     of pity and admiration.   The Matrons
        sob aloud.*

    1st Matron. O shame to Roman manhood!
Will no arm strike for her?

       Virg. I, I myself,
With these hands took her up, this virgin, this
Still tender girl, and plac'd her in my bosom.
Her feeble cry, the soft clasp of her fingers,
Whose little fold just met around my thumb,
Are present to my soul as fresh as then.
O Romans — fathers!   O mothers!   (she alas!
Has none — none now!) 'say, are these feelings proper
To me alone?   or speak I what all know,
Have felt as I?

   People. } All.
   Matrons. }

Virg. Could I feign these feelings?
Or does my language witness ——
      Marc. [*interrupting him.*] No one doubts
The emotion, nor the truth of him who vaunts it.
But I say, Romans — and I too dare address ye
As fathers — and ye mothers too, and wives —
These feelings are delusive ; for the true
Virginia expir'd, ere almost she had cry'd,
And this, the false, Virginius never took
Up to his bosom — never to avow her,
Though he have clasp'd her there a thousand times,
And fancied 't was the babe he had so rais'd.
Num. [*eagerly.*] Virginius then had no part in the cheat!
Marcus and Livia contradict each other !
App. But little ; for the main points are the same.[41]
Virg. [*looking round upon the crowd and seeing the impres-
      sion made by Marcus.*
      That shaft has miss'd. And yet I deem'd the point
Had pierc'd the heart of every Roman, at least
Of every Roman mother through and through,
As if they were but one, I shot so straight.
Covering her features again, he consigns VA. *to* ICILIA, *who
supports her as before, and the Matrons
instantly close round them.*
1st Matr. There are no Romans ; our degenerate bowels
Give birth to monsters, as Icilius said.
Icil. Better be barren, or in the unshapen germ
Wither your bodies' fruit, than suffer travail,
And give your paps to daughters, whose fresh bloom
Shall deck the slave-mart !
   8

1st Matr. Better wither all!

     [And the other women take up
       the cry, — " Wither all!"

App. [*to Virg.*] Let fly thy other shaft.

      Virg. 'T is at thy heart.
Come forward, boys. [*to Caius and Quint.*

    These youths were present, Romans,
When Appius' slave show'd tables from his master
Bidding his colleague keep me at the camp
For two days. [APPIUS *half-rises.*] Mark your ruler!
 But I then
Was on my way. Nor is this all. Three villains,
Hired to slay me, set on us near Rome ——

Hor. Of the same sort that took charge of Sicinius ——

       [*Commotion.*

Virg. And would have earn'd their pay, but for our steeds,
 We being unarm'd; and Quintus [*pointing to latter's*
 arm.] barely 'scap'd.

     [*App., turning quickly, speaks to*
      the soldiers behind him.

Icil. [*who has listened with fiery impatience.*
 Is this enough? Now, sons of Brutus, strike!

    [*rushes forward, with his poniard drawn —*
    Horat. and Lucret., on either side
    of him, in same manner.

2d Cit. Down with the murderer!

     1st Cit. For our freedom, strike!

App. [*pointing to Icil. as the latter turns about to encourage*
 the people.
 Thrust, soldiers, there!

Lucr. [*putting aside a spear leveled at Icil.*

Stain to thy order, Appius!
Lucretius fights now on the people's side.

Hor. [*same act.*] I told thee so, Aulus. — [*Turning fiercely on*
the people, who give way before the soldiers.

Traitors! what means this?

App. Death to thy hopes, Horatius. Soldiers, halt!
People! ——

Icil. O Rome! O Rome!

1st Cit. Icilius weeps!

Icil. [*indignantly uncovering his face, which he had muffled.*
⁴² Weeps? for ye will not let him shed but tears,
Even for liberty.

1st Cit. Yet Appius should be heard.

2d Cit. Perhaps so. But Virginius' tale ——

App. Is such —
⁴³ A fiction. Appius stoops not to say more.

Ica. [*hastily.*] If 't be a fiction, O how like the truth!
Citizens, I myself have known, have seen,
The importunities your decemvir offer'd,
Even in the common streets — worse still, the gifts
Sent to this maiden, to this Roman girl —
Plebeian chastity being a thing to barter,
Unlike Lucretia's. —

1st Matr. Hear her!

App, Peace, ye trash!

[*Icil. is seen to repress a violent emotion.*

Ica. It is most strange, till Appius' lures had fail'd,
His client's pretext never was put forth!

App. Woman, who art thou? But I need not ask.
Thou art the sister of the would-be tribune.
Thy tongue, like his, has motive to be false.
Icil. [*passionately to the people.*
    Must we bear this?
                App. Much more, if 't be too light.
Lictors, make room: strike none but who oppose.
Once more, Assertor, take, as right, thy slave.

The People still stand between the advancing Lictors and the party that surrounds VIRGINIA, *but give way, though slowly, sullenly, reluctantly, step by step, except the Matrons, who boldly oppose themselves to the armed men, and still hem her round.* ICILIUS *is seen approaching the group, his hand before his face. The Lictors, hesitating to stop him, look round to* APPIUS *for directions.* LUCRETIUS *and* HORATIUS, *with their eyes on the Lictors, stand ready to sustain* ICILIUS.

Va. Lucius! Now! now!
            Icil. I come, Virginia.
               Virg. [*to Icil.*] Stay.

Taking VIRGINIA *by the hand, he leads her by* MARCUS (*who, looking at* ICIL., *hesitates to oppose*), *towards the tribunal, followed by the* NURSE, *and supported by* ICILIA.

[*to Marc.*] Thy hand withhold a moment. — Appius, pardon
The outbreaks of a father's grief; and suffer,
Before I part forever from my child,
I question her apart, her nurse, and friend,

And put at rest my doubts.

      App. We grant thy prayer.
But be not long; the day draws to a close.

*The light here suddenly falling, as at the going-down of the
    sun, the stage becomes gloomy.
Virginius etc. take their way to the shops, followed closely
  by Icilius, who is beckoned on by Virginia.
    Virginius snatches a knife from one
      of the open windows.*

Virg. [*stabbing her.*] My child, return unto thy mother.
     [*Resigning her to the arms of Ica. and Nurse,
      while Icil. hangs over her, and bran-
        dishing the knife.*
          Appius!
 To the Hell-gods, with this blood, I devote thee!
Marc. He has kill'd his daughter! [*Burst of horror from the
     People, while Appius rises upright
       from his chair.*
     App. Seize on the murderer!
Virg. [*rushing to the people with the knife held up.*
 Romans! I have us'd a father's right, the law
And nature gave; sole refuge from pollution.
Hor. 'T is just. Down with the lictors!
      [*striking down the foremost.*
    2d *Cit.* Death to the Tarquin!
     [*wresting his spear from the next.*
1st *Cit.* [*almost at same moment.*]
  Throw Marcus and the woman from the rock!

*The Lictors and Soldiers, beaten down, stabbed, or their arms
wrested from them, fly, MARCUS and LIVIA with them —
some of the People pursuing.*
APPIUS, *descending from the tribunal, towards which the rest
are rushing, endeavors to escape.   Throwing down the
scaffold with its chair, they spring upon him,
VIRGINIUS (the knife still raised) with them,
followed by CAIUS and QUINTUS.*
NUMITORIUS *and the Matrons gather around* VIRGINIA, *who is
brought to the forepart of the Scene, — the tumult
and cries, and struggle against Appius, all
the while continuing.*

2d *Cit.* Down with the tribunal!
                              Hor. Leave to me! ——
                                        Lucr. To me,
      The tyrant!

ICILIUS, *pressing* VIRGINIA *a moment in his arms, springs after
them, beating back the crowd to get at* APPIUS, *who, striking down the foremost of his assailants with his sceptre, flings it away, and draws his poniard.*

      Icil. No! — Back! back!
                              App. To none!
                                        [*stabs himself.*
      Appius dies worthy of himself and name —
      And, dying, sends thee that, accursed dog!

Hurling the poniard at ICILIUS, *whom it misses,* APPIUS,
muffling his head in his mantle, falls and expires.

Icil. [*dropping his own poniard.*]

    'T is better thus. [*He returns, to hang over Virginia.*

Voice of Sp. Oppius within. } He shall have company.

Enter

VALERIUS *and* QUINCTIUS.

Val. We have heard. —— To escape the people, Spurius
    Oppius
Has slain himself.

Exeunt,

*slowly, and separately, in different directions, all the
Citizens, save* 1ST *and* 2D CIT., *who stand by the
body of* APPIUS, *but looking on the
party of* VIRGINIUS.

Va. [*opening her eyes.*] Is 't thou, Icilia? Kind!
    Where is my father? Did I dream the joy?
    Or is Rome — liberated?

              Virg. 'T is at last, my — child :

But at what cost!

              Va. I knew it. I am content.

Yet, is it — painful. Lucius — my beloved —
Receive — my last breath. Father, I — die — pure. [44]

Virg. Thou diest a Roman ; and thou diest free.

VIRGINIA, *putting up her lips to* ICILIUS, *her arms
extended to him, expires.*

ICILIUS, *having received her last breath, withdrawing his lips,*
resigns her to his sister, lifts his face a moment upwards
towards Heaven, then muffles his head with his mantle.
VIRGINIUS, *turning aside his face, covers it with his hand.*
The NURSE *is lying, gathered in a heap, at the dead girl's*
feet, with her face to the ground, wrapped in the
skirt of VIRGINIA'S *garment.*
HORATIUS, LUCRETIUS, *and the rest, stand in various attitudes*
of grief and awe, the MATRONS *sobbing, but low, be-*
hind, while faintly, from within the scene, is
heard, as far in the distance, the
cry of "Liberty !"
and the

Curtain falls.

NOTES

NOTES TO VIRGINIA

1.—P. 86. *The shadow of thy wings, three times this hour*—] This is the stage-reading. I have a memorandum, that in print it would be better to substitute the less pointed " day"; for the Romans, at this early period, did not divide the day by hours. — But " hour " must pass even here; since there is no other way to express the brief time of the conference, to which alone *Appius* refers.

2.—P. 86. *The people laid him out!*] For the Stage (as the language cannot be too perspicuous for an audience, who have not the time to pause upon a phrase), there may be substituted: " The people buried him!" or " A pauper's burial!"

So, in the passage above,—*If thou go down, my head, Be sure, rests not unmuffled,*—though Shakspeare's mention of Cæsar's action, when about to expire, has made the custom alluded-to sufficiently familiar to a mixed audience, yet, if deemed more directly explicit, the actor may recite as follows:

> " When Appius veils his head,
> Be sure my mantle hangs not from the shoulder.
> We fall together.
>
>   *App.* Now, no more. — One thing," *etc.* (as in the text.)

3.—P 87. *Thou might'st thank Cornelius then, When Lucius from the senate-porch made cry Unto the people, his arms about thee cast Sav'd thee from violence* ——] "Tum Appius ..... ad Valerium, negatum se privato reticere, lictorem accedere jussit. Jam Quiritium fidem implorante Valerio a curiæ limine, L. Cornelius [M. Cornelii decemviri frater] complexus Appium, non cui simulabat consulendo, diremit certamen. Liv. III. c. 37. p. 186 *ed.* Twiss (*ex recens.* Drakenborch.) *Oxon.* in 8°. 1840.

4.—P. 89. *While thou shalt help me to dispose my mantle* —] The Roman *toga*, which resembled greatly the Spanish *capa*, and in this form, though of smaller dimension, is still seen on the Italian priests in Rome, required, as does the *capa*, some care in the disposition of its folds. What pains were taken by the orators may be imagined without the story of Hortensius and the minute directions of Quintilian. *Appius* is not finical, even for that early day of the Commonwealth.

The object, however, for which I mark this passage, is to call the attention of the Actor to a point that is habitually neglected on the stage. The toga was an out-door habit. To make the Roman wear it in the house, *as a house-dress*, is almost as much out of costume as it would be in a comedy to dress the characters in-doors in Spanish mantles, or, indeed, in any sort of cloak. It is not worse, it is true, than Richard's crown and furred robe in Bosworth-field; but such absurdities should be avoided by any player studious of propriety, without which, effect is but unnatural, and illusion is impossible.

As to the precise cut of the Roman mantle, there is, it may be said, no positive indication. We have it represented, and the description supported by authorities, as *round*, as *semi-circular*, and even as *square*, that is, rectangular or having straight lines on all its sides, while some do not hesitate to maintain that it was stitched together from top to bottom.* It may safely be supposed, that while the mode of wearing

---

* Ferrarius, in making it to be round and closed (*De Re Vestiaria*, lib. i. c. 1. p. 619 *in Grævii Thesaur.* vol. vi.—Venet. in fol. 1732), would give us the

it was almost always the same, so far at least as the bringing of the
right side over the left shoulder, which was partly a necessity arising
from its length and amplitude, the cut differed according to the means,
if not the occasions of the wearer. Do we not see Spaniards who wear
the common French and English cloak like their national *capa?* Yet
these are square in all their edges; while the *capa*, to which I have
compared the ancient Roman mantle, is, when amplest, a perfect circle; the two front edges being laid together, the centre is the hole
formed by the collar. Take away the cape and collar, and you have a
toga. But when the *capa* is less full (and this is almost always the
case), it makes, spread out, a semicircle.* Without this circular sweep
of the bottom edge, it could not form those graceful or those majestic
folds which, when the right side is thrown over the left shoulder, make
this mantle conspicuous among the few that still survive the ugly fashions which the quick movements of a busier modern life have introduced. But for the authorities. Among the ancients, Quintilian says
distinctly that the toga was *round:* "Ipsam togam rotundam esse, et
apte cæsam velim. Aliter enim multis modis fiet enormis." *Orat. Inst.*
XI. 3., *Colon.* in 12° 1528, p. 517. Dionysius of Halicarnassus, that it

Mexican *poncho* (as I have heard it called), which is a circular cloak without
opening save in the centre, to admit the head and neck. As to his citation
from Gellius (lib. vii.), that in the earliest times the Romans wore nothing
whatever on their person but the toga, it would not follow that if then it was,
for obvious reasons, closed in front, it should continue to be so when worn over
another garment, and judging by the modern use of a cloak we might say just
the contrary. The same necessity, for closing in the first case, would exist for
leaving it open in the latter.

Aldus Manutius (*De Toga Romanor.*, ap. *Grævium* ubi. cit. p. 1192,) maintains the same strange opinion, using the same baseless argument derived from
the custom of a semi-barbarous antiquity. All the statues, so far as I know,
that represent the outer garment sewed up to the breast or neck, indicate the
læna, or *pænula*, traveling and foul-weather cloaks. See *note* 25.

* See "ADDITION TO NOTE," p. 200.

was semicircular.* He tells us that when the Etruscan ambassadors
accepted the conditions of L. Tarquinius, that is, of complete surrender,
they brought to him, a few days after, the symbols of sovereignty with
which they adorned their own kings, and among them the purple tunic
wrought with gold (χιτωνα τε πορφυρουν χρυσοσημον) and the variegated purple cloak or robe (και περιβολαιον πορφυρουν ποικιλον),
such as the kings of the Lydians and Persians wore, except that *it was
not square in form like that, but half-circular:* πλην ου τετραγωνον
γε τῳ σχηματι, καθαπερ εκεινα ην, αλλ' ημικυκλιον. And
he adds immediately: τα δε τοιαυτα των αμφιασματων 'Ρωμαιοι μεν
τογας, 'Ελληνες δε τηβεννον καλουσιν. (*Antiq.* III. 61.—p. 187,
t. i. *ed. Hudson. Oxon.* in fol. 1704.) †   Among modern writers, Sigonius,

---

* Winkelmann, who maintains that the form of the toga was round ("zirkelrund geschnitten,") committed the strange oversight to find in the passage
of Dionysius, presently cited, the adjustment or envelopment (*Umnehmen*),
otherwise *cast* of the mantle described by the semi-circular outline, not its
form.   His commentator fails not to remark this error of perhaps a too rapid
reading, or of the prejudice of theory or the near-sightedness caused by preconceived opinions ; and he adds : "Deutlich sieht man die halbzirkelförmige
Gestalt des Toga an den Statuen, wo sie zwey Enden (oder Winkel) macht,
das eine vor, das andere hinter der Person, welche die Toga trägt." *Gesch. der
Kunst des Alterthums, Buch* VI. c. 3 (*Werke,* 5r *Bd. s.* 72 u. 377.—Dresden, in
8° 1812.)

† From that wonderful people, the Etruscans, the Romans, in all probability, derived, not only the curule chair, the lictors and fasces, the purple and
the painted vestment, and, I may add, the sceptre with its eagle, of their rulers,
but also the *toga,* the prototype of which (in its rude and scantier shape, not in
its perfection,) may be seen in certain monuments of that ancient race.   See
Tav. 31 in Ferrario : *Costume ant. e mod.* vol. 5 (Firenze, 1828, in 8°) p. 163.
In another plate, *Tav.* 3. (*ib.* p. 62,) we have a group of figures, well-drawn, of
which one wears a *toga,* or mantle corresponding thereto, the part over the
left shoulder being grasped by the right hand, as if to hold it there, as is often
seen with those who wear the Spanish cloak. (cf. *Tav.* 5. ib. p. 74.) But the

(*De Judiciis* lib. III. c. 18.—*ap. Graev. in Thesaur. Antiq. supra cit.* vol. II. p. 814), gives us the choice between the semicircular and the quadrate form, though he appears to lean judiciously to the former, as the proper cut:— " Toga amictus fuit exterior, a tegendo, ut scribit Varro, corpore appellata. Hæc fuit lanea, semicircularis, tunica superior, ad talos fluens, eademque aperta .... Semicircularem docet Dionysius in Prisco, cum scribit, *togam pictam amictum*," etc. [as above]; " et Isidorus libro xix. scribens, *togam pallium esse purum forma rotunda; mensura vero togæ justæ esse sex ulnas.*" It will be observed that he does not remark the difference between the *round* of Isidore, and the *half-circle* of Dionysius. They are in fact, as I have tried to show, the same thing so far as the different amplitude of the garment allows it. " Contra vero quadratum fuisse monuit Athenæus lib. 5º, cum inquit: *Romani in Asia, ut vim Mithridatis effugerunt, ad templa confugerunt, et, quadratis vestimentis abjectis, pallia sumpserunt.* Togas autem eas fuisse, Cicero indicat in Oratione pro Postumo : *P. Rutilium,* inquit, *facilius certe necessitatis excusatio defendet, qui, cum a Mithridate Mitylenis oppressus esset, crudelitatem regis in togatos vestitus mutatione vitavit, &c.*" See the whole chapter, which is full of interest and instruction. However, without the supposed corroboration of Cicero, the citation from Athenæus would be obviously of no account, and I am not sure it would be difficult to explain away the testimony even of the former. It was one of the military cloaks that is intended by Athenæus.

centre and helmed figure, with the two lictors in tunics preceding him with their fasces, the first one holding also in his right hand a single rod, wears, if he represent a chief *Lucumon* or Etruscan king, the *trabea*, with its stud or button in the centre, which, by those who like the Abbe Magnetti (*Cost. Etrus.*, in *Ferrar.*, vol. cit. p. 67.) consider the *clavus* as such a stud, may be considered the origin of that ornament of rank with the Romans. Dionysius may have drawn on his imagination for the identity, in form, of the royal garment with the toga ; but it is sufficient for the argument, that he must have been familiar with the shape of the Roman mantle, and that, doubly defining it, by its Latin and Greek name, he makes it to have been half-circular.

As Cicero, like other Roman writers, uses "toga" often figuratively for *peace*, and makes it the very emblem of public tranquillity and freedom from warfare,* he could mean, one would think, in employing in that passage the phrase *togatos*, but to express the *gens togata*, the Romans, as a people the object of Mithridates' hatred, not in that particular instance where it would be even absurd to suppose they wore the mantle of civil life.† *Toga vero Romani in pace utebantur, in bello paludamentis.* (*Vet. Schol. in Pers. v.* 14.—where, as is often done, *paludamentum* is made synonymous with *sagum.*‡) *Toga* as a phrase was

---

* "Non dixi" [he is speaking in reference to his use of the phrase *Cedant arma togæ*] "hanc togam qua sum amictus . . . sed, *quod pacis est insigne et otii*, toga." *Orat. in L. Pison.* c. 30.—p. 70 Op. ed. *Bipont.* t. vi. Again, speaking of certain habitual ornaments of discourse,—"*togam pro pace.*" De Orator. III. 42. (p. 266 t. ii. *ed. cit.*)

It is unnecessary to accumulate evidence of a fact so familiar; I will add only, that in times of great danger, the Republic being in actual war, the mantle was changed in the city itself for the scantier and less stately military cloak (*sagum*). See sub-note ‡.

† Yet, taken in connection with what directly precedes it in the oration for Rabirius ("Fecerat temere,"—and so on, through the page,—144 t. vi, Oper.; *ed. cit.*) the passage is one of perplexity. Aldus Manutius (ubi cit. p. 1202) tells us that according to Plutarch the ancients *fought in the toga girded.* Referring to the passage, which is in Coriolanus, I find it unmistakable, even allowing for the time in which he wrote, when the toga had fallen into considerable disuse, and for what he avows to have been his imperfect knowledge of the Roman tongue. Ην δε τοτε τοις 'Ρωμαιοις εθος, εις ταξιν καθεσταμενοις, και μελλοισι τοις θυρεοις αναλαμβανειν, και περιζωννυσθαι την τηβεννον, ἁμα και διαθηχας αγραφους γενεσθαι, κ. τ. λ. (*Oper.* t. i. p. 217. ed *Xyland.* Francof. in fol. 1599.) My limits, already greatly extended, do not permit me to examine this question further. I will but add, that if the toga were short and scanty (as it must have been with the poor), it could have been girded, and thus made literally succinct, as with the troops in Plutarch. See sub-note below, which appears to furnish, in the assertion of Rubenius, a conjectural solution of the difficulty.

‡ *Sagum* and *paludamentum*, frequently put reciprocally for the same outer-

used constantly in opposition to war, the pursuits of war, and the habiliments of war; of which it would be superfluous to cite instances; and *togati* absolutely to express the Roman citizens, not soldiers, as in this very story in Livy, after the catastrophe and Virginius' appeal in the camp : "Immisti turbæ militum togati." III, 50 (t. i. p. 293. *Elser.*).

As to the size of the toga, the variety in which needs hardly any argument or citation of authorities, it is discussed by Aldus Minutius : (*ut supra* p. 1198.) The six ells assigned to its just measure, were of the ample cloak undoubtedly, and not of such as Cato wore. A Spanish mantle that is circular will contain seven yards of broadcloth. Cicognara makes the diameter of the semicircle about three times the statue of a man, and in the broadest part its width about a third.* That it reached to the heels, as Sigonius describes it, may be said to have been impossible, because impracticable, for ordinary wear. That error, like the description of its passing under the right arm, comes from the observation of statues.

The material was wool, as indeed with all the garments, except of the priests, during the earlier days of the Republic. It was without color (*pura*) for the ordinary citizen; but in persons of rank there was an insertion or embroidery of purple called the *clavus*.†

garment, corresponded with the Greek *chlamys*, and like it were fastened with a clasp or brooch, usually on the right shoulder, leaving the arm on that side bare. But it might be shifted, that is, the mantle be clasped to the left, or the clasp brought to the middle. Its length varied, and it may be supposed to have been worn both fuller and longer by men of rank, as in the *paludamenta* of the Emperors. Rubens (for it is the son of the great painter who is known as *Rubenius*) gives us the figure of the *chlamys*,—very much resembling a wide-bottomed petticoat of the present mode. He considers the *toga* as not differing much in form from this, the *chlamys*, except *in magnitude and its cast*. "Togam Romanam haud multum forma a chlamyde diversam fuisse, sed magnitudine solum et circumjectu, existimo." (*De Re Vestiaria* : lib. II. c. 8.— *Graev. Thes.* vi. 1018.) Will this help to explain the doubtful phrase in Cicero, and the one still more perplexing in Plutarch?

* *Storia della Scultura*, I. c. 5 : (*Venez.* in fol. 1813. t. i. p. 81.)

† Grævius, in the preface of his 6th volume, shows, as he himself says

As to the right arm's being left free, of which I have just spoken, it is probable that this was only the mode adopted by orators. Were one to speak in any cloak whatever, he would naturally, I might almost say necessarily, free the right arm precisely as we see it often (not always) in statues. But that it was so worn on other occasions, and especially in the streets, is not more probable than it would be were one, who had been in Spain, to assume that such was the mode of wearing the mantle there. The length alone would prohibit it, because when so worn it would touch the ground precisely as we see it in the *Augusto Togato* of Visconti, which nevertheless, and though in a rhetorical attitude, has the right shoulder covered by the mantle, the right arm being well freed by the depression and largeness of the fold.*

Rubenius does, beyond the possibility of skepticism, that the *clavi* were stripes inwoven or embroidered in the toga. "Clavos fuisse lineas ad instar fasciarum, oblongas quadratas, non rotunda frusta, aut pannos, capitibus clavorum similes, tam certis et liquidis argumentis probare mihi videtur Rubenius, ut ne Pyrrho quidem de hac re dubitare possit. .... Tunica laticlavia dicitur Graecis μεσοπορφυρος, *quæ in medio purpuram habet intextam*," etc. etc. See all on that page (it is not numbered), and, further on, the two following pages and part of the next.

A more modern authority is just as positive "that the terms arose from the figure of the *clavus* (a stud) on the dress." Fuss (*Rom. Antiq.*—Transl. Sect. 452., Oxf. in 8°. 1840. p. 521). He adds : "A passage in Horace, Sat 1. 6, 28, seems to prove that it was worn on the breast," and quotes :

> " Nam ut quisque insanus nigris medium impediit crus
>   Pellibus, et latum demisit pectore clavum."

To correct so strange a surmise, it is merely necessary to quote the gloss of Torrentius. "Demisit : *recto ordine descendebant insuti clavi, vel intexti*."

* See the representation of this very noble statue, probably of Greek art, in the *Museo Pio-Clementino*, (Roma 1784,) Tav. xlv. Tom. II. ; with note (*b*) p. 92. A copy of this sumptuous work will be found in the *Astor Library*. The figure is imitated on a smaller scale in Ferrario (*Costume*, cc. V. Tav. 7), where the want of accuracy of the designer has actually added to the majesty and *breadth* of effect which distinguish the original.

Merely adding, for the benefit of the actor, the judicious advice of Quintilian, not to let the side that is thrown over the shoulder descend lower in front than the middle of the leg nor behind so low as the hips, I will conclude this too-long essay on what was the distinguishing outer characteristic of Roman citizens, and continued so while Rome retained her liberty, by quoting from Cicognara: "Non eravi in Roma distinzione più onorevole della toga. Gl' imperatori la vestivono, e Cesare stesso era di quella coperto allorchè fu assassinato in Senato. (*Sueton.* in *Caes.* c. 82.) Settimio Severo, che arrivò alle porte di Roma in abito militare, smontò da cavallo ed entrò in città alla testa delle sue truppe dopo d' esservi rivestito della toga. (*Dion. Cass. Hist. Rom.* l. I. xxiv.)" *Storia ec.*, I. c. 5. p. 87. The last sentence is worthy of note as confirming by an example the essential character of the toga, as a civil garment only and robe of peace.

5.—P. 91. *Not at least Till Hymen's torch is lighted,* etc.] This reading, as being the simplest and most directly intelligible, is I think the best also for the Stage. But if a more florid and elaborate one be preferred, it may be adopted as follows:

> *Ica.* Not at least
> Till Hesper rising bids the five-fold torch
> Of Love be lighted, and the deck'd couch is spread
> Here in the hall, and thy cheeks' blushes, deepening
> Under the saffron veil, make pale the flowers
> That crown thy locks, and o'er thy yellow shoes
> Flows the white stole whose purple fringe I am weaving, —
> When girded, *etc.*

or:

> *Ica.* Till the star
> Of evening rising bids the five-fold torch
> Of Hymen kindle, *etc.* (as above):

while again, the text may be further simplified for general ears, by substituting after the colon in the fourth line:

> ... when deeper glows thy cheek
> Under the veil, and the long robe enwraps thee,

(or, as in the text, "and the fring'd robe is on thee,") *etc.*

6.—P. 93. *Full five denarii, has consum'd my all.*] Or read: "Full twenty sesterces, consumes my all;" which will be familiar enough. The denarius was equal to ten *asses* (the *as* representing at that time a pound of brass). And originally the verse redd, "Full fifty asses, *etc.*" But this would have had an equivocal sound for an audience.

7.—P. 95. *Alas, I weep not therefore*, etc.] For the Stage, omit from this verse to the half-verse, "*Va.* To this stranger," inclusive.

8.—P. 101. ... *he frowns*, etc.] For the Stage, if the Actor of *Icilius* be tall,—"he towers."

9.—P. 104. *Which soon will pale but one, and ported bare.*] For the Stage, may be substituted the more ordinary:

> Ere long to encircle one, and carried bare.

But the elevated language of the text is better suited to the occasion and the man.

10.—P. 105. *And made the street* Accursed *to this day!*] According to the well-known story, which is probably the exaggeration of the sequel of an atrocious deed, it was the wife of Tarquin, Servius' own daughter, who drove over the body of the murdered king. Dionysius tells the tale with considerable effect, which would have been heightened but for his mania of putting speeches into the mouths of all his characters; how, when the body was yet palpitating ($\sigma\pi\alpha\iota\rho o\nu\tau o\varsigma$), the fiendish woman forced the reluctant charioteer to drive over it in the narrow street, striking him, in her fury, with the foot-bench. The change in the name of the street is then told :— 'Ουτος ὁ στενωπος, ολβιος* καλουμενος προτερον, εξ εκεινου του δεινου και μυσαρου παθους ασεβης ὑπο 'Ρωμαιων κατα την πατριον γλωτταν καλειται. Dion. Hal. *Antiq.* IV. xxxix. p. 233 t. i. *ed. supra cit.*

Livy's account, " Creditur, etc." (*lib.* I. c. 48. t. i. p. 56, *Twiss ;* p. 71, *Bipont ;* p. 97, *Gronov.*) is worth reading, because, from a certain preciseness of detail, it carries you to the scene and with the actor. He proceeds : "*Sceleratum* vicum vocant, quo amens, agitantibus furiis sororis ac viri, Tullia per patris corpus carpentum egisse fatur," etc.

a.—P. 111. Venus Cloacina.] The origin of this strange title, according to Lactantius (*de Falsa Relig.* lib. i,—as cited in the Elzevir Livy, t. i. p. 189), was as follows : " Cloacinæ simulacrum in Cloaca maxima Tatius consecravit, et, quia cujus effigies ignorabat, ex loco illi nomen imposuit."

11.—P. 108. — in their tunics.] Under the *toga* was worn the *tunic,* which at first was without sleeves.† It was girt around the waist, and descended about to the knee : " Nam *infra* mulierum est, *supra* centurionum. (Quint. *Orat.* XI. ed. cit. p. 517.) This was worn by all ranks, and with the common people was their sole garment. But

---

* A note in Drakenborch's Livy (ed. *Twiss*) at the corresponding passage will be useful here. Speaking of the name in Livy, " *Urbium,* vulgo *Virbium,* qui haud procul Bovillis fuit, (Pers. Sat. vi. 55" [where see *Vet. Schol.*]) it proceeds: " *Orbium* videtur velle Festus ' cui nomen a flexuosis orbibus.' Huic cognomen Scelerati hæsisse probabile est ; certe non Cyprio Vico" [as in some edd. of Dionys.], ut constat ex Varr. de L. L. iv. qui *Scelerotum vicum* haud procul Cyprio fuit." See also in the elegant Elzevir ed. (Gronov.) of 1679, the note on the same term ; t. i. p. 97.

† When worn, they did not descend further than the elbow, usually not so far. "I soli plebei vili, e gli uomini infami usavano le maniche lunghe, come si vede dagli archi di Tito e di Constantino." Levati. *Cost. dei Rom.* in Ferrario : *Cost.* ec. V. 613.

as the knights and senators wore the toga with a stripe of purple, those narrower, these wider, so the tunic was, with them, likewise distinguished.* Hence *Icilius*, a little earlier in the text, says to *Lucretius :*

> " And they please me little ;
> As does thy *purpled tunic*, which they suit."

In the bust, supposed of Junius Brutus, (Visc. *Iconogr. Rom.* I. *Pl.* 2. and expl. ch. 2., p. 16 : *Paris*, in fol., 1817,) we see the tunic very full, making numerous plaits, as compressed by the toga.

In saying that this body-garment was the only dress of the common people, it must be understood, at all ordinary times ; for on solemn occasions it is not to be supposed that even the lower classes, except the very poor, were without the upper vestment which was the distin-

---

* *Tunica.* " Hæc angustior et brevior quam toga fuit, ac primum sine manicis, deinde manicata, ac cinctura constricta est.

" Cum ergo cives omnes Romani tunica uterentur, factum est, ut tunicæ ordines distinxerint : nam senatores et equites tunicam clavatam induerunt, plebs rectam" [*puram*,[a] h. e.—colorless) et sine clavis. Clavata tunica fuit, quæ clavos purpureos intextos habuit, aut latos aut angustos. Fuerunt autem clavi, quasi flores panno intexti [b] . . . . Cæterum tunica latos clavos purpureos intextos habens, quæ et *latus clavus* et *tunica lati clavi* dicta est, propria fuit senatorum atque amplissimi ordinis insigne." Car. Sigon. *in Græv. Thes.* ubi cit. c. xix. p. 820 sq.

See also the whole of that chapter. Sigonius quotes there so amply and so aptly that the interest it excites is unusual.

". . . De tunica lati clavi purpurea . . . satis aperta . . . significatio in hoc Ovidii versu :

" *Induiturque humeris cum lato purpura clavo.*" Ald. Man. u. c. p. 1206.

[a] " *Toga pura* fuit communis toga hominorum *privatorum*, eorumque *virorum*. Itaque etiam *virilis* est appellata. Ac *pura* quidem dicta, quod albi coloris esset, nulla admista purpura." Sigon. *ubi supra*, p. 816.

" Toga, pura, virilis, libera, *recta*, eadem erat." Ald. Manut. *ib.* p. 1192.

[b] See, above, sub-note † on p. 185, s :.

guishing garb of a Roman citizen.* Thus (a little below in the text), *Icilius* bids the *Citizens*, that is, the more substantial among them, *put on their mantles.* It was in fact, in that great city of the olden day, as you may see it now, in London for example, where grooms and several others of the lower classes go in their sleeved waistcoats in ordinary ; only, the Roman wore no shirt under his tunic, that being, even for the rich, the sanitary comfort of a later day which saw the introduction or the familiar use of linen and cotton. Nature is the same everywhere and at all times, rising above fashions or modifying their conditions. Keeping this fact in view, we shall seldom be mystified by the conjectures and disputes of antiquaries. In modern times, vulgar men, or men who love their ease more than elegance or decorum, take off their common coat in-doors and sit in their vest and shirt-sleeves. Wore they woolen tunics only, we should have in these the ancient Roman, who knew not the convenience, except in military life, of a succinct upper-garment.

12.—P. 113. *Why did I make that law ? What is plebeian, That flesh patrician may not mate therewith ?*] Ὡς δε ουκ ηδυνατο προς γαμον αυτην λαβειν, εκεινην τε ὁρων εγγεγυημενην ἑτερῳ, και αυτος γυναικα γαμετην· και ἁμα ουδ' αξιων εκ δημοτικου γενους ἁρμοσασθαι γαμον, ὁν αυτος εν ταις δωδεκα δελτοις ανεγραψε, κ. τ. λ. DION. HAL. *Ant. R.* XI. xxviii. (*Op.* ed. cit. t. i. p. 676.)

"Jam et processerat pars major anni, et duæ tabulæ legum ad prioris anni decem tabulas erant adjectæ." LIV. *Hist.* III. c. 37. (t. I. p. 186, ed. cit.)

Cicero speaks of this characteristic law in one of the defective chapters of his Republic (II. 37. *Nobbe,* ex recens. *Ernest. Lips.* 16°.

---

* "Itaque objicias licet, quam voles sæpe, palliatum fuisse, *aliqua habuisse non Romani hominis insignia* etc." Orat. pro Rabirio. The whole passage (p. 194, CIC. *Op.* Bipont. t. vi.) is worth reading, as illustrating the tenacity with which the Romans held to the wearing of the toga as characteristic of their people, even in the days of Cicero.

1827): a chapter which incidentally refers to the subject-story of this Tragedy. "Ergo horum ex injustitia" [Decemviror. *sc.*] "subito exorta est maxima perturbatio et totius commutatio rei publicæ: qui, duabus tabulis iniquarum legum additis, quibus, etiam quæ disjunctis populis tribui solent connubia, hæc illi ut ne plebei cum patribus essent, inhumanissima lege sanxeruut; quæ postea plebeiscito Canuleio abrogata est: libidiuoseque omni imperio et acerbe et avare populo præfuerunt."

13.—P. 115. *'T is Virginius' daughter!* Num. *Gods! we are too late*] The passage may read thus :

> 'T is Virginius' daughter !
>
> > *Icil.* Gods! —— [*springing forward in the di-*
> > > *rection of the sound.*
> > *Num.* We are too late. [*following,* etc.

But it is more consistent with the character of *Icilius,* that he should not exclaim, but act at once, as I have made him in the text; — where, if preferred, *Numit.'s* part may read, "O! we are too late."

14.—P. 118. *Romans! freemen! brothers! Yè know me ; I have never spoken false. This is Virginius' daughter ;* etc.] Between the second and third lines of this appeal, I had written two other verses. They may be restored, if judged advisable ; the passage reading thus :

> —— I have never spoken false.
> Look on this tender maid, half-dead with shame
> To be so branded. Has a slave such mien ?
> It is Virginius' daughter ; *etc.*

15.—P. 119. *If thou dare touch her, though it be the form,*—] Or, more directly intelligible perhaps, thus :

> If thou dare touch her, though the form require it :

(*Marcus,* namely, putting forth his hand to touch the shoulder of

Virginia, as the formality exacted on such occasions.) But what *Marcus* says, himself, presently, may render the meaning plain enough:

———————— let me wave the form.

16.—P. 119. *Now, by the manes,* etc.] The actor may read: "Now by the ashes," *etc.*; though the former word should be sufficiently familiar.

17.—P. 120. *By the same law, assert her to be free, And as her guardian, in the father's room, Demand the right to lead her where I will.*] Or:

> By the same law, assert her unto freedom,
> And as her guardian claim the natural right, [or,
>   claim prescriptive right.]
> She being born free, to take her whence she came.

But the legal phrase, "assert her unto freedom," though more strictly Roman, would not be directly understood from the stage.— The last line of the text: "Demand the right, *etc.*," may be redd,

> Claim natural right to reconduct her home.

18.—P. 124. *Arrest,* etc.] The naturalness is marred in this and the preceding line *metri grat.* Omit for the Stage the last word in either verse. But in the second may be redd: "Seize him, bind, or slay!"

19.—P. 125. *But who are surety that the girl appear?*] This verse, with the four in connection, directly before and after it, may be thus modified:—

> *Num.* My son, that was not wise.
> See! they have taken alarm.
>   *Marc.* Be 't, great decemvir:
> I ask but justice. Meantime, that the girl
> May be forthcoming, let the friends find bail.
> *Val.* Here! Lucius Valerius.
>   *Hor.* And Horatius, here!

9

People. { And here !

          And here !

                    And all of us !

Which perhaps would be the better reading for the Stage, because it expresses more distinctly that requirement of the Roman law, which we have, among so many others, borrowed ; the word "bail" exciting at once in the minds of the audience a familiar image.

Or again :

> See where the pander, *etc.*
> *Marc.* Be 't great decemvir ! Meantime, let the friends
> Give surety that the maiden re-appear.

Or :

> I ask but justice. Meantime, that the girl
> May be forthcoming, let the friends find bail.

20.—P. 127.   App. *Waits no one more for justice?   Lictors, move.* (Rises, and *etc.*]   Otherwise, omitting this last verse, where *Appius'* "Waits no one more for justice ?" might excite a smile :

> APPIUS, *looking from side to side for a moment, rises slowly,*
> *and as he turns, about to descend the tribunal,*
> *the Drop falls.*

21 —P. 128.   *'T were best not ask me.* (carelessly.]   Or : " I am not Pontiff, [*coldly.*"   But this would need more knowledge of the Roman religion than the audience in general can have. — For " Think'st thou there be Furies ?" may be redd, " Believ'st thou in the Furies ?"

22.—P. 130.   *I made thee note the daughter's beauty—*] —" Virginia's beauty " is preferable : but from the Stage, the enunciation of " Virginius," almost directly after, would be unpleasant, from the want of a sufficiently sensible difference between the sounds.

23.—P. 131.   *Torture his pride !* etc. etc. to end of Scene.]   Or, omitting these five last lines, make Marcus' *Exit* at "thrown away," and Livia's after "Thou shalt see," (two lines above.) This is more in the true spirit of tragedy (as I conceive it); in which any sarcasm, that shall excite even a smile in the audience, is misplaced.

24. - P. 135. *Whose tutelar-gods thy mother's girlhood knew—*] This line may be omitted ; and so, which is the original conception, it better suits the rapidity of *Icilius'* present manner. "Await with him thy sire," may read, "Await thy troubled sire."

Otherwise again, the whole passage may read thus:

> And the black gore drip downwards!— No more sorrow !
> Come, my Virginia, let us seek the hall.
> There, by thy uncle's tutelar gods, with him
> Await thy father, while Icilius goes
> To stir Rome's ashes.— Why this sudden change ?
> Have the gods heard our anguish ? Let the shadow
> Now passing from my heart be better augury,
> And thy own grim forebodings pass away
> Like the night's dreams.

25.—P. 136. Draws his hood, *etc*] That is, of the *penula* or traveling-cloak. This was a thick, rough, or even shaggy, woolen outergarment or surtout, used as a protection against the weather. Hence often worn in the theatres, like the *lacerna ;* especially in winter. We read of it most frequently as a defence against rain. The pompous lines of Juvenal to that import (I. v. 79.) will readily be remembered:

> —— " fremeret sæva cum grandine vernus
> Jupiter, et multo stillaret pænula nimbo :"

as also the witticism of Galba, when asked to lend his cloak of that description : "Non pluit, non est opus tibi ; si pluit, ipse utor."*

---

* See Oct. Ferrar. *De Re*, etc. Pars II. Lib. II., which is devoted to the subject. (p. 823 sqq. Graev. *Thes*. VI.)

Penula. "Hæc ex lana alba, aut ex gausape fuit confecta, pluviæ atque

26.—P. 139. *The third day after that is long enough !*] This verse may be omitted.

27.—P. 142. —— *were alone Icilius' only sorrow :*] "Icilius' heavy sorrow"—if it be wished to avoid the *apparent* tautology,—for such it is only at first sight: but the original reading, which is that of the text, is far preferable in every respect; and it alone expresses my meaning.

28.—P. 142. —— *that they love their wives.*] —"that they love their homes [*or*, hearths.]" For the Stage, perhaps; as the mass of an audience catches instantly and eagerly at the faintest shadow of the comic, (which, by the way, is, in acting, the saving grace of many a bad tragedy;) and, as I said before, the least pleasantry I deem to be out of place *here.*   .

itineris caussa, non togæ, ut lacernæ, sed tunicæ superimposita." Can. Sigon. De Judiciis, III, 18.—p. 819 *Græv.* vol. cit.

Pænula—"habitus hibernus ac viatorius, et ad propulsandos imbres, ceterasque asperioris cœli injurias, peridoneus. Fiebant autem pænulæ ex crassiori lana, non ex tenuiori prolixiorique ut togæ." Jo. Bapt. Donn *Diss. de Utraq. Pænula* ; in *Græv.* vol. cit. p. 1151.

"Erat et alia pænula, capitio adjecto, de qua Plinius l. xxiv., ubi pænularum capitibus centunculum comparat: *Itali*, inquit, *centunculum vocant, rostratis foliis, ad similitudinem capitis pænularum, jacentem in arvis.* Bart. Bartholin. *de Pænula.*—p. 1172. *Græv.* etc.

… "Strictior est et ejus ora quæ collum ambit, tam laxe tamen patens ut caput exeri possit, operiri aut involvi. Unde Pomponius in Penicea : *Pænulam in caput induce, ne te noscat:*" (which is precisely the act of *Virginius*).— *Id.,* *ib.* p. 1172. … "Pars ventrem spectans aperta est, alioquin vestimentum clausum et rotundum esset." *Ib.* He adds a descriptive figure.

"La penula era un mantello di grossa lana adorno di frangie, aperto solamente nella parte superiore per farvi passare la testa. Quello de' soldati avea il color rosso, quello de' cittadini bruno. Di dietro eravi un cappuccio, col quale coprivano il capo ne' tempi piovosi." Levati, *ubi cit.*

29.—P. 142. *I seek to restore the tribunes. Appius said it.*] This variety in the rythm is used to give a sudden and brief rapidity to the enunciation. If the Actor prefer, it may be redd: "I would restore the tribunes," *etc.*

30.—P. 142. *Alas for me! their power suspended trials.*] Or: "Tribunes! Alas! their power could put off trials."

31.—P. 149. *—'t would cost me merely life.*] Or, with an allusion to *Virginia,* "but *my* life." And for the last words of *Valerius,* to which *Icilius* makes reply, may be redd:

—— "to keep back Spurius Oppius.
Courage, Icilius! when the sun goes down,
Rome will be free :"

which pre-indicates the time of the catastrophe.

32.—P. 150. *— that shall make thee his, Renders thy sire the proudest in all Rome.*] ——"that confirms thee his, Will make thy sire, *etc.*"

33.—P. 151. *All other shrines, were not her temple here?*] "All other homes, were not her mansion here?"

34.—P. 152. *Justice no more shall lend her snow-white pall To hood Oppression ——*] The dress of the Roman women consisted of the stole (*stola*), a sleeved garment, which corresponded to the tunic of the men, but descended to the feet,* and the "pall" (*palla*), which was the Pallium of the Greeks, and, worn over the stole, as a mantle, corresponded to the toga of the men. Of its shape there is dispute, as in

---

* "La tunica lunga con lunghe maniche, come vedesi nella figlia di Niobe, è quella precisamente che i romani poi chiamarono *stola.*" CICOGN. *Storia della Scult.* I. c. 5.—p. 77 t. i.

regard to the form of the toga. Winkelmann supposes it to have been round, and Ferrari to have been semicircular; but Cicognara maintains that it was in cut a parallelogram.* That it was, or may have been, rectangular, any artist may ascertain for himself by trying a sheet, or better a light blanket, which will enable him to imitate easily the modes of wearing this dress as it is seen in statues. With a very natural action the pall was frequently drawn over the head, sometimes merely to the forehead, sometimes so as to conceal the features (as with *Virginia* in the entry to Act v. Sc. 3),whence the expression in the text ; which however may be redd from the Stage :

> "Justice no more shall lend her snow-white robe
>   To hood Oppression."

There is a fine line of Horace (*Serm.* I. ii. 99) which describes with a single touch both the stole and pall :

> "*Ad talos* stola *demissa,* et *circumdata* palla."

The toga was worn by women only under disreputable circumstances, of which the Satire cited furnishes more than one illustration.

On the color of the *stola*, see the note of Baxter and Zeunius on the 36th verse of the same Satire, (p. 299, ed. Lond. in 8°, 1809.) It cannot be doubted that it varied at different times, and not only according to the rank but to the age of the wearer. A maiden of Virginia's youth, of the more respectable class of the plebeians, would hardly wear anything but white. See note 10, p. 106, *Tav.* xx. *Antichità di Ercolano.* (fol. 1757.)

Finally, on the Palla, consult Octav. Ferrar. : *Analecta de R. V.* c. 26.—p. 1103 sq. in *Græv.* vol. cit.

35.—P. 153. *And Publius' own are fulgent with new hope.*]   "And Publius' quiet mien is full of hope."

---

* *Storia,* cc. *ubi supra.*, p. 79, 80.

b.—P. 159. — in a mourning-cloak —] The *Pallium* (*palla*, "pall") described in note 34.

36.—P. 161. *But, being taught in time Her falsehood with, etc.*]

> " But, when certain proofs
> Taught me to know her falsehood with that man,
> Yon Claudius, plaintiff here, I flung her off,
> As I would fling a viper, (see! she trembles!)
> Never having, *etc.*"

And above, for *brought from taken Antium*, "taken in the Volscian war."

37.—P. 164. —*and honor now But little known, man trusts man's word no more*—] Or, —"man plights his word no more:" which is more accurate in construction, though less tragic (stern and nervous) in sound.

38.—P. 166. — *Wherefore Wear ye else hidden arms?*] "Else, Why wear ye hidden arms?"

39.—P. 167. —*Such the law Of great Valerius makes deserving death.*]

> " And therefor
> May by the great Valerius' law be slain
> By any hand; law natural and just."

But the text has the advantage of brevity.— For *makes* in the text, may be redd "made." But it is less forcible.

40.—P. 167. *There sits your Tarquin—— App. But thou stand'st not Brutus.*] Perhaps this play on the word, though bitter and stern on the part of the speaker, might cause a smile in some of the audience. It may read then: " But thou art not [*or*, art no] Brutus."

41.—P. 169. *Virginius then had no part in the cheat! Marcus and Livia*, etc. App. *But little,* etc.] The first line may be omitted; which restores the part to its original conception. And again, for the Stage, all three of the verses may be thrown out, as impeding the action.

42.—P. 171. *Weeps? For ye will not,* etc.] It may be pointed, "Weeps;" — which allows the actor to give another tone to the expression. I think the reading of the text better suits the character, although the energy, and fierceness even, of the exclamation, make the difference scarcely important.

43.—P. 171. *A fiction. Appius stoops not to say more.*] From here to *Lictors, make room* — to be omitted on the Stage.

44.—P. 175. —— *Lucius — my beloved — Receive — my last breath. Father, I — die — pure.*] *Virginia's* dying words might read thus:

<blockquote>
"Lucius — my beloved ! —
T was at thy hand —— But it is fitter thus.
Receive, etc."
</blockquote>

But *Icilius* is made to express himself too nearly in the same manner with regard to Appius : *'T is better thus.*

ADDITION TO NOTE 4, ON THE FORM OF THE TOGA.

P. 181.—I should have added here an undernote to this effect :—

Any rectangular piece of cloth may form a square, a circular, or a semicircular cloak, according to its amplitude, on which depends the number of its gathers at the shoulders. The Spanish mantle owes its curve to this arrangement and nothing else. Take out the plaits and it is quadrilateral. It would follow then, that, could we suppose the same condition obtained with the *toga*, that is, that it was gathered at the shoulders, the curvilinear sweep of the bottom edge would be the result, not of its cut, but of its disposition. But if cut, or more probably woven, not drawn into shape, it must have made not the half of a circle but a narrower segment; for thus only could its widest part equal a third of its diameter. A cloth so fashioned I have essayed on a layfigure, and found it easy therewith to imitate the drapery of the *Augustus*. The right side envelops twice the form, passing in the first involution *under* the right arm, and finally over it at the shoulder: a hint that may be of service to the artist, as well as to the actor. The effect was superb.

BIANCA CAPELLO

MDCCCLV

CHARACTERS

Primary

FRANCESCO-MARIA DE' MEDICI, *Grand Duke of Tuscany.*

CARDINAL FERDINANDO DE' MEDICI, } *his brothers.*
DON PIETRO DE' MEDICI,

MALOCUORE, *a Gentleman of the Grand-duke's household, and his confidant.*

PIETRO BONAVENTURI, *at first a Clerk in the banking-house of Salviati in Venice, but subsequently the Grand-duke's Favorite and Intendant.*

LUCA SENNUCCIO, *his fellow-clerk and friend, and subsequently of the G. Duke's household.*

CARLO ANTONIO DEL POZZO, *Arch-bishop of Pisa, — at one time Auditor of the Treasury,* } *both of the Grand-duke's Cabinet.*
OTTAVIO ABBIOSO, *Coadjutor-Bishop of Pistoia and Florentine Secretary at Venice,*

BIANCA CAPELLO, *at first wife of Bonaventuri, subsequently Grand Duchess of Tuscany.*

DONNA ISABELLA DE' MEDICI, *the Grand-duke's sister.*

SIGNORA MALOCUORE, *wife of Malocuore.*

Secondary

PAOLO GIORDANO ORSINI, *Duke of Bracciano, husband of Isabella de' Medici.*

BARTOLOMMEO CAPELLO, *Senator of Venice, Bianca's father.*

VITTORIO CAPELLO, *her brother.*

GRIMANI, *Patriarch of Aquileia, her uncle.*

TIEPOLO, ⟩ *Venetian Senators, special Ambassadors from the*
MICHIELI, ⟩ *Republic.*

BACCIO BALDINI, ⟩ *Court Physicians.*
PIETRO CAPPELLI, ⟩

SCHERANO, ⟩
MASNADIERE, ⟩ *assassins.*
MALANDRINO, ⟩
SGHERRO, · ⟩

CAGNOTTO, ⟩ *armed servants of the Favorite.*
BRENNA, ⟩

DONNA ELEONORA DI TOLEDO, *wife of Don Pietro.*
DONNA VIRGINIA DE' MEDICI, *the Grand-duke's half-sister,*
betrothed and subsequently married to Don Cesare d' Este
Bonaventuri's MOTHER.
AIA, *Bianca's Governess.*
Count Ulisse Bentivoglio. *A Page in Bonaventuri's*
household. Two Assassins.

Mute Persons

PELLEGRINA, *Bianca's Daughter, wife of Bentivoglio.* DON CE-
SARE D' ESTE. *Senators. Magistrates. Lords and*
Ladies of the Court. Venetian Nobles.
Pages. Soldiers. Servants.

SCENE. *In the First Act, in Venice; in a portion of the Fourth,*
in Rome; for the rest of the play, in Florence, until
the catastrophe, — which takes place at Caiano,
in the neighborhood of Florence.
COSTUMES. *Those of the latter half of the 16th Century.*

BIANCA CAPELLO

Scene I. A room in the Apartment of Bonaventuri
in the Casa Salviati in Venice.

BONAVENTURI. SENNUCCIO.

Senn. Capello's daughter? Thou art doubly mad!
Bonav. All passion is but madness. Why not mine?
Senn. All passion is not madness — not as thine.
　　Thou art in impulse, act, and object mad.
　　To love the flower of all Venetian maids,
　　That was not sane: why! art thou not, as I,
　　But Salviati's servant, and low-born? —
Bonav. What has? ——
　　　　　Senn. To dare to make thy passion known,
　　That was still madder. —
　　　　　　　Bonav. Could I will it else?

Can ? ——

Senn. But to seek —— What dost thou seek in fine ?

Bonav. Nothing. Wilt hear me speak? Thou art no more
    Luke my companion, friendly although rough,
    And counseling like an elder brother ; thou
    Speak'st without pity, hast no sympathy,
    Though 't was for that, and through the show of that
    Alone, I utter'd what no human ear
    Should otherwise have learn'd. Thou did'st seduce me
    By thy great urgence and thy tone of love
    To throw myself upon thy offer'd breast,
    And then brok'st from me, with a shout and laugh.

Senn. A shout, Pietro[1], if thou so must phrase it,
    For I was sore amaz'd ; but not a laugh.

Bonav. Yes, with a laugh. For what is it but scorn
    That makes thee treat my passion as insane ?
    I look'd for sober counsel, — for reproof ;
    But yet for pity, — not for mockery.

                    Senn. No.

    Nor hadst it. Canst thou not allowance make
    For my surprise ? It seem'd so strange a thing,
    When I beheld thee pining and cast down,
    Thy sparkling eyes grown heavy like a girl's
    Sick of her maidhood, and thy jocund laugh,
    That had at times contagion even for me,
    Turn'd to a melancholy vacant smile,
    As if thy soul were in the topmost clouds,
    And oft in answer to my happiest speech
    Heard thy inapplicable words, or met,
    As often quite, thy start, and stare, and " Luke,

Forgive me! Do not think me rude! I am
Scarce well ": it seem'd so strange a thing,
To learn at last thou wast heart-sick for one
So high above thee, and so rarely bright,
It was as though thou sighedst for the moon.—
Bonav. Endymion did.
     Senn. That was in fable.
        Bonav. Not
In fable though, the Moon return'd his sighs.
That was the natural sequel of true passion,
Which fires in turn.
     Senn. Thou hast the fable wrong.
It was the Moon lov'd him, who slept through all.
Thou may'st be handsome as the Latmian boy.
Like him, thy moon consoles thee but in dreams.
Bonav. Not so, by Heaven! for I am wide awake,
And —— [*checking himself.*]
Senn. Darest not say, that thou art lov'd in turn?
Bonav. I dare not say it, but ——
     Senn. Thou look'st it! Now,
This is sheer lunacy! Moonstruck Pietro!
Art thou then well awake?
     Bonav. I am awake:
Awake to find that I have dream'd of things
Not less unreal than Diana's kisses;
As of thy heart for instance, and the place
Methought I held in it; awake to learn,
And learn to my dismay, that souls as calm
And as profound as thine may stir with envy.

Senn. Pietro! — But so be it. It is well
That I should read my nature. It may be
That thou divinest right. Our friend's self-love
Jars harshly on the quick sense of our own.
'T is Heaven's foresight. — But, if envy's gust
Ruffle the surface of my graver spirit,
Thy vain presumption surges fathom-deep.

Bonav. Vain? and presumption? It is kindly said!

Senn. 'T is said, at least, in no disdain of thee.
Capello's blood flows from the mountain rill;
Thine is like mine, the puddle: so men think.

Senn. But what of these distinctions knows the heart,
Or asks? Love is no herald; flesh and blood,
Not gules and argent, are his lore: nor can
The Doge's bonnet, did its jewel'd band
Gleam on Capello's haughty forehead, throw
The terror of his function round his child.
She is herself alone; lov'd for herself.

Senn. 'T is thus thine eyes behold her. But for hers ——

Bonav. They look not through her father's robe of state.
Besides, I am not sure Bianca knows ——

Senn. Bianca? Really! ——

Bonav. Wherefore not? I would
I had not so betray'd me! But thus far
Since thou hast brought me to confess, hear on.
Hear on? No! read! Read there!

Handing a note to SENNUCCIO, *after kissing it with rapture.*
Then, eagerly watching his countenance as he reads,
BONAVENTURI *continues triumphantly:*

Art dumb? Is that

Diana's beam? And am I yet asleep?

Senn. I see no signature — no name without.

Comes this indeed from her? from her to thee?

Bonav. To me from her.

         Senn. It passes all belief!

Is there no fraud? Women have snar'd ere now.

What means this mystery? [*indicating a place*

                              on the note.

        Bonav. First give it voice. Read out.

Let my ears drink the rapture that my eyes

Have ten times in the hour past reel'd with; let

My heart renew its triumph. Read! Read all!

Senn. [*reading.*

  "Surprise — I would not say distrust or fear —

Made me, perchance, seem harsher than I meant.

I would amend my fault, if one have been.

Does thy petition, in thy friend's behoof,

Bear to be urg'd again, so let me hear it:

That with prepared ears I may decide,

If with my quality and maiden shame

It suit to grant it. She who bears thee this

Will tell thee more. Thou mayst confide in her,

As I do in thy nobleness." — And —— Well?

Bonav. Wilt thou without rude hindrance hear me through?

    •   SENNUCCIO *nods gravely.*   .

Resolv'd to speak or die, I chose an hour

When Blanche's governess came from her prayers,

And told her that a case of life and death

Depended on the favor of her ward;
Whose intercession in a friend's behalf
I must implore in person.   The good dame,
By my strong urgence mov'd — how could she else ?
I pray'd as to a saint, — at last consented
That on the morrow I should be receiv'd
Into their barge, and to her lady's ear·
Breathe out my supplication.

                   Senn. And thou went'st ?
Pietro I ——
Bonav. Hush I — I went.   Bianca's hand —
'T could be no other there, so small, so white I
From the Capello's gondol-window wav'd
A kerchief.   'T was a minute.   In the next,
I stood before her — knelt.   Her veil was dropp'd,
Even as I entered, by her guardian's hand.
Senn. 'T was well the hag had some small conscience.
                   Bonav. Luke I ——
At my mute look and motion of reserve,
Bianca made the dame some steps retire,
Then softly bade me rise and speak. [2]   O me I
The voice took from me all my power.   Perhaps
The innocent young creature redd the cause
Of my fresh agitation, if already
Looks, gesture, attitude had not betray'd
My soul's true object; for her own sweet speech
Trembled a little, as, with downcast mien,
She bade me gain composure, and once more
Enjoin'd me rise, if I would have her hear.

My thoughts came back. I told her the deceit
My friend's despairing passion made me practice ;
That not upon her father's lips, but hers,
Hung the decision of his fate; and then,
When I had pour'd forth all my passionate thoughts,
Which no more broke in the utterance, but rush'd
One rapid torrent, of such musical flow
That my own senses vibrated, and love
Took from the echo of itself new force, —
Then did I pray that I might see the face
That had wrought such sweet mischief. She complied.
O Luke ! ——

  Senn. Take breath, Endymion.

     Bonav. Would'st thou hear?

Senn. Ay !   But expect no sympathy.

     Bonav. Not now.

I end the tale but to excuse myself. —
Transported, madden'd if thou will, by charms   ·
Which gained by nearness, and which pudency
Color'd to make transcendent, I avow'd
My friend and I were one. And now in haste
Comes up the governess, and with reproaches
Lets down her lady's veil and bids me go.
I rose — for still I had knelt. "And shall my friend,'
I ask'd, "dare then to hope? " — "Hope all men may,'
Bianca said : "They who are right, hope always."

Senn. A most sententious maiden ! — Well, so far,
The mystery is solv'd. But this remains.
Think'st thou the lady knows thee not her peer ?

She writes, " Thy nobleness." What means that phrase?

Bonav. For one so patient, thou art much in haste.

Give me the note. — Thou hast heard I left abruptly.

I fear, alas ! she knows not what I am. [*with dejection.*

Senn. Fear, say'st thou ?   By St. Luke! 'tis nobly said !

I too did fear, Pietro. [*extending his hand, which Bona-*
venturi does not touch.

Bonav. [*haughtily.*] What then?

Senn. This:

Thy honorable nature had succumb'd.

No! [*as Bonav. is going.*

in this mood thou leav'st me not.

Bonav. [*endeavoring to free himself.*] Why stay,

When from thy coldness and distrustful thoughts

I fly to Paradise ? and not to play

The Serpent, as thou ——

Senn. As I do not think.

• Thou shalt stay till thou hear'st me ; for 'tis thou

That wrong'st me, not I thee.   Do I not know thee?

Daring, impetuous, yet of kindly heart,

Who among men hath honor, if not thou ?

But what is human honor?   This one thinks,

Not for wide worlds he would commit a theft,

Yet plots, cabals, o'erreaches, undermines,

And calls it policy.   This, who the rare

And precious gift enjoys to never lie,

Save in surprise or fright of shame, belies

His conscience daily by complaisant smiles,

And in the exaction of his self-love feigns

Desires he feels not! Affluence clips the wings
Of honesty, which flies distress; [3] and longing
Indulg'd melts virtue that was cold as snow.
Thou art as open as the broad sun-light,
And all a man; yet what ensures thy soul,
When passion makes it agony to part,
And happiness, and pride, and dread of shame,
And pity itself, all urge thee to defer?

Bonav. My present action. She who brought this billet —
Given me this morn at mass — a fortnight gone
Since in the gondola I knelt and sigh'd —
Comes at the night's fifth hour — 'tis now at hand —
        [looking off the scene.
To lead me to Bianca — to her home.

Senn. At the Capello's palace?

    Bonav. At the palace.

Senn. Whither thou goest, to? ——

    Bonav. Tell Bianca all:
To end the dream which laps, perhaps, her senses,
But is no dream for mine.

    Senn. This thou wilt do?

Bonav. I will. *[with dejection, yet firmly.*

  Senn. Now Heaven make thee blest, Pietro!
Happen what may, thou 'lt bear no self-reproach
On the charg'd conscience. Yet, ah be advis'd!
Subdue this love? To what end can it lead?
Know'st thou not Venice and the dreaded Ten?
Let but her sire denounce thee to the Signory,
Thy life is not a summer's day.

Bonav. So be it.

Clock within strikes Five.

Hark, from the clock-tower ! [*Exit precipitately.*

         Senn. Rash, but gallant heart !
Thou goest downright to manifest destruction :
For my cold counsel tempers not thy pulse.
Thou hast call'd it envy.   Envy !   Can it be ?
So.   Let me sift myself.   I would not make
One of another class with those I sketch'd ;
Men who sin not themselves, nor play the fool,
But grudge the mirth and joy of those who do.

         .   [*Exit — thoughtfully.*

SCENE II.

In the Casa Capello.   A room in Bianca's Apartment.

BIANCA *and the* GOVERNESS.

*Bianca walking up and down in agitation.   She stops to
look off the scene.*

Gov. 'T is but two minutes.   Think!
                      Bian. 'T is but the street
Between us.   Two are twice too much.   Were I
As he, I should not be so long.   And yet
     She ceases to address her attendant.
How ardent was he!   Had he not been so,
I had not ventur'd.   But what will he think?
Gov. What matters?   He is noble; then, must see
How you have suffer'd.   .
           Bian. Yes, could he but know
That for the last ten days I scarce have slept,
Fearing a thousand things, and hoping more ——
Why came he not to the house?   He must have seen
How well he pleas'd me.   Could he else, so made?
Gov. That may you say.   And such a generous hand!
Pure, all pure gold, the purse he gave me leaving.
It is a right rich house.
           Bian. Four minutes more!

O he is laggard!   Hark but! —— On the stair!
Now! — Now! — The door, good nurse!

Enter BONAVENTURI.

BIANCA *runs up, as if to throw herself into his arms, but
stops, sinks on a seat, and extends her hand, which* BONA-
VENTURI, *kneeling, takes and kisses.*

                           Bonav. O gentle lady! —
Dare I once more? ——   'T is what I scarce had
     hoped!
Bian. You speak to chide me.   Have I been too bold?
Bonav. Bold?   'T was an angel's impulse!   But for this,
     How could I, so unworthy, dare again? —
     I could but silent suffer, as till now,
     Through the long weary fortnight, since the hour
     I knelt and ventur'd in another's name
     To tell you I ador'd you, I have suffer'd.
     But this one minute, were it now to end,
     Repays me, O for all! for all! [*kissing tenderly and
                         rapturously her hand.*
                      Bian. Alas!
And I ——   But rise. [*withdrawing gently her hand.*
                — I fear'd —— I know not well
What 't was I fear'd.   Is it, I was unkind?
I would not be, believe me.   If in error,
In the surprise, the —— if I said too little,
Or, O! too much, forgive me, and forget
All that is wrong in what I said or wrote,

For it has much annoy'd me.

         Bonav. This for me?
I have not merited that thou shouldst lose
One half-hour's rest, shouldst feel one moment's care,
For such as I. Forgiveness? Let me pray,
Once more upon my knees, to be forgiven
For the deceit through which this hour is mine.
Thou smilest. Best, as brightest of thy sex!
Hast thou been conscious of my long, long love,
And find'st it not so criminal? Indeed,
I could no longer bear it; I had died,
Had I not spoken. [*He takes her hand. Bianca, in*
                  her reply, folds the other over his.

         Bian. Wherefore died? Seem'd then
Bianca so ungentle, when thine eyes
From thy sad window watch'd her going out,
And waited her return? Didst thou not think,
Vain man! the eloquence of those wistful looks
Made echoes sometimes in the maiden heart
That knew as yet no love but that of friends
And parents? Henceforth thou wilt not despond?
Thou hast stolen an easy way to Blanche's heart!
Live then to guard it; live for *her*, live *with* her.

Bonav. Forever! O such life were one long dream
Of Paradise, with no forbidden fruit,
No serpent, and no —— Must I not despond?
The dream already breaks; the cherub stands
Before the portal with the flaming sword,
And Heaven's decree admits of no reversal.

Bian. What mean'st thou?

        Bonav. Can this night endure forever?
Wouldst thou permit, or could I dare request
Again admittance to thy chamber?

        Bian. No!
Why shouldst thou need?   My father ——

        Bonav. O my God!

   * *Springing up, he comes forward, and* BIANCA *fol-*
      lows him to the front of the scene.

    The GOVERNESS *also comes nearer, though keeping*
     still in the background.

Bian. What is it ails thee?   In my father's name
Should he no terror.   Thou art not his foe?

Bonav. O no!   But in thy father's blood is that,
Though both are mortal, will not mix with mine.

Bian. Yet thou art noble ——

        Bonav. Noble?

        Bian. And thy house
Is one whose stem might be entwin'd with ours.

Bonav. My house?   Whom tak'st thou me for? — O my
     fears!

Bian. Wo's me! — Art thou not Salviati?

        Bonav. No!

Bian. Nor of his kin?

       Bonav. Alas! nor of his kin.

Bian. O Heaven! — Speak out!   Thou would'st not tor-
     ture me
Who have been kind to thee?   Say what thou art.

Bonav. Bonaventuri, Salviati's clerk.

BIANCA *sinks on a chair, which the* GOVERNESS
has brought her, and covers her face with both hands.
BONAVENTURI *kneels softly before her.*

Oh dearest lady! whom I have so wrong'd
Not of my will, think not too hardly of me!
Not by surprise, not from reluctant lips
This truth was wrung; believe me, O believe!
I fear'd your error, and I came to tell,
To tell you all.   Do not be angry with me!
Bonav. Alas! I have no anger, only sorrow,
Sorrow for both of us. — [*She drops her hands.*
— Bonaventuri! —

[*with a faint smile.*

Thou seest I fear not to pronounce thy name —
What I have said can never be recall'd;
What I have done, that will not be forgotten :
If it will soothe thy anguish at this parting,
To know I share it, be it even so.
And now — farewell! [*extending her hand.*
          Bonav. Not yet!   In pity, no!
Thou canst not so dismiss me!   Think, O think,
Of the long hours where hope shall never more,
Never, make day for me!   Think of the past,
The month on month my yearning heart hath hunger'd,
Feeding itself upon the single thought
Of such an hour as this, which thou wouldst shorten
Thou dost not seem to scorn me: let me then
Lie at thy feet, and, for some minutes still,
Dream I 'm in Heaven.

Bian. To awaken where?
Since part we must, why struggle to obtain
A respite that at best can be but brief?
Bonav. Because it is my life, and all beyond
Is death and darkness.

    Bian. Hast thou then for me
No thought? Canst thou bear nought for my sake?

       Bonav. [*rising quickly.*] Yes;
An age of heartache, will it give you ease.
I was but selfish : I will go. I go. [*moving sadly away,*
     with his eyes still on Bianca, who rises.
Gov. [*laying her hand on Bonaventuri's arm.*

 Come then, young man, since you are no one now.
It is high time that you were gone.

      Bian. How now!
Aia, know better thine own place, and mine;
And, where I honor, learn to show at least
Some sign of reverence.

  Gov. [*low, to herself.*] What a change is here!
She was a child this morning!

      Bian. Mind her not:
I am the mistress here.— Look not so mournful!

       [*giving her hand.*
And yet I cannot bid thee not remember.
Bonav. Could I obey?— Wilt thou remember me?
Wilt thou mourn for me, if—— Bianca! (so —
Permit me —'t is the only time — to call thee)
Whatever happen, thou wilt not condemn me?
Thou wilt not mix my errors with my birth,

And deem me all unworthy ?

        Bian. Seem I such?

What mean'st thou ?

        Bonav. Heaven bless thee !· and — Farewell!
As he is going, BIANCA, who has seemed a moment
    stupefied, suddenly hastens to him.

Bian. Bonaventuri !

        Bonav. Why command me back ?

I thought it past.

        Bian. [*taking his hand, looks fixedly and anx-
iously in his face.*] What didst thou mean by that ?

There is a desperation in thy look   '

That should not be there.   Art thou not a man ?

Is love the only object of man's being ?

There be far nobler aims ; and thou art young,

Ardent, and bold.   Live that I may not blush

To have shown thee favor, live because thou hast

Thy life thou knowest not why, and hast no right

To squander it as if it were thy choice.

More, thou didst lay it at my feet : 't is mine,

If thou concede it not, as fits thee rather,

Thy country's, and thy fellow-men's, thy God's!

Why art thou silent ?   Why that stony look

Of passionless despair ?   Thou dost not love me !

Thou wouldst not else ——

        Bonav. Bianca ! [*slowly.*

        Bian. Promise then

Thou wilt do nothing desperate, thou wilt

Do nothing till thou hear'st from me.   Thou canst

Never more enter here ——

      Gov. [*who has looked on Bianca all the*
while with amazement.] Not by my will!

Bian. Aia! —   But thou shalt hear from me, thou wilt
Write to me by the messenger, and send.
Dost thou then promise — solemnly?

        Bonav. I do —
By all God's holy angels! — thou art one.

Bian. Stoop! — With this kiss [*kissing him solemnly on the*
             forehead.
      thou hast Bianca's — friendship.
I vow it — hear, Heaven!   So long as thou do nought
To forfeit it.   Now go at once; go quickly.
The Mooress waits without to lead thee down.

BONAVENTURI *kissing passionately* BIANCA'S *hand, presses it,*
clasped, a moment to his heart, then moves to the
door, his face still turned on BIANCA.

Gov. [*as she conducts him out.*
   Mary be prais'd! here never to come more.

       [*Exeunt Bonav. and Gov.*

BIANCA *gazes a moment fixedly on the door, then wrings*
her hands in a paroxysm of grief.

Bian. Now he is gone, I am a child again.
O Mary Mother! St. Mark! and gentle Luke! [*kneeling.*
All angels and good saints! pray, pray for me!
Aid me against myself; I have no strength
To make the sacrifice which Heaven commands.

She buries her face in the cushion of the chair, sobbing
bitterly. — Scene closes.

SCENE III.

A room in Sennuccio's apartment, in the Casa Salviati.
SENNUCCIO *sitting at a table reading.*

Enter BONAVENTURI.

SENNUCCIO *looks up, then resumes his occupation.*
BONAVENTURI *looks at him for some moments, then lays*
before him an open letter.

Bonav. Read.
   Senn. From Bianca? [*looking at the signature.*
     Bonav. Ay.   But read aloud.
Senn. [*reading.*

 " Thou ask'st in vain. There are no means. Not one.
My governess is proof to prayers and gold.
She threatens even, if I give not o'er,
To expose us to my father.   What to do?
I am so watch'd, by day as well as night,
I cannot meet thee elsewhere, and here now
Would put thy life in peril and my fame.
Write me no more such letters, O in pity!
They burn into my brain.   My nights are frightful;
And from brief slumbers and distracting dreams
I wake to weep, to ponder our sad lot,
To see perhaps thy wan face at the casement,

Think on thy anguish, which redoubles mine,
And deem sometimes 't were better both were dead.
I thought myself more strong when thou wast by,
But in thy absence find myself the weaker.
Have then, I pray, compassion on us both."
Thou wilt have, wilt thou not?

      Bonav. It is too late.
I have already written, three days since.

Senn. And was that generous?

      Bonav. It was simply just.
I had compassion on herself and me.

Senn. Explain.

   Bonav. For that I come; and for thy aid. —
I wrote to say, I would receive her here,
Here in my rooms, in Salviati's house.

Senn. [*starting up. They both come forward.*
  Art thou distracted?

      Bonav. Desperate alone.
I never spoke more sanely in my life.
My plan is for salvation. [*Senn. about to interrupt.*
      Hear! then judge.
I told her I would watch for three whole nights,
Until the day broke. Coming, she should be
Sacred before me as an enshrin'd saint
Before its votary. This I truly vow'd,
By her dead mother, by her living self.
But coming not, I cast off hope forever,
And with it my young life, then nothing worth.
Two nights have pass'd in vain. This early morn

I saw her at a window.   O so white!
So suppliant with those melancholy eyes!
Whose deep-sunk and impurpled orbits show'd
Long watching, passion, and the pine of care, —
That my fast purpose trembled.   But it holds.
The third night comes : and with it — comes Bianca.
I feel it in my soul.

    Senn. Thou tak'st her for ? ——

Bonav. Capello's child, high-thoughted and most pure ;
 Yet a deep-loving woman.   She will trust me.
Senn. And thou?

    Bonav. Will keep my oath.   I swear it here,
As I have sworn it on my knees to God.
Witness ye saints ! my sister, now in Heaven,
Would not be more immaculate by me
Than she shall be this night !

      Senn. What then your aim ?
Bonav. To marry her.   Thou 'lt aid me ?

       Senn. No !

        Bonav. Thou wilt.
Thou wouldst not scruple to give life to both.
Senn. Ay, must I do it wrongly.   But this life !
 To take her from the lap of luxury, to expose her,
This delicate child, soft-nurtur'd, and high-plac'd,
This daintiest flower of all Venetian land,
To the bleak winds of penury, transplanted
To an ungenial and a barren soil :

   BONAVENTURI *walks about impatiently.*
Is this —   Stop ! listen to me ! — this your life ?

Better to slay her outright, and to die for 't!
That were a crime, but 't would be truer mercy.
But this is idle talk: for, say she come,
How know'st thou she is reckless as thyself?
'T is a long leap, a marriage!

      Bonav. She will take it,
When there is no way left her but to leap.

Senn. Ha!

 Bonav. Wilt thou aid me, Luca?   'T is not much.

Senn. Let me hear further.

     Bonav. When Bianca comes,
She leaves the portal of her house ajar,
So that she may steal softly back unseen.
Now, were it slily clos'd behind her ——

       Senn. Well?

Bonav. There is but left, her ruin or to fly.
Luke! dearest Luke!   I will be all my life
Bound to thee, wilt thou do me this slight office.

Senn. Hast thou then done? — Is this indeed thyself?
Speak'st thou of real purpose?   Art thou truly
Pietro Bonaventuri?   If thou art,
Then am I Luke Sennuccio; and no man
Durst ever call on me before to do
A thing so base.

    Bonav. Have patience!

      Senn. Hear now me.
If thou do not abandon this vile plan,
I will report thee to the lady's sire —
Or no! I will not put in risk thy life;

I will expose thee to Bianca's self.

Bonav. [*haughtily.*] Who gave you right to hold this talk
    to me?

Senn. Nature, and threaten'd innocence, which finds
    In every true man a defender.
                    Bonav. Luke!
I thought thou wast my friend.
                    Senn. I am thy friend.
Thou never hadst a truer.   I dare say
Thou never wilt have one so true again.
For I will not, to pander to thy passions,
Stain thy immortal soul.   I will not suffer
What doubtless now to thy distemper'd blood
Seems venial craft, but one day will appear,
When the film leaves thine eyes, atrocious guilt.

Bonav. Thou didst allow me honor.
                    Senn. I do still.
Said I not too, alas for human honor?
Alas, that somewhere it has aye some flaw!
Passion, ambition, indigence, all serve
To lend it pretexts to excuse its fall.
Thou, in the hunger of thy famish'd love,
Dost clutch at bread that is not fairly thine.
Thou shalt not have it.
                Bonav. Thou dost bear me hard.
Thou art no lover, and thy cold resolve
Cuts off the last resource of both our lives.
For Blanche will pine to death, nor I survive.

Senn. So all youth think.   And very few think right.

The storm blows, and the lily stoops her head,
But lifts it soon, and with the calm revives.
But, be it otherwise : hast thou not heard
Thou shalt not evil do that good may come ?
Be honest, do thy duty : the result
Is with the All-Powerful, not the feeble will
Of circumscrib'd and narrowsighted men.
Pietro ! end this matter as it may,
Thou art not sinless, knowing from the first
Well who thou art, which knew this virgin not.
Thou hast repair'd that error, like the brave
And honest soul thou art.   Wilt thou fail now ?
I will not think it.   Get thee to thy chamber.
Ask if thou lov'st Bianca or thyself.
And on the altar of a true affection
Burn up thy guilty wishes.   Angels will
Inhale with joy the incense, God approve
That truest hero, him who conquers self.

*Bonav. [Throwing himself on Sennuccio's breast, and with
emotion.*

O Luke ! had I thy spirit !

Senn. [caressingly.] And my blood ?
Virtue, believe, is not to know not sin,
But the soul's victory when tried by sin.
Be thou thus virtuous, I will say thy love
Honors Bianca, were she born a queen.

[Exit Bonav.

Luke, *leaning with his bent hand on the table, gazes
on him seriously as he retires.   And Scene closes.*

SCENE IV.

In the Casa Capello.

A room hung with portraits. On a table, two lighted candles.

CAPELLO. GOVERNESS.

Gov. I meant, your Excellence, to speak of this.

Cap. Hast thou then notic'd this sad change? Since when?

Gov. 'T is some weeks gone since first my lady droop'd.

    I thought it nothing serious, still believing

    A little time would make all well again. —

Cap. Complain'd my daughter? Sought she for no aid?

Gov. Alas! your Excellence, 't is not the body:

    This is some sore distemper of the mind.

Cap. What mean'st thou?

                Gov. I would pray to be forgiven

    If I offend; but my young lady ——

                    Cap. Speak!

Gov. I fear, has something heavy on her heart.

Cap. Mean'st thou, in fine, my daughter is in love?

Gov. May it please your Excellence, 't is nothing less

Cap. Be but the object worthy of her love,

    I were well pleas'd that it were nothing more.

    Who is it then?

              Gov. Your Excellence must know

    My lady would not make of me her friend.

Cap. Thou art her governess: if, as I am loath
    To even conjecture, there is wrong in this,
    Thou only art to blame. Thou hast my child,
    Daily and nightly, under thy sole care.
    What can transpire that thou shouldst not observe?

Gov. Heaven is my judge, that I in this have done
    My proper duty. Till the last two days,
    I hop'd that all was well. But yesterday,
    Nor less the one before, the livelong night,
    My dear young lady never press'd her bed,
    Walking unquietly from time to time
    Her chamber through.

              Cap. And where wast thou the while?

Gov. Twice went I to the door. She thank'd me kindly,
    But bade me leave, as wanting not my help.

Cap. How is 't to-night?

             Gov. She has retired early;
    And all is quiet in her chamber. Haply
    She will sleep well to-night, being so much worn.

Cap. 'T is likely, very likely. God so grant!
    I will not break this salutary rest.
    But on the morrow bid her be prepar'd
    For solemn question. — O my darling child!

    He ceases to notice the GOVERNESS.

Let not my colder age efface the sense
Of my once passionate youth. When thou wast born,
I pray'd *that* error of the old might not
One day be mine. Yet is the lesson hard
For a fond parent's heart! The child is his,

But not her passions.   At the age when most
She needs his guidance, when new-born desire
Makes the first object welcome, and the soul
Takes cognizance of only things extern,
Then may he least command; then, child no more,
And yet not woman, she escapes his hand,
Before her unfledg'd sense has power to fly.
Hast thou done so, Bianca?   Is this *love*
Which fevers thy young blood, then this unrest,
This secret sorrow marks a sense of shame,
Or unrequited or forbidden passion.   See! ——
  Turning to the pictures.   In so doing, he observes
              the GOVERNESS.
Thou needst not wait, good Aia.   It is now
Past midnight.   Listen at my daughter's door,
Ere thou retirest; but disturb her not. — [*Exit Gov.*
          Regards again the pictures.
Next to my father Carlo the ambassador's
Hangs thy sweet image, my Bianca!   'T is
One of the best from old Vecelli's hand.
How his soft pencil and his dulcet grace
Have beautified and made the canvas live!
The blood is in those cheeks! those eyes are moist!
From those just-parted delicate lips I seem
To feel the warm breath, and my own in turn
Might almost wave those airy threads of gold
That shape thy ringlets!   Magic power of color!
Yet Titian vow'd thou didst surpass his art,
As did the light its symbol on his board.[4]

Such do not sigh in vain.   Thou sorrowest then
For a forbidden passion which is shame ;
And my old house —— Thou shalt not dim its pride!
Forget thou the Capello, and a veil
Shall hide thy forfeit station, like Falier's,
Who too forswore his birthright.   'T is a thought
To keep me waking.   Let me drive it hence.

He lifts one of the candles towards the picture.

One nearer look, my child, before I go.

Scene closes.

Scene V.

*A street, with a canal crossing it above; where, by a bridge
which spans the canal, are obscurely seen, in the faint
morning-twilight, the prows of gondolas. Forward,
on either side the street, facing each other, the
Casa Capello and the Casa Salviati.*

*From the portal of the latter
Enter*

BIANCA *and* BONAVENTURI,
*the latter having a small dark-lantern,
which he masks.*

Bian. See! the gray dawn! Farewell! A last —
Wo 's me, I cannot say again — Farewell!
Bonav. [*pressing her to his breast.*

    Haply, 't is not forever. Heaven bless thee!
Thy word remember.

        Bian. Never, never, never
To be another's, if not thine. Farewell!
Embracing. BIANCA *crosses over to the palace on the right.
But almost instantly, coming back in terror:*
    Ruin! ruin! O God! the door is clos'd.

Bonav. Hast thou no key?

    Bian. None, none! And if I had,
I durst not use it for the noise.

      Bonav. Stay here.
I will essay.   Perhaps the door will yield.

Bian. No, no!   Try not.   There is no help but flight.

Bonav. Whither?

    Bian. Hast thou no parents?

      Bonav. Ay, but poor.

Bian. No matter; I can work.   They shall be mine.
Come Bonaventuri!   Come, my husband!   Come!

Bonav. Alas, Bianca! all my worldly means
 Lies in this little purse.   The rest was given,
 How gladly! for that first blest scene with thee
 Which costs thee now so dear.

      Bian. Be it small or great,
It must be.   My few rings will eke it out.
Tarry not.   Every moment here is fraught
With more than death.   I cannot face again
My father.   Come.   Art thou a man?   Must I
Entreat thee to do that, which not long since
Thou wouldst have thought salvation?

      Bonav. 'T is for thee.
Wilt thou meet poverty and honest shame——

Bian. Rather than what awaits me here?   That, that,
 Canst thou ask that?   O linger not!   Each minute
 Is so much lost to flight that must be quick.
 For they will follow us.   It is thy death.

Bonav. Come then, Bianca; now mine, life or death!
   To the first gondola. Once out of Venice,
   The first priest, if thou wilt, shall make us one.
Bian. Yes. O my father!
                 Bonav. Hush, Bianca! Come.

              He takes up the lantern.
They move up the scene in the shadow of the houses.

              The Drop falls.

Act the Second

Scene I. A chamber in the Pitti Palace at Florence.

The Grand Duke
seated, leaning on a table in a pensive attitude. Malocuore *standing apart, a little before him.*

Mal. [*in a tone of deferential inquiry.*
    My lord the Duke is not so well to-day.
          A pause.
With still more deference.]
    Will my lord pardon his poor servant's zeal,
    And give command the hunt shall not take place?
G. D. [*without looking up.*
    For my ill-humor why should hundreds lack
    Their custom'd pleasure? Let the order stand.
          Again a pause.
Mal. 'T was from the last hunt that my liege came back
    With that strange sorrow which still wounds our hearts.
          A longer pause.
G. D. Thou art a courtier, Malocuor. Men say
    Thou hast sharp eyes, seest quickly and seest far.
    Thou boastest of thy zeal in our behalf.
    Forget thy art.[5] What whisper stirs the court
    Touching our strangeness?

Mal. Some ascribe the cause
To depravation of the humors, bile,
Infarction of the spleen, — such natural ills;
Some to the weight of heavy cares of state ;
Others — your Highness bids that I should speak —
To discontent with your Archducal spouse.

G. D. [*hastily.*

They do me wrong : I hold her — in esteem.

Mal. Which often is the antipodes of love.

G. D. And to which guess does Malocuore lean ?

Mal. The last, with some admixture of the first.
Your Highness' malady is of the heart.

G. D. Ha ! — Men say well: thou hast keen eyes.

       Mal. Would then
The royal patient deign to state his case,
Perhaps the surgeon might propound a cure.

   The G. D. rises and walks to and fro.

G. D. [*after a pause.*

Hear then. —— But can I trust thee ?

       Mal. Shall I prove
That I am worthy ? Shall I state, myself,
Your Highness' symptoms, with the when and where,
And how, of the attack ?

     G. D. What know'st thou ? Speak!

Mal. 'T was at the last hunt. As the cavalcade
Swept through the suburbs, and the people flock'd
To door and window to behold their Prince,
In a small cottage with a vine-clad porch,
That stood secluded where the highway turns,

Lean'd from a narrow casement next the roof,
A fair young creature of some eighteen years,
So strangely beautiful, and with a mien
So far above the seeming of her place,
The Great Duke, starting, drew his bridle short,
To gaze ——
    G. D. Art thou the Devil?
                      Mal. I am but
Your Highness' humble subject — with sharp eyes.
G. D. No more! Thou hast thy monarch's secret. He? —
Mal. His subject's instant aid, so he will deign
Graciously to command it.
              G. D. Instant? Then
Sawest thou not, with all thy sight, what I
Saw and will vouch. This is no peasant maid,
Simple and uninstructed; far less one
Of that most numerous class in every life,
Whose vanity throws out perpetual lures,
Tempting temptation. Else the glance that pierc'd
Had made me whole. But thou dost not believe
In virtuous women?
           Mal. Ay, as in wall'd towns.
Many are strong, but none impregnable.
A vigorous siege and obstinate resolve
Will batter down or bring a Troy to terms.
Where open combat fails, some wooden horse
Lets in the troop that makes the stronghold ours.
Is it your Highness' will, this very day
The chance is given you to assault the place.

G. D. What sayst thou?

     Mal. Be it not ascrib'd a fault,
That I have dar'd anticipate your will.

G. D. Who gave thee orders?

     Mal. Will my lord but hear?
I have ventur'd only to make clear the approach,
By which your Highness might lay siege in form.

G. D. Speak plainly, Malocuor, and leave thy cant.
I like it not.   Here is no vile intrigue;
And shall be none.

     Mal. Returning from the chase,
The Sovereign lifted up his eyes again,
Unto the cottage-window.   But no more
The star was burning there that made the day;
And over his visage came like darkness.   This,
When I saw this, and mark'd from day to day
The sadness lessen not; when, furthermore ——

G. D. [*impatiently.*

 Well, well! we have admitted thou hast eyes.

Mal. Pardon, your Grace! — My spouse, by my command,
Made easily acquaintance with the dame
Who is this angel's mother, then herself.
She has seen her often, finds still some pretence
To do her kindness, — though, unlike the dame,
The daughter is both proud and strangely shy.

G. D. How speaks your spouse her bearing otherwise?

Mal. Modest, reserv'd; but, like her voice and mien,
Above her sphere.

G. D. And beauty?

Mal. Marvelous.

G. D. [*taking his hand.*

Ah, Malocuore! And this priceless maid? ——

Mal. So rarely worthy of a monarch's love;

Has then my lord no wish to see her near?

G. D. Wouldst drive me mad? Speak on!

Mal. No wish to be

Beside her — and alone — and even now?

G. D. What! what! Thou didst indeed promise instant
aid!

Mal. This very hour my spouse will bring her home.

G. D. To thine own house?

Mal. To mine: my sovereign's house,

Will he so grace it.

G. D. And this very hour?

He rests his hand on MALOCUOR'S *shoulder.*

Dear Malocuore! This is too much joy!

What shall I do to compensate thy love?

Thou hast indeed thy keen eyes us'd right well. —

Thou wilt attend me. — Saidst thou not, this hour? —

Bid come our Chamberlain. — [*Exit Mal.*

How bright the day!

Sitting down by the table.

It seems to me as now I first had life.

Rising, he passes through a door above, and

Scene closes.

SCENE II.

*In Malocuore's house.   The dressing-room of Signora Malo-
cuore.*

BIANCA.   *The* SIGNORA.

The latter displaying her jewels and finery.

Sign. You are a strange fair creature.   One would think
   These toys had been your playthings all your life.
   Yet that is not a long one either.
                        Bian. Why
   Should usage only breed indifference ?   Rather
   It is the innate relish or distaste
   For such things makes them valued or despis'd.
   Age pranks itself therein like lighter youth.
Sign. You are a young philosopher.
                        Bian. I know
   The difference betwixt folly and good sense.
   It were not wise in me to covet what,
   Even were 't attainable, would not fit my place.
Sign. That place may better; and these jewels then ——
Bian. Would still have little value in my eyes.
   I dress to please my husband; and his taste
   Is well contented with this simple garb.

Sign. In sooth, it does not misbecome you.   I have known
                                             [*significantly.*

A sovereign prince to admire as plain a robe.
Pray let me hang this chain about your neck.
Thus, you are lovely.   Do not take it off.
It well relieves the ivory of that skin.

Bian. [*tranquilly removing the chain.*

But is in painful contrast to the rest.
Signora, to oblige my husband's mother
More than yourself, I have let you bring me hither.
Thanking your courtesy, suffer me to leave.

Sign. [*looking off the scene, as if hearing something.*

A little longer.   I have yet to show you,
Gentle Bianca, what is worth this all.
                                   [*Exit.*

Bian. It must be greatly so, if thou wouldst dazzle
The rich Capello's child.   Capello! Father!
Mourn'st thou Bianca yet?   Or has just anger
Stifled all sorrow for thy truant girl?
Who has one only grief, the thought that thou
Art unforgiving and yet unconsol'd.*

Enter

the GRAND DUKE — *eagerly,*
but becomes at once embarrassed, while BIANCA *looks*
surprised, but steady.

G. D. Pardon! I —— [*stammering.*
             Bian. Signora Malocuore

Has stepp'd out for a moment.

     G. D. The Signora

Shall be excus'd. Her absence gives me room

To make, without the encumbrance of a third,

The acquaintance of the loveliest of her sex.

Bian. This cannot be the master of the house.

G. D. The master's master, and your beauty's slave.

Bian. Ah! — It is —— 'T is! I see now. The Grand

  Duke ?

G. D. Francis of Medici, who —— Do not stoop!

 'T is I should rather kneel, wouldst thou permit,

 Fairest Bianca.

    Bian. Speak not so, my lord!

That tone becomes not either you or me. —

I have an earnest prayer to make your Grace.

'T is a small matter, but concerns me much.

G. D. Rise first. Now, what is there that thou canst ask,

Saving his honor and his people's weal,

That Francis will not grant ? Think it then granted,

So thou wilt one accord to me in turn,

Bianca, and my love ——

    Bian. My lord! my lord!

I am — a marry'd woman.

    G. D. Marry'd ? Well!

Am I not marry'd too ? Alas! the heart

Cannot be bound so easily as the hand.

Bian. But the will may, and should when reason bids.

G. D. Reason now bids me to obey my will.

 The flame thy beauty kindled thy sense fans.

I had not heard thy speech, when on my eyes,
Lovely Bianca, ——

        Bian. Pardon me, my liege.
That I dare interrupt, impute it solely
Unto my duty, to you and to myself.
If I could ever listen, plac'd as now,
To such wild words as these from such as you, —
As I do not believe I ever should, —
Yet is my will not free as yours; my heart
Is, like my hand, my husband's.

        G. D. Every word
But adds new motive to my passion, showing
How rightfully 't is plac'd.   Thou shouldst be silent,
Wouldst thou not foster feelings, which, in sooth,
Needed no nourishment.

        Bian. Then let me hence.
Such protestations — pardon me, my liege —
Demean yourself, your august spouse, and me.

        [*Offering to go.   He stops her.*
G. D. Art thou insensible?   Thou art not vain.
But hast thou no compassion?

        Bian. I have more.
You are my Prince, albeit I was not born
Your subject.   Men report, and I believe,
You are among the noblest of crown'd heads.
My eyes have noted in your form and mien
What women value; and my ears have found
Sense in the tone and purport of your speech.
Thus amiable, thus gifted, so high-plac'd,

You cannot lack for dames in all your court
Fairer than your poor handmaid, noble too,
Who would joy in your homage, and respond
Haply unto your love, if — let me dare
To speak thus — you will do yourself that wrong
To offer it.

      G. D. And are they such as thou?
Thy very words prove otherwise. If such,
They would not listen more than thou. No, thou,
Thou only, who, believe me! since these eyes
First saw thy fatal beauty, hast alone
Been mistress of my senses and my thoughts,
Thou only, fair ——

      Bian. My lord, I must, I can not,
Will not listen longer. All the honor,
The reverence that I owe you, that I render;
But my first duty is to God. Permit me
Thus to perform it. [*her hand on the door.*

      G. D. [*stopping her.*
      No. If it must be,
'T is I will go. Bianca, have me not,
I pray, in disesteem. Let Francis hold
The next place in thy bosom, if thou canst,
To thy most happy husband. Thou shalt not
Say I abus'd my privilege. In love
I am like other men, and, loving so,
Like any gallant man I take my leave.

      [*Exit, bowing with sad deference.*
Bian. A noble prince. Not conscious, surely, he

Of this vile plot.   Ah! the arch-plotter comes.

Enter the Signora, *with a casket.*

Sign. I have kept you too long waiting.   Pardon. — Here
　　Is what will wake your wonder. [*opening the casket.*
　　　　　　　　　　　Bian. That was done
　　During your absence bravely.   Shut the box.
Sign. What!   Have you seen the Duke?   I thought as
　　much.
　　He often takes us by surprise.   I hope
　　You have seiz'd the occasion, to present your prayer ?
Bian. Was it for *that,* you urg'd me to come hither ?
Sign. No.   But I promised access to His Highness:
　　And I am happy, have you us'd this chance.
　　Sweet, look not grave: and do not haste away.
Bian. I do not like surprises: and this one
　　Has brought me no advantage.   I will not
　　Trouble you longer.
　　　　　　Sign. Nay, you shall not go
　　As you were angry.   I shall see you home.
　　　　　　　　　　　　　[*Exeunt.*

SCENE III.

An Antechamber in the house of Malocuore.

Enter
from one side the G. DUKE, *as passing through,*
escorted by MALOCUOR.
The G. D. *stops short, laying his hand on his follower's arm.*

G. D. I have seen her, heard her, touch'd her.   All my nerves
Tingle with pleasure.   Yet my heart is sad.
Mal. Is it that all is won?   Accomplish'd hope
Often brings sadness.
　　　　　G. D. Since it nothing leaves
To feed expectance? or, the goal once reach'd,
We find the prize not worth the strain and sweat?
My longing is unsated, *my* bright prize
Grows brighter on my vision, like the sun
As day advances.   Yet my heart is sad:
For — all is lost.
　　　　　Mal. Then is it the first time
Your Highness has been vanquish'd.
　　　　　G. D. The first time
Defeat is dearer to my heart than victory.
Thou look'st surpris'd.   I tell thee, Malocuor,

All thou hast said, all that thy spouse has told,
All that in heat of fancy I have dream'd,
Fall short to picture beauty, sense and worth,
That have no rivals save themselves.   She is
The loveliest, best, and wisest of her sex.

Mal. May I infer, the most obdurate too?

G. D. What else?   I said, "the best": and she is wed.

Mal. 'T is the first trial.   When we shake the tree,
The apples fall not.   But we lend our strength
To newer efforts; and they drop in time.

G. D. That is your over-ripe, and worm-gnaw'd fruit.
Bianca's stem is tough.

    Mal. Let royal favor
Pour sunshine on the treasure of the tree,
The crude pulp mellows, and the stubborn stem,
Now useless, withers up.   Invite the lady
To grace your Highness' Court.

      G. D. That would I gladly.
But not to rot the virtue I admire.
The tree shall bear its honors in our midst,
And its fruit give out fragrance undespoil'd.
'T is something still to see her, hear her, know
That she is near me.   Once beyond my reach,
I should be wretched, fearing she were lost.
Know'st thou her husband?   To be lord of her,
He should be not ignoble.

     Mal. Not in mien.
The man is fair to look on, and well-spoken.
My lord might give him place about his person.

G. D. See it be done. Promise him what thou wilt,
  So it be not a place of public trust.
Mal. Your Grace shall be obey'd, and, more — be happy.
    They resume their way through the antechamber,
      MALOCUORE *ceremoniously conducting, and Exeunt.*

SCENE IV.

*A poorly furnished chamber in the house of Bonaventuri's
  Parents.*

BONAVENTURI. *His* MOTHER.

Moth. 'T is as thou sayest, Pietro, and our luck
  Is surely blossoming. And glad am I,
  If only for Bianca's sake, 't is so.
  To see that delicate creature, night and day,
  Toiling with those soft hands, that ne'er were made
  For menial labor, makes my heart bleed.
                    Bonav. Yet
  She does not murmur.
            Moth. More an angel she.
  An angel is she. Oft I wonder, son,
  Though thou art brave and comely, thou couldst win

So rare a maiden.   But I wonder not,
Once won, thou gav'st up all to make her thine.
Bonav. She gave up all too, mother ; and that all
   Was more a thousand times.

                    Moth. The heavier then
Her loss.   I fear she feels it so.   Her brow,
Methinks, grows sadden'd, and her cheek more pale.
I would she had less care on her young heart.
Bonav. What can we do ?   Our money is all spent.
Until the Duke's protection be procur'd, ·
I dare not stir abroad to seek for work.
I wonder that Bianca was so bold
To gaze from window when the Court rode by.
Moth. 'T was but an instant, from the upper floor.
Thou shouldst not blame her.

              Bonav. And I did not.   Yet
The risk was great.   And therefore I rejoice
In this court-lady's favor.   If nought else,
The Duke may shield us.   That is one care less.
Was not that wheels ? [*listening.*

         Moth. [*opening the casement.*
         The gracious dame herself,
In her brave equipage, has brought her back!
Bonav. She comes.   Bianca!   ·

        Enter BIANCA.
    She throws herself into her husband's arms.

           Bian. O, let us begone!

Bonav. Whither? What is the matter? Has the Duke
Refus'd his safeguard?

      Moth. Have you seen His Grace?

Bian. Yes, I have seen him, and will not again.
O Bonaventuri! O my husband!

      Bonav. Speak!

What is it?

   Bian. Ruin! Ruin, if we stay;
Hope, safety, happiness, all things in flight.
Let it be instant!

    Bonav. Whither? And the means?
Venice can reach us elsewhere. As well here.

Bian. No! not as well. This place is bann'd of Heaven.
The world elsewhere is all for us to choose.

   Bonaventuri *folds his arms about her as
she hangs on his breast, —* the Mother *looking on in
speechless wonder, and*

     the Drop falls.

ACT THE THIRD

Scene I.   As in Act II. Sc. II.

SIGNORA MALOCUORE.

Enter,
in festival dress, MALOCUORE.
He flings himself weariedly on a couch, without removing
his hat.

Mal. 'T is monstrous!   Florence stands agape.   Fools ask:
    Is this a Prince?   or some great hostile king's
    High servant sent to ratify a peace?
    And wise men answer low: "Bianca's brother."
    Just as thou seest me, wearied unto death,
    So see a hundred nobles, dragg'd in state
    To swell the triumph of Vittorio, son
    Of a Venetian Senator. [*flinging his hat off in disdain.*
               Sign. And who
    But thou to blame?   Of all thy fine-wove schemes
    To advance thyself, and stretch thy purse and mine,
    What is the upshot?   O'er thee, step by step,
    Strides Bonaventuri; and the prude, his wife,
    Rides over me and all.
            Mal. Peace!   Fret me not.

I am not now in mood.

    Sign. To list the truth?

'T is wholesome though. Thy aching bones are part

Of thy just penance; and my knotty facts

Shall lash thee to new virtue.

     Mal. Well; proceed.

Only hear me in turn.

    Sign. Bianca houses

Not in the suburbs in a cottage now,

But near the *Trinità*, in palace-walls

That shame our own: her low-born husband rolls

In wealth beyond his trading master's, holds

His head above the nobles, with a pride ——

Mal. Will one day hurl him headlong. But his spouse

Is gentle still. Why shouldst thou carp at her?

Sign. She treats me with an insolent disdain,

Or looks me over.

    Mal. Ay; she knows thee well.

Sign. Ha!

  Mal. Was 't not thou that pander'd to the Duke?

Sign. At whose base prompting? If my palm is black,

Thou art in to the elbow. Was it I

That brought her to the Court? I had left her poor.

Her natural pride now swollen by all this pomp,

With courtiers cringing at her dainty feet

Who scarcely kiss'd the crown'd Joanna's hand,

She trifles with the Duke, and plays the chaste,

While he, the more she frowns, the more adores.

Is not that so?

Mal. It is; but shall not be;
Though I deem not, as thou, Bianca feigns.
Sign. What new plan toward ? [*disdainfully.*

            Mal. Thou knowest the hopes I built
On the bold Favorite's amour with the Princess?
Sign. The base was quicksand.   So the fabric fell.
The dissolute Duchess makes the wife's cheek pale,
But not her heart.   It still beats for her lord,
Or seems to.

        Mal. I have what will change its pulse. [*Going.*
If she resist this! —— [*holding up for a moment, at a*
                              distance, a sealed letter.
            —— Even then I hope.
A mine will spring the tower which stands a siege.

                                [*Exit.*

Sign. Subtle maligner !   Thou mayst fathom man,
But hast no plummet to explore our sex.
Thou think'st I know thee not.   Thou had'st better
    trust me !
Thy dallying with the Cardinal I see.
Beware!   A crafty priest has double craft.
The mine thou digg'st against Bianca's faith
May split the rock whereon the miner stands.

                 [*She turns, as going.   And*

    Scene closes.

Scene II.

A room in the Old Medici Palace (the residence of
Don Pietro.)

Isabella.   Eleonora.

Isa. Content thee. That I fling away my hours
On Francis' pet, is not the man is bold,
Or young, or handsome — though I weigh the worth
Of all these qualities — but that I hate
His wife.
    Eleo. [*in great surprise.*
      I thought thou favoredst the Capello!
Isa. As thy dear lord, my brother does. In heart
I loathe her.
    Eleo. And for what?
              Isa. Because I loathe her.
What matters it? Not always do we know
Our cause of hate.
    Eleo. Not always care to know.
Isa. Or care to know. Be it as thou wilt. So say,
I am her rival; say, that men desert
Calypso's isle of dainties for the web
Of chaste Penelope; is 't not too much
The hypocrite should make both thee and me

Odious before our lords, and in the court
Teach men to estimate our freer lives
By her stiff model?   Harmless as a dove
Fools may esteem her; but the serpent's wisdom
Prompts her mock coyness.   If Joanna, whom
My brother Ferdinand so loves (because
Her weak spine promises the Duke no heir
That long shall live,) in her now-coming throes,
Which threaten peril, die, behold a chance
Bianca may improve!
     Eleo. Thou art not serious?

Isa. Our sire was, who in his later day
Married Camilla.   She was not the peer
In beauty, worth, or birth of this Capello.
Francis has cloister'd her,[6] but not the less
Will do as his sire, mad for love as he.

Eleo. Ah! this is why the Cardinal and my lord
Precipitate the ripening of our plot.

Isa. It will not do.   Bernard' Girolami,
The two Capponi, linger yet in France;
The Alamanni, Machiavelli, all,
Though eager, wait their secret coming, ripe,
Yet unresolv'd.   The Cardinal —— But hush!
Here comes a doubtful friend.   Eleonor',
Watch well your lips.

    Enter MALOCUORE.

      What passes in the town,

Good Signor Malocuor?

     Mal. May it please your Grace,
The storm breaks not as yet ; but thunder rolls
At the horizon. Now the peace is over
Between the Cardinal and our Sovereign Lord,
His Eminence' agents stir the popular mind
With satires on the adventuress, and psalms
In praise of good Joanna, whose near death
Must come of Victor's triumph ! [9] The Capello
Will not go down to future times a saint,
If my lord's foes can help it. — Going hence,
Left my lord Cardinal any charge for me?

Isa. None. But be watchful. Thou wilt hear from him
Perhaps from Rome.

    Mal. I humbly take my leave.

        [Exit — by the
side he had entered. The two princesses Exeunt by opposite side.[10]

SCENE III.

Room in the Pitti Palace.   As in Act II. Sc. I.

GRAND DUKE.   DON PIETRO DE' MEDICI.   DUKE OF
BRACCIANO.

The Grand Duke seated.

Brac. Your Highness has a twofold stake in this.
　　　Your sister is my spouse, your insolent favorite —
　　　So let me call him — is her open lover.
　　　Does Isabella's conduct shame your House,
　　　His prodigal pomp and measureless assumption
　　　Wound your chief nobles' pride, and tempt your people
　　　To mutiny, clamorous that they are not heard.
Don P. My liege and brother: Bracciano's words
　　　Express his wish and motive: my resolve
　　　Is fix'd.   Eleonora shall not make
　　　My name a byword.
　　　　G. D. [*rising.*] That thyself hast done.
　　　Thy wantonness and license are unmatch'd.
　　　Nor canst thou fling one stone against thy spouse
　　　Should not rebound on thee.
　　　　　　Don P. My luxury
　　　Is not fed from thy treasure.   For my spouse,

The Archduchess' wrongs are not so secret.

                            G. D. Ha! —

Brother, the cleft betwixt us yawns too wide
To need distension.   This much is to say:
I would not have the Duke of Alba wroth.
Eleonora's death ——

             Don P. May drive him mad.
What then? it is my quarrel, none of thine.
I reck not the Toledos.   Mov'd I not
Don Pedro in this matter?   With what boot?
He let not even his sire, Garzía, know,
But screen'd his strumpet sister in my spite.[11]

     The G. DUKE *walks up and down a few moments*
       in anxious thought, then, turning to the
          DUKE OF BRACCIANO:

G. D. Orsini, will it not suffice for thee
    To shut up Isabella?   Cloister'd life
Leaves her repentance, yet concludes thy shame.
Brac. But gluts not vengeance.   Sure, my liege o'erlooks
    The Orsini's honor.
            G. D. Not so, Duke, not so.
Have not the Medici shed blood enough
Of kindred veins?   Wouldst thou exact this too?
She was my father's darling.   It is hard.

     Walks up and down with signs of agitation.
       Then, addressing both:

For Bonaventuri — Let me frankly speak:
I trust to both your honors — If I wink
At his egregious folly, think ye then
My pleasure goes with my forgiveness? No,
He should have died ere this; but men would say —
I slew him to ascend Bianca's bed.

Don P. We will provide for that, so thou wilt promise
To hold us not to answer for the deed.

The G. D. stands thoughtful for a moment.

G. D. Pietro, our brother Don Giovanni died
Like righteous Abel. The assassin fell,
Stabb'd by his father, in his mother's arms.
I will not imitate my brother's crime,
Nor my stern father's vengeance.

                     Brac. And for me?

G. D. My sister is thy spouse. I cannot punish
What, plac'd as thou, I might myself have done.
           [*He bows in sign of dismissal, and*
                Exeunt Don P. and Brac.

The GRAND DUKE *looks after them a*
moment thoughtfully, then moves slowly towards the
chair — and scene changes to

SCENE IV.

A magnificent room in the palace of Bonaventuri.

Enter BONAVENTURI,
leading in with great animation SENNUCCIO,
who follows with marked reluctance.

Bonav. Welcome once more! A thousand, thousand times,
Welcome to Florence! Make this house thy home.
Command me every way. Why art so grave?
Thou wouldst have fled me in the public street.
Couldst thou then think Pietro could be else
To Luca than Pietro?
     Senn. Yea. And there
Perhaps I did thee wrong. But elsewhere too?
Why didst thou flee from Venice? That bad scheme
Thou wouldst persuade me to? ——
     Bonav. [*changing color.*] Dost ask me *here*,
If I be lawful master of my own?
Senn. No; for thou art not. Thou didst steal thy wife.
Bonav. Sennuccio, I bear much from thee.
       Senn. Is 't not
True thou didst rob the old man of his child,
When thou didst suffer me to think thou wouldst not?
Bonav. But not to beggary I bore her. Lo!

The amends is ample, and the sire appeas'd.
This day thou sawest her brother, like a prince
Attended, ride in triumph to my house;
Where he now gladly dwells.

       Senn. The more his shame,
Knowing how it was got.

      Bonav. Thou dar'st! ——

        Senn. Not say
One word that is not truth. Wilt thou maintain
This palace was given by the Duke to *thee?*

Bonav. I do. It is my meed, and fits my place.
I have risen in his service step by step.
All know I am his Favorite.

      Senn. And thy wife?

Bonav. His Grace adores her. But that hurts her not.

Senn. No? Yet they say in Florence ——

      Bonav. What is said?

Senn. [hesitating, then, slowly.
She is to Francis, what Camilla was
To Cosmo ere he wed her.

      Bonav. 'T is a lie!
The atrocious slander of the Grand Duke's foes,
Led by the intriguing Cardinal. Bianca
From the first warn'd me — still would have me fly.

Senn. Yet thou remainest? —[*looking at him with aston-*
            ishment.

    Let me see thy wife.

Bonav. Gladly. Come now. Thou then wilt do me right.
Thou then ——

Enter a PAGE.

Well?

Page. Be not angry, sir! The note
I was bearing to the Duchess, by mischance,
Or stolen, is lost. I am sure 't is not my fault.
I miss'd it only when I reach'd the door.

Bonav. Thou art very careless. Get thee back at once.
Tell to her Highness thy mishap, and say,
I will be shortly with her Grace. [*Exit Page.*

           — Now, Luke.

       [*about to lead him off.*

Senn. Stay yet. What is this Duchess? I have heard
Strange tales to thy dishonor. Men assert,
The dissolute Isabella——

         Bonav. [*with confusion, yet with vanity.*

            O a freak!

Her Highness shows me favor.

           Senn. As she does

Her lord's own kinsman. Have a care! Thou goest
Straight to thy fall. Beware the Orsini!

         Bonav. [*impatiently.*] Come.

As he is leading SENNUCCIO *off,* BONAVENTURI *stops.*

Say nothing of this letter to Bianca.

Senn. She then?——

      Bonav. Still loves me dearly. It might grieve her.

Senn. And is that true? Then thou deserv'st to fall.

              [*Exeunt.*

Scene V.

Another Apartment in the Same.

Bianca *discovered in a dejected attitude.*

Bian. And this is splendor! this is pleasure! this
  The world calls happiness!   Would I could exchange
  All that is now for what alone was ours,
  When in that humble home I toil'd all day,
  As never yet my father's handmaids toil'd!
  Then slept I well; my check was pale indeed,
  But not with sorrow; for my husband's heart
  Was all my own.   [*Comes forward.*
            And is it no more mine?
  Haply, his vanity alone is mov'd.
  Wealth, luxury, the notice of the great,
  All swell his pride.   Alas! he will not see
  There be distinctions which are far from honor.
  Sure of my heart, which well he knows is his,
  He glories in the Duke's mad passion, and counts
  Its harvest only, reckless that the world
  Deems it is gather'd from his partner's shame.
  He comes.   And with a stranger.
      Enter Bonaventuri *and* Sennuccio.
              A grave face

That pleases me.

 Bonav. Bianca, welcome bid

To Luke Sennuccio, my old Venice friend.

Bian. All of my husband's friends are welcome here.

 But a true friend, as I have heard you call'd,

 Sits next my heart.   From heart then welcome, sir.

          [giving her hand.

Bonav. Adieu, awhile.   Bianca, I have wrung

 Consent from Luke to make his quarters here.

Senn. But ——

 Bonav. Nay, revoke not!   I shall hold thee bound.

 Keep him engag'd, love, till my soon return. *[going.*

Bian. Why must thou go?   Must it be every night?

Bonav. 'T is nothing — a mishap.   'T is not for long.

          [Exit hastily.

  Sennuccio *looks after him with indignation,*

   and with pity on Bianca.

Bian. [*observing the look.*

 Pray, mind me not.   I ought not to be vex'd.

 I —— [*Recovering with an effort.*

   Sir, you are fresh from Venice.   Left you then

 The Adriatic in my brother's train?

Senn. No, I have idled in my native town

 Some days.

   Bian. And came not once to see my lord?

 O Signor!   And he thought so much of you!

Senn. I knew not that his feelings were not chang'd.

 The gay, rich courtier, favorite of the Duke,

 Was not my fellow-clerk of former days.

Bian. You do him wrong; his heart is still the same.
Have you not found it so?

        Senn. But could I know it?
What gave me right to press on his new fortune
The reminiscence of a rusty time?

Bian. Old friendship, and the knowlege you had had
Of his brave heart.

      Senn. Alas, Signora! when
I saw in mien the outward man so chang'd,
Needs must I credit what the people said.

Bian. What said they?   Tell me!

       Senn. Can you bear the truth?

Bian. Your quality of plainness I have heard of;
Oft, for my husband's sake, have wish'd it near.
I hear nought but from lying lips; my eyes,
They serve me, painfully and well.   What say
The folk of Bonaventuri?

      Senn. Let me first,
Signora, put a question.   Is it true,
That you have pray'd your husband flee from here?

Bian. It is, I think, my daily prayer.

      Senn. And why?

      A pause.

Bian. Here is not safe for either him or me.

Senn. [*solemnly.*] It is not safe for either you or him.

Bian. What mean you?   Ah! 't is this that I would ask.
What say the people of us; of us both?
The wrong they do my honor can I help?
It is his will, and I submit to bask me

In the hot sunshine of the Court. But oh!
For the old shadow of my humble life!
Not for my father's roof — I would not be
Other than wed, — but for the humble shadow
Where liv'd my husband all in all to me,
For I to him was all! [*weeps.*

        Senn. And is it now
Too late for this?

        Bian. For him — not me. He loves
Too well the pomp of this most wretched life.

Senn. Wretched indeed! where every breath he draws
Is deadly-perilous to himself, and blasts —
Pardon! — the good name of his spouse.

        Bian. 'T is frank.
This thou hast heard. This is the common fame
I too have learn'd to read in all I see;
For not a whisper yet invades my ears.
I read it in the wicked eyes, that flash
Malignant triumph when not bent on mine,
Then suddenly, when my gaze encounters theirs,
Look meek as angels', or grow loving-soft.
I know how busy are the Grand Duke's foes.
They sow thick calumnies, and the poison-seed
Will sprout when I am dead. Bianca's name
Shall be enroll'd with all that in her sex
Is impudent, artful, — it may be, debauch'd;
And all because the husband that she lov'd
Was weak.

        Senn. And selfish.

Bian. No, no; say not that!
His heart is good: he knows not that I suffer.

Enter a PAGE.

Page. The Signor Malocuore.
    Bian. Let him wait. [*Page about to go.*
Senn. Rather, I take my leave. [*going.*
     Bian. Go not, I pray.
Believe me, I have not known such relief,
Not since this weary prison-life at Court.
Or, if you will go, you will soon be back?
You will not disappoint my husband's hope
And mine?
  Senn. I will not: for you are sincere.
Lady, for your sake, here a day or two
I will sojourn.
   Bian. So you shall make these walls
To me more sufferable. [*Exit Sennuccio, bowing with
     an air of deep respect and sympathy.
   To Page.*] Show the courtier in. [*Exit Page.*
A brave good man! How his unburnish'd gold
Makes vile the tinsel of such knaves as this!

Enter MALOCUORE.

Mal. Most excellent lady! if I should intrude ——
Bian. At this unwonted hour for him, what brings
  The Grand Duke's confidant?

Mal. The present matter
Looks rather to your honor'd spouse, than you.
Taking from his vest a letter.
This writing is his hand, I think.   The address
Is known to you. [*gives it.*

BIANCA *regards the letter with agitation;*
MALOCUORE *watching her with malignant pleasure.*

Bian. [*with an effort.*] How came this to your hands?
Mal. What matters it?   The purport you will find
Concerns you nearly.
         Bian. [*recovering, and with sternness.*
         Brought it you for that?
And hop'd you I would read it? [*flings the letter on a
                       table.*
         Mal. Hop'd you would,
In justice to yourself, here ascertain
The measure of your wrongs.
         Bian. [*with increasing severity and with scorn.*
         That with your master
I might consent to right them!
         Mal. The redress
Lies with yourself, Madonna.   But, to know
How grossly you are cozen'd by your lord ——
Bian. Sir, touch him not!   It is a dastard's part
To vilify the absent.
         Mal. [*discomposed.   Then, gravely:*
         I have done

My duty toward a lady whom I honor,
My lord adores, and my own spouse holds dear.

　　　　　　　　　　　　　　[about to go.

Bian. And has your duty further prompted you
To ope this missive? [*lifting it.*

　　　　　Mal. [*commanding himself.*

　　　　See, madam, for yourself.
The silken thread, the seal, are still unbroken.

Bian. Then shall they so remain. [*She holds the letter in the*
　　　　　　　　　　　　　　flame of a candle.

　　　　　Mal. What would you do?

Bian. Destroy forever what 't would shame my lord
To think I knew of, and prevent in you
The hope that in your absence I would read it.
'T is done. You know me better now. Good night.

　　　　　　　　[*Exit — with an expression of*
　　　　　　　　　　　deep despite — Mal.

Oh Bonaventuri! And for thee, for this,
I gave up all! [*clasping her hands in anguish.*

　　　　My heart! my heart! my heart!

　　　　　　[*Buries her face in her hands,*
　　　　　　　　　sobbing. And

Scene closes.

SCENE VI.

A street, having others crossing it.
It is starlight.   On the right, a whiter portion of the sky
shows the moon to be rising.

Enter
SGHERRO, MASNADIERE, SCHERANO, MALANDRINO,
and other ASSASSINS.

Sgher. Scherano, Malandrino, get you quickly
To the Orsini palace, for the task
That 's laid out there.   The knave that keeps to-night
The gate will smooth your way.   Whisper my name. —
Make a clean job.   You are to use no weapons.
Ply but your fingers.
                    Malan. Captain, let me stay.
Here is more manly work.
                              Sgher. But pays no better.
Why, thou art nice!   Is not Bravone gone
To Cafaggiolo, with the bold Lucchesan,
To rid Don Pietro of his Spanish wife?
Malan. But hast thou men enough?   The fop, they say,
  Is full of mettle; and the two stout fellows,
That follow him, look as they would use their swords.
Scher. One of them may.   The other is bought off.

Sgher. Which makes us six to two.   They must indeed
  Be devils to match us.   To thy proper work.
                    [*Exeunt Scher. and Malan.*
  Here comes a lantern.   'T is our game.   This way.
The Assassins secrete themselves in one of the cross streets.

                    Enter
  BONAVENTURI, *preceded by* BRENNA *with a lantern,*
    and followed by CAGNOTTO: *both well-armed.*

Bren. We are beset! [*falling back on the others.*
      Bonav. Stand by me, men.
                  Bren. [*running off.*] Not I!
  They are two to one. [*Exit.*
          Bonav. Base coward!
                  Cagnot. Traitor rather:
  He has carried off the light.
                  Bonav. We shall not need it.
  The moon is o'er the houses' tops enough
  To let us see their blades.   They are on us now.
  Back to the wall, Cagnotto.

    During this dialogue, the ASSASSINS,
who had spread themselves out so as to prevent escape,
    come forward, SCHERRO *in advance, to the two,*
      who stand with their backs to the wall.

      Sgher. [*to Cagnotto.*] Get thee gone.
  One is our man.   That is not thou.

Cagnot. [*cut'ing him down.*] It is
For thee.

An Assassin. Thou hast made me Captain. Thanks!

     [*wounding Cagnot., who falls.*

Cagnot. Master, I have done you service. See me paid.

         [*Dies.*

Bonav. [*running the assassin through.*

  'T is done, my brave. So. [*disabling another.*

      Halt, you other three!

What would you? Money? Take it. Let me hence,
And ten times o'er the amount is yours to boot.

Masn. Coin thy blood into ducats if thou wilt,

 'T is in thy veins alone we seek them. Thus.

All three remaining Assassins rush on BONAVENTURI *at once,
who, after an animated resistance and repeated
wounds, falls.*

Bonav. Bianca! Thou 'rt — aveng'd!

    Masn. The Orsini too.

Quiet? [*leaning over the body.*

Assass. This will make sure. [*raising his weapon.*

    Masn. No! 'T is enough.

He has fought bravely, and our work is done.

  *The Moon, now risen over the houses' tops,
  throws its light upon the group.*

The Assassins disperse, leading off their wounded comrade, and

    Scene closes.

SCENE VII.

In the Orsini Palace.   The bedchamber of Isabella.

ISABELLA *asleep.*
Beside the bed, on a stand, a taper and a silver hand-bell.

Enter, a-tiptoe,
SCHERANO *and* MALANDRINO.
They speak in an under-tone.

Scher. Shall I awake her ?
                              Malan. No, 't is better thus.
Going to the bed.] A most fair creature !
                              Scher. Let us wake her then,
And hear her prayers. What ho ! Your Highness ! Up !
Isa. Who are you ?   Ah ! [*she starts up and rings the bell.*
                              Scher. Cry, ring.   There are no ears.
The Duke has taken especial care of that.
Isa. [*wildly.*] Has my lord sent to murder me ?
                              Malan. Even so.
Isa. Let me escape !   I am not fit to die.
I will make you richer far than he will do.
My brothers too will heap wealth on you both.
Scher. Which of them ?   Don Pietro's wife even now
By her lord's will is going where you shall go.

Isa. [*sinking back.*] Accursed House of Medici!

       Scher. Ay, so

Say I! Amen! I would we were well-rid

Of all the race.

     Isa. Have mercy! Take this ring.

'T is worth a thousand ducats.

      Malan. [*taking it.*] 'T will not save you.

Scher. Quick to your prayers. Your lover by this time

Is well carv'd up.

     Isa. Troilo Orsini?

     Malan. No,

Bonaventuri.

Isa. [*falling back again.*] God is just!

 Scher. [*pressing a pillow over her face.*] Why so;

'T is a good prayer. — Thou dost nought, Malandrino!

Malan. [*sullenly.*

My hands were made to clutch an iron sword-hilt,

Not to choke women.

     Scher. Only take their rings.

'T is nice distinction!

     Isa. Oh!

     Scher. What! not yet done?

Thou art strong, to be so fair. [*A pause. He lifts the*

            pillow.

    Still now.

      Malan. Come then.

I'd rather kill ten men than do this over.

      Exeunt — Malan. looking back

    upon the bed, as he moves.

SCENE VIII.

In Bonaventuri's palace.   As in Scene V.

BONAVENTURI *lying on a couch.*
At his head, one on either side, the Court Physicians
BALDINI *and* CAPPELLI.   BIANCA *kneeling*
by the Couch, holding his
hand clasped in hers. SENNUCCIO *standing at*
the foot.

Bian. Thou shalt have justice!   Thou shalt hear it vow'd
By his own lips!   Thy spirit shall go down,
Unto the biding-place of all the dead,
Appeas'd!   Vittorio will bring back the Duke.
He has pray'd me test his friendship.   I have kneel'd
But once for favor; I will kneel once more,
•   And thy poor bleeding wounds, belov'd Pietro,
Shall cry with me for vengeance. —
                    Bonav. [*feebly.*] He will come —
Too late: my life — ebbs fast.
                    Bian. Have mercy, God!
Sustain him yet awhile, renown'd Baldini!
Master Cappelli,[12] is all art in vain?
Bald. [*feeling the wrist of the hand Bianca abandons to him.*
Alas, Signora! all that art can do

Is now to watch its own prognostications
Fatally realiz'd.

   Capp. [*feeling the other wrist.*

    If your honor'd spouse,
Lady, has aught at heart he fain would utter,
Let him be quick. This draught will give him strength,
Yet a brief space. [*Bonav. drinks.*

   Bonav. Bianca! ——

     Bian. [*kissing his hand.*

    Speak, beloved!
Thy will shall be my law.

     Bonav. [*reviving.*

     Canst thou — forgive me ?

Bian. Thou hast done no wrong; none that I ever ponder'd
 With aught but sorrow — sorrow for thyself.

Bonav. Thou knowest not all. That night — we fled from
  Venice ——

Raise me. — Still higher, Doctor. Thank you. — Then,
When on the stairs I left you — to make sure,
I said, that all was safe — I stole away
To — shut the portal of your father's house,
That barr'd return for aye. Breath! breath, O God!

   BONAVENTURI, *panting.* — *A brief pause.*

Bian. Be sooth'd. 'T was passion made thee to forget
 Duty and honor. I have not repented,
 Save for my father's sake, to have fled from home.
 I have liv'd happy, till — till ——

Bonav. Till I wrong'd thee.
I am justly punish'd. Seek not — to avenge me.
Sennuccio —— Oh! — The draught! the draught,
    Cappelli!

             Drinks again. Pause.

Quickly! My last sand 's running out. Bianca —
Take to thy heart — Sennuccio. A true friend,
He did abhor my — treachery. Let him be —
Warmly commended — to my lord the Duke.
He will — well serve him — as I — ne'er have done.

        Enter VITTORIO CAPELLO.

Bian. [*starting up eagerly.*
    Is his Grace coming?

              Vitt. News had reach'd the Palace,
The Lady Isabella and the spouse
Of Don Pietro suddenly were dead. —
Bonav. Murder'd! — Heaven's justice! — Murder'd!
    Falls back, gasping, into the arms of the attendants.
                Vitt. The Grand Duchess,
Hearing, was seiz'd with travail premature,
And cannot live beyond the hour.

    The Physicians, already in excitement,
hastily resigning BONAVENTURI *to* SENNUCCIO, *make for*
the door, but pause on the sill, as BONAVENTURI,
springing up half-erect, exclaims to BIANCA:

Bonav. My star

Is set! I see — ascend the whitening sky,

Lord of the day — thy planet! Hail, Grand Duchess!

Falls back.

Thus — Bonaventuri's murder — is aveng'd —

And thou — art recompens'd. [*Dies.*

Senn. It is all over.

With a piercing shriek, BIANCA

throws herself upon the body. The PHYSICIANS,

one instant more lingering, hurry from the scene.

VITTORIO, *with hands folded, looks from the foot of*

the couch upon the corpse, and SENNUCCIO

at the head bends over it, and

slowly

The Drop falls.[13]

ACT THE FOURTH

Scene I. A saloon in in the Pitti Palace.

DONNA VIRGINIA *and* SIGNORA MALOCUORE.

Sign. How does your Highness like her for a sister?
Virg. Well.
   Sign. Well? But for a mistress?
                    Virg. Even as much.
I find her nothing chang'd. Our Sovereign Lady
Is the Signora Bonaventuri still.
Sign. Ay, so I think her. She can never be
Aught but the widow of a banker's clerk.
Virg. But that is not my meaning. She was ever
More than the Favorite's wife. A noble lady,
Who still has been the pattern of our sex, —
Whose virtues have no rivals but her graces, —
And those scarce match'd. My brother has done well.
Did not the proud Republic this day crown her
Their royal daughter, she were still his peer.
Sign. You do surprise me. Have her witch's-arts
Enchanted too your Highness? "
                 Virg. You forget,
Signora Malocuor, of whom you speak.
The Grand Duke's bride, Bianca, has no **arts**

Save those which nature taught her.   I had thought
The rabblement alone believ'd such tales.

Sign. I did but jest.   I was, knows not your Grace?
 Donna Bianca's first and fastest friend.
 Well pleas'd am I to find your Highness' heart,
 So far as the young prince, Don Cæsar's right
 Permits, is given so well.   But may I ask,
 Does the Grand Duchess give hers in return?

Virg. She does to all who love her.   Even her foes
 May boast her kindness.

     Sign. Yet your Highness' mother —
Pray pardon me — is pining, cloister'd still.

Virg. That is my brother's fault, not hers.

     Sign. She has
The power however to move that brother's heart.
She us'd it for the Cardinal, her foe.
Why not for you?

    Virg. My mother was as kind,
And for the Cardinal did what she has done,
Open'd the royal coffers.   Why has not
The Cardinal, who pretends to love my mother,
In gratitude mov'd the Duchess to this act? ·

Sign. Haply for that he knew it were in vain.

Virg. I will essay.   In this high festal time,
 Fill'd to the brim with joy and happy pride,
 The Duke's heart may flow over ——

    Sign. But not hers.

Virg. [*without noticing the interruption.*
 — And the rich superflux make glad the heart

Of Cosmo's lonely widow. — Do not stir.

      [as Sign. attends her going.

I need you not, Signora. [*Exit.*   .

Sign. [*returning, after seeing Virginia ceremoniously through*
   the door.]   Why not say :

" Of the Grand-duchess dowager " ? Artless fool !
That hast a child's heart with a woman's head.
The daughter of Camilla, thou dost well
To take Bianca's part : thy upstart dam
Was such another mushroom, vain and proud,
And beautiful as she. Come but the day
That Ferdinand shall mount his brother's throne,
The fate of the new Duchess is like hers, —
Or haply worse, for the proud Churchman hates her.
And yet — methinks — he loves her too, with love
After his fashion, like his father's son.
I must watch this. Camilla freed or not,
St. Mark's new daughter shall not win thereby. [*Exit.*

SCENE II.[15]

A hall in the same.

Enter,
from opposite sides,
DON PIETRO *and the* ARCHBISHOP OF PISA.
The latter stopping ceremoniously for the Prince to pass,
DON PIETRO *goes up to him.*

Don P. Well met, Archbishop. 'T is a glorious day
For the Capello.
   Archb. And for you, my lord?
Don P. Even as you see. I, with the bastard John,
Marshal'd the guard of honor at the Gate
Right willingly. By Heaven! it was a show!
You, who with Abbioso and the rest
Met at Firenzuöl the pompous train,[16]
Can witness that. And when the pageant pass'd
Between our glittering lines, amid the roar
Of cannon, and the peal of all the bells,
I thought how Cardinal Ferdinand would wince:
And that was joy for me.
   Archb. Alas, my lord!
That you will visit with this evil will
Your pious brother!

Don. P. My pious brother! Is 't
Of Cosmo's son you speak?   Or think you well
I take for holy all a Churchman's cap,
Mitre or hat may cover?   You do right
Perhaps to love him.   'T was his hand that laid
The first step in your scale of fortune.   What
Have I to thank him for?   That he was got
Before me?   He has cause to dread, and hates,
Bianca: she may bear Francesco sons.
I have no cause for either fear or hate.
Dies the Grand Duke without heirs male, upstarts
My Cardinal brother, doffs the purple, and takes
His coveted place.   Sometimes he makes me blind
To his dark views, and presses me to marry.
But now and then comes daylight, and I see
Clearly — as now.

    Archb. Your Grace will yet admit
His Eminence is sincere, when once consider'd
'T is not the Duke's new marriage is oppos'd,
But marriage with the Intendant's widow, unmeet
For Cosmo's heir and Cosmo's ancient blood,
Unmeet to follow union with the House
Of Hapsburg.   To succeed the late Grand Duchess,
The Emperor Rodolph gladly had bestow'd
A child of Archduke Charles.   Such match had pleas'd
My lord the Cardinal.

    Don P. Think you so?   What then?
What is our blood that it should scorn Capello's?
Is it so many more than tenscore years,

Since Averado, son of the Lucchesan,
Portion'd his mighty fortune, got by trade,
Between his six sons? whence arose our House.
Not then the triple flower-de-luce emblaz'd
The middle roundle of our shield in chief.
Our power was all, — nor that without dispute;
Our rank a usurpation; and our title?
Why, know not all men, fifty years agone
Our beast still ramp'd where gleams the lilied crown?[17]
God's might! the throne of Clement's bastard son,
Founded by perfidy on public wrong,
Is all too new, that his unlineal heirs
Should in the second generation vaunt
A scarce-acknowledg'd royalty.[18] 'T is trick!
By holy John, as patent as this hand!
Did Ferdinand scorn Camilla? Yet was she
No equal of Bianca. Lo, this day,
Adopting her the daughter of the State,
The proud Republic crowns our Duchess queen,
Peer of the Queen of Hungary and her
Who sat in Cyprus. Why is he displeas'd?
Because her lord is Cosmo's eldest son.
Camilla could not bear a male should be
His senior. No, Archbishop, it is not
The Archduchess Ferdinand would choose, but one
He knows the Grand Duke would not choose.

Archb. My lord,
I cannot credit this. The Cardinal Prince
Is holy.

Don P. You may say so. But you are
A man, Del Pozzo, of no common mind.
You know the Cardinal is a worldly prince
And an unmatch'd dissembler.

Enter ABBIOSO.

Is 't not so,
Good Bishop?
   Abb. Pleases it your Grace to speak
Of what and whom?
   Don P. Of my pure brother, pious
Cardinal Ferdinand. Holdst thou him a saint?
Abb. My opinion of the Cardinal is known.
I love him not.
   Don P. With reason. Late at Rome
He holp to make St. Peter's Vicar loath
To hoist thee to the half Pistoian see:
Ah, Abbioso? Get thee quickly hence
To the Lagunes. In thy new function there,
Bland Secretary, serve thy liege lord Francis,
Near the Pregádi.[19] Here thou shalt not quarrel
With Holy Church.
   Archb. I would, your Grace, that none
Might quarrel here. Our sovereign is the lord
Of his own will. What pleases him to do,
In his born right, that should content us also.
And with a virtuous and high-bred fair dame,
As is our Lady, even the Cardinal must

In time be pleas'd.

    Don P. So let him be or not.

Philip of Spain approves.   Though Austria murmur,

Spite the whole College and the Pope to boot

Others will show like sense. — But time calls off.

We must prepare us to attend in pomp

The solemn crowning of the titular Queen,

And the renew'd high nuptials. How will like

Your Cardinal that?

     Abb. He has sent *one* gentleman

To watch the game and make report; himself

Too busy with affairs of Heaven to come.

Don P. An impotent insult. Laugh you not, Archbishop?

Archb. I know nought impotent in the hand or head

  Of the lord Cardinal. [*Exit Don Pietro.*

    Abb. No; nor in his fangs.

The Medici are venom'd serpents all.

Archb. Have care, Ottavio! I am known no traitor,

  Or thou hadst never risk'd that thrust.

      Abb. I hope

The new-create Grand Duchess may not prove

Its point prophetical. Let her, I say,

Beware the Cardinal Medici's venom'd fang! [20]

       [*Exeunt at opposite sides.*

SCENE III.

The Grand Duchess's Apartment in the same.

BIANCA, *magnificently arrayed, but without the royal mantle.*
VIRGINIA, *who has her hand in Bianca's.   On their*
right, a little behind, Bianca's daughter PELLEGRINA *with*
her husband BENTIVOGLIO.   *On the left, at a like dis-*
tance, SIGNORA MALOCCORE.

Enter
CAPELLO, *with the* PATRIARCH *of* AQUILEIA.
Behind them, VITTORIO.

Bian. It shall be so, Virginia.   Doubt it not.
   VIRGINIA *retires beside the* SIGNORA — *on whom she*
    .   *looks triumphantly.*
  O my dear father!   Uncle!   May I deem
  This day makes full requital for the past?
[21] The sorrow that I caus'd thee, the dishonor
  Brought, though I meant it not, upon thy House?
Cap. No more of that, my child.   'T was not thy crime.
  The good Sennuccio has disclos'd me all.
  Know'st thou, Bianca — did thy brother tell thee,
  How I had hung thy picture all with black,
  That day I lost thee? how the veil was drawn,
  When the Duke's favor shining on thy spouse

Made him thy equal?   But when Sforza came,
Praying the Senate to receive as son
Of Venice the Great Duke himself; and when,
Like Catharine Cornaro, thou wast made
The Child of the Republic, and a Queen ;
Then did I cause a crown surmount the frame.
But 't was not needed: Titian, had he liv'd,
Had pointed to the air of native pride [22]
That dignifies thy beauty, and had said :
" Superfluous decoration!   Nature gave
A better diadem.   And that I drew.
Lo, where in every trait the destin'd Queen ! "
Is it not true, Grimani ?   O my child !
Thou wast my darling ever, my best joy ;
Thou art my glory now, my House's pride.

Patr. The will of Heaven works oft by humble ways.
That jewel his bold subject stole and wore
The Duke hath made the centre of his crown.
Keep thou, O gem, thy lustre without flaw !
So shall the people bless thee. — Francis comes.

Enter
the GRAND DUKE, *attended by* SENNUCCIO.
The G. D. is splendidly attired, but without his robes of
state. SENNUCCIO *also, like all the other*
persons present, is in full costume as for some
extraordinary occasion of Court-festival.

G. D. Good morrow, friends.— Bianca! My fair Queen ! —

SENNUCCIO, *with* CAPELLO, *&c., takes his*
place with the other personages in the background.
How well this pomp becomes thee! Thou art now
A jewel fitly set. And yet, believe,
Thy lustre shines not more in Francis' eyes
Now than that morn, when, from the little window,
Like a rich picture in a sorry frame,
That sweet face dawn'd a moment on his gaze;
Not more ador'd than when, a twelvemonth since,
Thy heart first open'd to the houseless love
That long had knock'd in vain to be let in.
Yet do I joy, for thy sake, joy for mine,
[23] Joy for the offspring, hope of which I nurse
For my throne's heritage, our love's glad contract
This day shall ratify before the world,
And thou, whose worth needs not the gilt of rank,
Shalt by thy country, even for that worth,
Be dower'd with those distinctions which alone
The world will value. Thy true crown is here.
                              [*his hand on his breast.*
Bian. There will I strive to wear it. But, my lord,
We who live in the world, and for the world
Live chiefly, must our living even so rule
That the world shall not say we live not well.
That we do right, should satisfy ourselves,
And may, we hope, the Almighty; but, for men,
One thing is needed more, — that, doing right,
We seem to do so. [24] When Your Highness' brother,
The Cardinal Ferdinand, found me at your side

In your sick hour, not knowing we were wed,
His wrath was rous'd.   Even so the hard-judging
    world,
Untaught, had frown'd on my best act of duty;
And your own love, that should have rais'd its object,
While blessing, would have robb'd her of her fame.
But for this cause, believe me, dear my lord,
Bianca had been happy unacknowledg'd,
Blest in thy love, content to be thy spouse.
²⁵ Twice happy am I now my fatherland,
Not for my merits, but to honor thee,
Hath given me, for the thousand gifts I owe
Thy matchless love, to make some small return,
Lifting me to thy side more like thy mate.
Thou shalt not find me derogate.   Was I aught
As humble Bonaventuri's wife, I shall
Be ten times more, high-plac'd as Francis' spouse,
Endeavoring so to live, as not to shame
Thy crown, nor that which Venice this day gives.

G. D. But worthier in thyself, than didst thou wear
A crown imperial.   Come; the hour is nigh
Shall tell the world, not me, what thou deserv'st.
Sweet, let us to the robing-room.
                              Bian. Yet first
I have a grace to sue.   Wilt grant it, love?

G. D. What canst thou ask, that Francis will not grant?

Bian. Virginia's mother, twelve long years confin'd
    In a dull cloister: set her free, my lord,
    And make Virginia happy, and herself.

G. D. Knowest thou what this mother was? In league
    With Ferdinand, using aye in his behoof
    The power o'er Cosmo's doting heart she never
    Once turn'd to good account, fomenter still
    Of discord 'twixt us brothers, and betwixt
    Our sire and us, now let her out thou add'st
    Another to thy secret foes and mine.
    But I have never yet deny'd thee aught.
    I will not now, this happy hour. — Virginia!
    That day thy hand is given, as thy heart,
    To the young lord of Estè, shall thy mother
    Revisit the gay world.   Let her beware
    So to employ her freedom, that the gift
    Be not revok'd.   Nay, kneel not unto me;
    Kiss the Grand Duchess' hand.   And bid thy mother
    Remember it is she unbars the door,
    Not Ferdinand. —

As Virginia *attempts to kneel to* Bianca, *and kiss
her hand,* Bianca *draws her to her bosom, and kisses her on
the forehead.*

Ah, gentle love! — Now come.

Exeunt Omnes: the G. D. *and* Bianca *leading;
behind them the* Patriarch *and* Capello; *behind these*
Virginia *and* Vittorio; *then* Pellegrina *and* Bentivoglio;
and finally Sennuccio *and* Signora Malocuore.

Scene IV.

A cabinet in the Cardinal de' Medici's palace at Rome.

The Cardinal, *walking to and fro with signs of
discomposure.* Malocuore, *standing.*

Card. Go on.
    Mal. I fear your Eminence will lose
Your patience.
        Card. Patience?   Hast thou liv'd so long
To wear a beard, and know'st not, what affects
The heart with sudden sorrow, or wounds self-love,
Falls with as passionate impulse on the sense
As news that flatters vanity?   By how much
Hate is of more vitality than love,
By so much lend I now the readier ear
In that thy theme offends me.   On! go on!
Mal. When the Ambassador, Count Mario Sforza
Of Santa Fiora ——
        Card. Spare me.   Need'st thou specify
His titles?   Add then, Francis-Mary's minion,
And the Venet —— his Venice woman's tool.
Mal. — Brought back the State's diploma of paternity,
My lord despatch'd the Prince, Don Giovannino,
To thank the Senate.
        Card. A boy but twelve years old!

Apt messenger for such unworthy errand!

                       Mal. Then,

Two of her foremost senators were sent

By Venice, Tiépolo and Michiéli,

To invest her daughter with the parent's rights.

With these ambassadors came ninety nobles,

Both of the sea-girt city and the main;

Such a proud troop as never the Republic

Even in her palmiest fortune sent before.

What but like pomp should answer it? The Court,

The Cabinet, all Florence boasts of great

Or noble, throng'd to meet the imposing train;

Whereof, not least conspicuous for glad zeal,

Shone out my lord, the Prince, Don Pietro.

         Card. [*stopping in his walk.*] Ah!

Say'st thou? 'T is most likely.

In an under but bitter tone, and re-
            suming his walk.] Renegade!

Mal. All the Capello's house and kin were there,

From the Grand Duchess' sire and uncle down

To the last gentleman that boasts their blood.

You had thought them monarchs, conquerors at the
        least.

Thunder'd the cannon, and the bells rung out

From every tower, as the Sovereign's guests

Enter'd the Sovereign's Palace.

               Card. Who?

                   Mal. The House

And kin of Senator Capello.

Card. All?

Mal. To the last gentleman that boasts his blood.

Card. What! Not enough to house the sire and brother?
    Must the herd batten where my father fed?

Mal. The sire goes back: but not the brother; who gets
    A pension his male issue will inherit, —
    His daughter to be dower'd.

              Card. Holy Paul!
This passes all endurance. What! must I,
His father's son, be scanted and put off
In my emergence, that a foreign vermin
May pierce the fisc at will? — What more?

                          Mal. 'T is said,
The expenses of the marriage, reckoning all,
From the first mission to the crowning-rite,
Will make three hundred thousand ducats told.

Card. That while a dearth is pressing sore the land,
    And his born subjects pine for simple bread!
    O Lord, how long shall the crown'd sons of pride
    Abuse their loan'd prerogatives, and make
    The sad earth doubt Thy justice?

                    Mal. And for one
Not meriting such fortune.

           Card. [*roughly.*] Who is that?
By Heaven, thou! ——
Correcting himself.] Thou mistak'st me much. I meant
Not to impute the fault to her.

          Mal. [*insinuatingly.*] I thought
Your Eminence had hated the Grand Duchess.

Card. Should that prevent my knowledge of her due?
    Her natural gifts of —— To the tale. Proceed.
Mal. [20] The Ambassadors express'd the Senate's joy,
    That the two cities, henceforth close affin'd ——
Card. Pass all that, — as in time it all will pass.
Mal. And giving to the daughter of the State,
    In the paternal name, a most rare jewel ——
Card. And that. Come to the crowning act.
                         Mal. The crown?
Card. Conferr'd this day, I think.
                 Mal. About this hour,
In the Great Hall, most lavishly adorn'd,
Before the Eight and Forty of the Senate,
The Grand Duke, on his throne, receives the Duchess,
Who enters royally array'd, led in
By the Ambassadors, the whole gorgeous train
Of Venice nobles following. She takes
Her seat beside him. The diploma redd,
And ratify'd, of the conceded honors,
The diadem is set on her fair brow,
The nuptial ring is interchang'd anew,
And, wearing still the crown, the titular Queen,
Her lord beside her, marches to the Church,
The heroine of a triumph ——
            Card. [*musingly, and resuming his walk.*
                'T is too late
Now to regret. I should have lik'd to see it.
Mal. Ay, it will prove a rare burlesque.
                Card. Burlesque!

What mean'st thou? She will well become the crown —
I mean in beauty and in gentle pride.

Musingly.

Methinks I see her now; her gliding step,
Which scarce was motion, settled to a pace
Of quiet majesty; her radiant smile,
So proud yet sweet withal, though beaming still,
Yet less diffusive in its light; her eyes ——
Ah, there the ethereal fire, which Earth subdues
With its most tender passions! that soft flame
Which might convince an infidel, for there
The Soul and Heaven give out immortal signs ——

During this spoken meditation, the CARDINAL
has turned his back on MALOCUORE. *Now starting, as if
recollecting himself, he faces suddenly about and sees
MALOCUORE watching him intently, who at once
drops his eyes; and the* CARDINAL *resumes.*

Thou seem'st to think it strange I can admire
What all men must admire.   'T is not to love.
Besides this lady still has been for me
Most amiable and wooing.

      Mal. I have thought ——
But pardon me, your Grace.   I did forget.
Card. What wouldst thou say?   I pardon no reserve.
Mal. Yet, my lord's station, and our Holy Church ——
Card. Is 't that?   Were not the Apostles flesh and blood?
Thou 'dst speak, I see, of me and of Bianca.

What hast thou seen? Speak out! Thou hast thought
   — thou saidst —

Mal. I have thought at times, my lord, your brother's spouse
   Measur'd your fair proportions with an eye
   Of capable relish.   The Grand Duke is comely;
   But my lord Cardinal's youth and finer features ——

Card. Thou art a serpent.   Think'st thou I am Adam?
   I hanker not for the Forbidden Fruit.
   Dream'st thou I do?

          Mal. My lord would not, I see,
   Admit me to his confidence.

          Card. Because
I have no secret.   The Venetian is
My brother's spouse.   That he has made this choice
Displeases me, because it wrongs our House,
And mars its influence with foreign Courts.
Therefore I view her with such evil will
As may beseem a Christian and a prince
Of Holy Church.   I do admire her too, —
Esteem her worthy even of a crown,
Were that not what it is.   But love her! —   I
Forgive thee, Malocuore.   We will talk
Further anon.   [*Exit Malocuor.*

The CARDINAL *looks after him a moment with an expression
      of triumph and disdain.*

        Make *thee* my confidant! —
I will, so far as suits me; not so far

As make thee, dog! my master.   No, let fools
Unlock their hearts to knaves.   The key to mine
Lies only in my keeping, and shall ever. —
And to betray a love I shame to own
Even to myself!   Not that Bianca is
My brother's spouse.   [27] My father lov'd my sister:
And his last wife methinks was fond of me.
And but I was too young, perhaps in turn
I had lov'd her too.   I put her though to use.
She was my reservoir; I drew from her
The gold Francesco could not, and for which
He hated me.   But I should shame to own
I love his Favorite's widow, when for like love
I scorn him, as I hate him doubly too,
If aught indeed can double hate like mine.
[28] And her too I shall use — if not for pleasure,
For profit.   What imply those words that came,
Wrapp'd with the picture I had pray'd to have?

> *Takes, from a drawer of an open*
> *writing-table, a miniature, incased, and a*
> *letter.   Opening the latter he appears to read*
> *in it.   Then:*

[29] *She cannot live without me?* [pause.

                    — *Lives in me?* [pause.
Is it the simple passion of her nature
Lends her these phrases; for her way is loving
And tender unto all; or? —— We shall see.
This coronation over —— Would the crown

Were fire to burn her temples, though I would
So gladly feel them beat against my heart!
This over, she shall see me at her wish. [*pause.*
[30] No, it were better first to write. I will —
Will test her kindness. She shall use her hold
On my weak brother's heart to unlock his treasure.
I need fresh means. His hand, which never shuts
When a show 's promis'd or an artist sues,
Closes, perhaps instinctively, to me,
As if he felt his gold would prop the lever
That shakes his throne.   Ah! when that throne shall
    crumble
To pieces at my touch, to be rebuilt
For a more resolute ruler; when the wrong
Which nature did me when she made him first,
Though I was meant for government —— As yet
See I but darkly what my soul bids do
To rectify this wrong; but what I do
Shall be so done 't will not need doing over.
When I throw off this purple which I hate ——
But where wilt then *thou* be? [*gazing on the miniature.*
                    Or being, *what,*
What wilt thou then be? — Mine thou shalt be,
    or! ——
I hate thee as I love thee [*kissing passionately the glass.*]:
    't seemeth now,
As I gaze on that proud, yet winning smile,
Which woos yet mocks me, seems it to me now,
As I could kiss and choke thee at one breath.

Accurs'd enchantress! Such my tools have made
The credulous crowd believe thee. And thou art!
Thou art! But thy enchantments are all here.

*Gazing on the miniature a moment, he
closes the case, and walks up to the writing-table, to replace it,
and Scene closes.*

SCENE V.

Florence. The Great Hall in the Pitti Palace.

The GRAND DUKE, *wearing the grand-ducal crown
and robes, and seated on his throne, surrounded by the Senate
of Forty-eight, and the Magistrates in a semicircle on
either side. Within the crescent, on his right,* DON PIETRO, *the*
DUKE OF BRACCIANO, DON CÆSAR D' ESTE, ARCH-
BISHOP OF PISA, ABBIOSO, *&c. On the left* DONNA VIRGINIA,
PELLEGRINA, SIGNORA MALOCURE *and other ladies.*

The Hall, magnificently draped, is hung with banners, &c.,
and the whole Court is in sumptuously festal and
solemn array.
On either side a line of soldiery extending up to the
throne, with banners of arms, &c., among
which those of Venice are
conspicuous.

A grand burst of music,
and Enter.
in royal robes, her train borne up by two Pages, BIANCA
conducted by the two Venetian AMBASSADORS,
and followed immdiately by BARTHOLOMEW CAPELLO *and the*
PATRIARCH, *and en suite by* VITTORIO, *and a long train*
of Venetian nobles gorgeously appareled.

G. D. [*descending the steps before his throne.*
　　　Our well-belov'd, right royal Duchess!　Sit
　　　Bodily at our hand, who in our heart
　　　In spirit art ever thron'd. [*Places her on the throne and*
　　　　　　　　　　　　　　　　sits beside her.
　　　　　　　　　　Rever'd Capello!
　　　Our lady's noble father; thou, grave Patriarch,
　　　Her honor'd uncle and ours; be seated near.
　　　　　　　　　　[*They take their places on his right.*
　　　Our sometime Auditor, most Reverend Sire
　　　In God, Archbishop Antony of Pisa,
　　　Read the diploma of St. Mark's adoption,
　　　For which cause sit we here.

Archb. [*reading.*

In the high name.

Of the august Republic, we the Doge
And joint Pregadi, wishing to attest
Our deep sense of the many and rare virtues
Which render worthy of the highest fortune
Blanche, daughter of the Senator Capello,
Whom the Great Duke of Tuscany has wed,
And to do honor to the Great Duke's self,
Adopt her as the daughter of the State,
Conceding unto her the rank and title
Of Queen of Cyprus, with all high prerogatives
And honors which to the adoptive parent
Of right belong.

G. D. Speak ye, the Ambassadors
Of Venice, Excellent Signori Tiepolo
And Michïeli, is that your Senate's voice?

Tiep. It is.

Mich. We ratify it, and pronounce
By virtue of our warrant, in the name
Of Holy Mark, the Lady Blanche Capello
True and legitimate Child of the Republic.

Tiep. In whose high name we place this royal crown
On her fair brows.

The AMBASSADORS *crown her,* — BIANCA
advancing and standing up.

Both. { Long live the Queen Bianca!

Venetian }
Nobles. } Live Queen Bianca!

            The Guards, presenting arms, and their stand-
ard-bearers waving all the banners, join in the
cry. A burst of music.

         Patriarch. 'T is the Senate's wish
Of Venice, and the Great Duke lends consent,
The high espousals solemniz'd before
Between His Highness and the Lady Blanche,
Born daughter of Bartholomew Capello,
Should by His Highness this day be renew'd
With the Queen, daughter of St. Mark. Advance,
Ambassadors, and give away the bride.

         The Nuptial ring is exchanged
in the customary form, and the PATRIARCH, *spreading*
his hands over the pair, appears to repeat the
prayers and benediction. Then aloud:

Heaven on these nuptials shower perennial joy;
And give the fair engrafted plant to glad
With long fecundity the sovereign stock;
So after ages, happy in its shade,
May bless, as I do now, the parent seed!
G. D. Now to the Church, to offer thanks to God.
And meetly close this high auspicious day.

The Characters and other persons
form in procession, which passes down and from the scene
in the following order :
PATRIARCH OF AQUILEIA *and* ARCHBISHOP OF PISA.
BIANCA, *with the crown on her head, led by the* GRAND DUKE,
and having her train borne up by the SIGNORA MALOCUOR
and another LADY OF THE COURT, — *the Gr. Duke's train*
borne by two PAGES.   *Then* DON PIETRO, *with* BAR-
THOLOMEW CAPELLO; DONNA VIRGINIA *with* DON CÆSAR
D' ESTE; *the* DUKE OF BRACCIANO *with* VITTORIO; PEL-
LEGRINA *with* BENTIVOGLIO ; SENNUCCIO
and ABBIOSO ; SENATE.
Then the train of VENETIAN NOBLES ; *then the* INFERIOR
MAGISTRATES; *and finally the* GUARD, *which have*
presented arms as the procession passes between
the lines. Music playing throughout, until

the Drop falls.

ACT THE FIFTH

Scene I.   A room in the Grand Duchess's Apartment.

BIANCA.   CARDINAL.

Card. Nay, it is so.   Your modesty disowns
　　Your kindness' due.   I know my brother's heart:
　　One may wring aught from it but gold.
　　　　　　　　　　Bian. My lord,
　　You do him wrong.   A freer hand or heart
　　Can boast no monarch: few so free.
　　　　　　　　　　Card. Well, well;
　　I will not argue — not with you.   Once more,
　　A thousand thanks.   I would I could believe
　　I ow'd your kindness to a dearer feeling.
Bian. Than what, my lord?
　　　　　　　　Card. Than that which you profess.
　　Oft in your letters you have call'd me dear;
　　And when you bade me hasten from dead Rome
　　To give new life to Florence and to you,
　　It was with such a magic of sweet words
　　As lent even to your picture sweeter charms.
　　May I believe them real?
　　　　　　　　Bian. My poor words?
　　O yes!   Indeed, save dear Virginia only,

Who of my lord's near blood can be to me
That which your Highness' talents, winning way,
And suavity of speech have render'd you ?

Card. And is that all ?   Alas! your pictur'd lips
Give back no colder answer.
                    Bian. Does your Grace
Then question them?   When, at your prayer, I sent
My poor resemblance, pleas'd to think you held
In some regard your brother's wife, I sent
Truly my heart with it.   Did your Grace in turn
Give truly yours ?
               Card. So truly, and so wholly,
I come to seek it.   Give me back my own.
Or satisfy the sweet yet painful void
That leaves my breast no respite.
                  Bian. My lord Cardinal!
This language in a Churchman ——

               Card. Seems it strange ?
Has not a Churchman senses?   Are they proof
To that delicious sickness whose contagion
Seizes the spirits of all other men ?

Bian. My lord! my lord!   Either yourself are mad,
Or you think me so.   If you not remember
What your position calls for, at the least
Forget not what belongs to mine.   [*Turns to go.*
               Card. Yet stay !
Beauteous Bianca! hear me yet one word.

Bian. My lord, a thousand — in another tone,
And of another import.

Card. 'T is to say,
    You disavow the affection you have own'd,
    And bid me to forget what I have learn'd.

Bian. It is to say, I bid your Grace remember
    I proffer'd but a sisterly regard;   ▾
    Which still is yours, if you will take it fairly;
    But, to pervert it to a guilty thought,
    Is to charge *me* with folly, and yourself.

Card. Why guilty?   You have said, my speech and ways
    Won from you liking.   Was 't in nature then,
    I should not yield the body of my soul
  · Captive to beauty, wit, and grace like thine?
    That magic which entrances all the world
    That come within its circle, which has wrapt
    My eldest brother for so many years
    In such infatuate passion that fools say
    Thou usest philters, shall it have no spell
    For a more sympathetic spirit like mine?
    Yes! fairest of all ——

Bian. [*who has looked steadily on him, throughout his appeal,*
        with a scorn gradually increasing.
                    Must I understand
    By this, your Eminence would make love to me?

Card. Ah, look not thus! though even scorn shows beau-
        tiful
    In that angelic face.   Saints look not down
    On their poor worshipers with gleaming eyes:
    And I am such; I love not, but adore.
    Thou art a Gorgon now; but not the terror

Of those haught looks can frown me into stone;
For my blood boils with passion.

    Bianca moves to touch a hand-bell.] Yet fear not!
Ring not! I have but words: words which shall out,
Though, could I now go back, I would not breathe
    them.
Bianca, I adore thee; with a passion
Which makes the love of even my brother tame.
I am more young than he, my heart less worn.
Look on me, and compare us. Is he comelier?
Has he?——

    Bian. My lord, is this mere gallantry?
Or comes it truly from your inmost soul?
Card. From the hot heart of my impassion'd spirit.
I swear it by my habit, by the Church,
By the high God in Heaven, and what for me
Has all of Heaven in one thought — thyself!
I love thee with a passion!——

                Bian. Hear me then.
Were I so meanly, loathsomely ingrate,
As to forget all good I owe my lord;
Could I be, what as yet I ne'er have been,
So intemperate of blood as at one time
To love two men; could I so far forget
My duty unto God and unto man,
As, with a double adultery, to yield
My body to my lord's own brother; still,
Still would I shrink, as from the touch of plague,
From taint by such a traitor — traitor, ay! [31]

Traitor unto thy God, thy Church, thy brother!
The hooded snake, which bites even unassail'd,
Shall be as welcome to my breast as thou!
     She takes up the bell; but at the moment

                Enter VIRGINIA.

O my Virginia! thou art come in time.
Card. [*who at first springs towards Bianca, as though he
          would strangle her, turning about, and with clenched
          hands, mutters :*
Death! 'I should sink to this! [32]   [*Exit.*
                         Virg. What troubles thee,
Sweet sister?   Thine eyes blaze, albeit thy cheek
Is fearful-pale.
          Bian. The Cardinal and I
Have had high words.   I do repent me much
I strove to reconcile my lord and him.
But thou look'st sad too.   Is it all for me?
Virg. Alas! My mother! They have taken her back
To her old cloister.   Dare I pray once more
Thy influence with my lord and brother?
                              Bian. I fear
'T will be in vain.   Yet, for thy gentle sake,
I will essay.   And happily now comes
The Duke.   Thou wilt not go?
                    Virg. 'T is best.
What could my tears with him, if thy prayer fail?
                                   [*Exit.*

Enter GRAND DUKE.

G. D. Virginia? Flies she me? Thy darling friend
Should feel her presence here is joy to me.

Bian. She had a grace to ask, and, dear my lord,
Would trust my pleading rather than her own.

G. D. Knowing I could refuse thee nothing, ha?

Bian. My lord is ever gracious; but this quest
I fear will try him. 'T is her mother's cause.

G. D. Pray, do not plead for her. I have no heart
To say thee nay. But now —— Dost thou remember,
I gave Virginia warning that her mother
Must not abuse her freedom? Yet her home
Was made the haunt of traitors, who paid court
And offer'd mock condolence to the widow,
That they might shame their Sovereign, teaching men
To call me tyrant and set her in honor
Above my own thron'd Duchess. Chief of these
Were my born brothers; and of these the chief
Was Ferdinand. Thou changest hue! I mark'd,
On coming in, thy forehead was o'erclouded,
And thy pal'd cheeks show'd traces of a storm.
What has befallen?

        Bian. What never must again.
I have borne, my lord, from the o'erweening prelate,
What makes me sorry you are not still foes.

G. D. Ha! Has the ungrateful traitor dar'd renew
His old despite?

        Bian. It were not wise, my lord,

Even were it noble, to accuse the absent;
Nor, speaking to my sovereign and my spouse,
Can I forget the reverence due his blood;
But this in brief — and it is much to say:
The Cardinal-Prince in me sees but the widow
Of Bonaventuri, in himself the son
Of Cosmo.

    G. D. The old devil of his nature;
A rampant arrogance that gets the better
Even of his practis'd craft. It shall be tam'd.
His visit over, let this ill-starr'd union
Be never more renew'd. He but abuses
My trust, as thy sweet nature. Florence is full
Of plots and treason of his foul engendering,
Hatch'd into life and foster'd by the means
I lent him at thy instance. Malocuor
Begins to give me doubts; and Pietro falls
Visibly once more in the traitorous mesh.
Hast thou not mark'd this?

              Bian. No, my lord: till now
I doubted not the Cardinal was restor'd
To godlier feelings.

    G. D. Such he never knew.
And Pietro is the fool of his own passions,
Which Ferdinand plays with, with a master hand,
For his ambitious aims. — Yet be to both,
Until the banquet and the hunt are over
Which end this luckless visit, gracious still.

Bian. Still, as befits me ever to our guests

And to thy brothers. But to seem again
That which I was, when, deeming I had won
His heart in turn, I held the Cardinal dear,
That can I not.

    G. D. And that I would not have.
Be, as Heaven made thee, open as the day,
And leave to those, whose thoughts bear not the light,
To mask their visages. — But I am come,
Not to condole with thee, nor yet to praise thee,
But have thy sentence on the gem they are adding
To our art-treasures, for whose wasteless wealth,
Thus gather'd, coming time shall laud my name.

Bian. The new-found statue ?

    G. D. 'T is now clean'd, and shows
A prodigy of beauty, scarcely flaw'd.
How Benvenuto's eyes had glisten'd over
Its grand yet fine proportions ! — Come, love, come!

Bian. O my dear lord, I should but mar your pleasure.
Hold me excus'd. A weight is on my soul
I cannot lift; a presage of dire evil.
The shape I see not, but the thing is there.

G. D. It is a shade then. Wears it Ferdinand's hat ?

Bian. [*gravely.*

 I have said what Ferdinand never will forgive.

G. D. And thus that gentle heart is made uneasy,
      [*folding his arms about her.*
 Sorrowing for wounds it has made another bear,
 Albeit in self-defence.

    Bian. That is not all.

The Cardinal's face was black with gather'd hate.

G. D. He is a serpent.　Fear not therefore thou.

The cygnet is beneath the parent's wing.　　·

　　　　　　　　　　[pressing her closer.

Can the snake reach it?　Fie, thou timid swan!

Summon thy ladies, and be with me straight.

　　　　Kisses her hand, and Exit.

Bian. But with a heart thy dear love cannot lighten.

Would it were morrow and the Cardinal gone!

　　Moving to the table, lifts the hand-bell, as to ring it;

　　　　and Scene changes to

Scene II.

A room in Malocuore's house.

Malocuor

*walking slowly, with an air of deep meditation,
his hand on his chin.*

Enter

Signora Malocuore — *her face radiant with triumph.*

Sign. What wilt thou give me for the news I bring?
Mal. [*gazing at her for a moment sharply.*

'T is something fatal; something —— Thou shalt have
A carcanet of diamonds, bring'st thou such
As shall destroy the Duchess, and perhaps ——

[*checking himself.*

I will not tell thee that.

Sign. Perchance I know.

Thou plottest for the ruin — it may be
The murder of thy lord, to place the Card ——
Mal. [*in alarm and threateningly.*

Wilt hold thy wicked tongue? How know'st thou?
Walls
Thick as our own have ears.

Sign. That know I well:

Our mistress's for instance.

     Mal. Ha! —   Speak out.

But whisper. 'T is? ——

    Sign. [*pausing* — *then slowly.*

     The Cardinal loves Bianca.

Mal. [*peevishly.*

 That is old news for me.

    Sign. But not so old,

The Cardinal has avow'd his passion, and been ——

Mal. [*eagerly interrupting.*

 Say but rejected, thou hast made us both.

Sign. Rejected; with such virulence of scorn,

 But that I heard, I had not thought her mouth

 Could breathe such accents.

    Mal. [*rapturously.*] This is Heaven!

       Sign. Hell rather.

Mal. Ay, Hell for them; but a brave Heaven to me.

    Two slow taps heard at the door.

 Go now; there comes, and in the nick of time,

 One I must deal with.

    Sign. [*going.*] Have a care!

       Mal. Be sure. [*Exit Sign.*

        by another door.

Now, no more doubt! [*exultingly.*] 'T is ripe! ——

        Come in.

    Enter

  by the first door, MASNADIERE.

Masnad. Your Excellence has order'd ——

Mal. [*bringing him forward.*
      Come this way.
And speak more low. — Thou hast a nimble tongue
As well as poniard. Knowest thou a man
Thy mate therein ?
      Masnad. Your Excellence, I do.
Mal. Canst thou malign a person of high rank
Even in his very teeth ? and foil his thrusts,
If he push questions home ?
        Masnad. I have foil'd home-thrusts
Of sharper stuff than words, and done more hurt
To persons of high rank than with my tongue.
Mal. Know'st thou the tavern of the Golden Lilies ?
Betake thee thither then —— Soft ! I must see
This mate of thine. Go, bring him hither straight.
But not that way. I'll show thee now a room,
Where I can teach you two and not a soul
Know of the lesson. There a secret stair
Leads to a little garden-gate, whereby
Thou 'lt bring thy fellow. Follow. Softly ! So.

Leads off, on tiptoe, and with finger on lip,
Masnadiere *by a small door to the*
further part of the scene.

SCENE III.

A room in the Cardinal's Apartment at the Pitti.

CARDINAL.   DON PIETRO.

Don P. I know not that.   If, the last time, 't was feign'd,
    Why feign'd she not the birth too?   Why resort
    To visceral pangs, at peril of her life,
    To end a pregnancy, which, if 't were shamm'd,
    She would have clos'd by simulated travail
    And a supposititious offspring.
                   Card. Why?
    Because she knew I had set a watch on her.
Don P. If she knew that, she could have chang'd her
    creatures,
    And so avoided it, did she deceive.
    'T were harder for her to o'erreach in this
    Her lord than thee.   Now, by the gods! I think
    'T was poison given her to prevent a birth.
Card. Thou dost not hint I gave it?
                 Don P. Faith! our sire
    Was thought a subtle poison-mixer: Strozzi,
    Who had tried the like on him, had cause to dread him.

Thou hast, I know, his art.   Say, thou dost use it;
That is thine own affair.

    Card. Art thou gone mad?
Dost thou forget my habit and my place?

Don P. No, I remember priests may do for God
What laïcs do for Satan.   How much more
A *prince* of Holy Church!

    Card. A scurril jest;
Which I might take for earnest, were 't my will.
But for thy sake, my brother, I can bear,
With the Lord's grace, even that.

    Don P. [*scornfully.*] For mine?

      Card. Thine only.

Don P. Hark!   I 'm thy junior, Ferdinand; but no babe,
To bite on coral.

    Card. And I hold thee none.
Let the witch foist on her besotted lord
Some peasant or strumpet's bantling, who shall climb
Our father's throne, what is my loss?   Hurt pride.
The purple bars me from succession; but thou,
Wounded in honor, art shut out from the crown,
Which is thy natural right, failing Francis' heirs.
More, thou art wrong'd in the present: our sire's wealth
Must make the nest warm for the cuckoo's brood.
What!   Thou art touch'd at last?   Why so! why so!
'T was well reminded.   Wilt thou not awake?
Promise me thou wilt marry, dear Pietro!
'T is the sole hope for Florence and for me,

Who count our House's honor next to God's.

Don P. Why press that point? 'T is time when I succeed.

Card. And shouldst thou die? What hope then for our
  House?

  Shall this pernicious harlot's purchas'd seed

  Mount to my father's heritage? Perish rather

  She and her prematurely dotard spouse

  By one quick blow together!

                    Don P. Sayest thou, brother?

  How happens it that thou, who wast but now

  In amity with the Duchess, art fallen out?

Card. Because but now she has wrong'd me with sharp
  insult,

  As lately thee. Thou lov'st her not?

                    Don P. Why no.

  She might have had my Spaniard at the Court.[33]

  But that the girl was not made welcome, is that

  A cause to foul her Highness with gross names?

  Troth! I believe I honor her in heart

  The more she did not.

                    Card. So not I! It was

  The rankest hypocrisy. The harlot soul

  Loves most the form of chastity. Out upon

  These whited sepulchres! The flowers that prank

  Their outward wall draw beauty from corruption,

  And lade the churchyard air with scents that bring

  To wise minds thoughts of rottenness.

                    Don P. My mind

Is dull then as my eyes. I see but beauty
And smell but sweetness in Bianca. Yet,
God wot, I love her not.

    Card. Well. To the point.
I have certain cause to think the fresh maternity
Our Duchess threatens is but assum'd. Wilt thou
Be diligent as I to thwart her aims?

Don. P. Why yes, so far.

    Card. 'T is for thy good, not mine.
The honor of our House, there, there alone,
I vie with thee in interest. We will talk
Further of this. Meantime, spread thou by stealth,
But largely, what I have told thee. Thou mayst
 safely.
Think of our father's throne, and of his wealth
Squander'd on bastards. With that spur, devise;
And make her fame as odious as thou canst.

Don P. I will think on 't; but, 'sooth! I like it not.
 'T were manlier far to poison her outright.

       [Exit Don P.

Card. And would she were! to save thy brains the pain,
Thou shallow libertine! — and me perhaps
The odium of the deed. — I could not prick
Thy honor to the leap; I touch'd thy purse.
Well — there thou art not far wrong. — But who
 had thought
I could so blind thee! *Thou* succeed! *Thy* heirs!
The purple bar my natural rights! A word,

The Pope gives dispensation; [34] and my vows
And habit alike are cobwebs.   They shall mesh
Thee as some bigger flies.   Then break thou through,
If thou have power!

Enter MALOCUORE.

            Ha, Malocuor! — Come forward. —
Why art thou dull?   Why, man! the sun looks bright
That dawns upon our fortune.   Saidst thou not
The people famine-stricken were astir,
Rous'd by the Duke's exactions? that the nobles,
Fir'd by the sequestration of the goods
Of the conspiring twenty of their order,
Are disaffected? (little do they think
'T was of my prompting!) and Camilla's lot
Is made to appear a grievous wrong?   Hear now: —
The Queen of France has charg'd — thou know'st well
     why —
Troilo Orsini's murder on thy master,
Who is as innocent of his death as thou.
St. Mark's portentous star is on the wane.
Thou shak'st the head!   Why, what is this?
                       Mal. My lord —
Could I dare speak ——
            Card. Thou mayst say what thou wilt.
Hast thou not heard I pardon no reserve?
Mal. A strange report is running through the town,

The Cardinal-Prince — forgive, your Grace! — made
    love
Openly to his brother's spouse, and was ——
Card. 'T is false as Hell! a devilish juggling lie!
But what if it were true? Say on.
                              Mal. And was ——
Instantly and with scorn rejected.
                              Card. Death!
Where gott'st thou that? Where? Quickly! Stam-
    mer not!
Or! ——
    Mal. Everywhere and anywhere. Aloud
In the open marketplaces, in the taverns,
'T is told with laughter. Men exalt the Duchess
As a Penelope, and deride your Grace.
Card. Villain! thou liest!
                              Mal. Give me then to death.
But if I do not? ——
                              Card. Then shall die the inventor.
Mal. That is the Duchess' self. She told her ladies;
And, ere you might count ten, ——
                              Card. O, that her neck
Were 'twixt these fingers! — But I 'll not believe it!
Thou art impos'd on — or imposest. I will
Have instant proofs! Dost hear me? instant proofs!
Proofs, dost thou hear me! proofs, I say!
                              Mal. And shall.
Card. But on the instant! I will have no stop.

Mal. Will your Grace venture then to come with me?

Card. To bring the source of that infernal slander
Home to that — woman? Whither not? To Hell,
Must I there seek it.

   Mal. Could your Grace procure
A close disguise.

  Card. At once.

    Mal. [*turning to go.*
    I will be back
Similarly metamorphos'd —

   Card. In five minutes.
Go. I will have this proof, or — 'ware thy soul!
         [*Exit.*

MALOCUOR, *looking after him with a sinister smile,*
raises his hand exultingly, and Exit by the
door where he had entered.

Scene IV.

A large public room in the Tavern of the Golden Lilies. Various groups of common men, artisans, etc., with soldiers intermixed, drinking at separate tables. At a table in the foreground, standing by itself,
Masnadiere *and* Scherano.

Scher. Who is this man of rank he is to bring?
Masnad. I know not, I; and care as little. Most like,
 The Cardinal's self.
    Scher. That is a daring thought.
How should it stead him, what we have to say?
Masnad. Much, an' thou weigh'st the matter. Was't not
   thou,
 With Malandrino and myself, wast sent,
 To stir the people, when our Lady's brother,
 Vittorio, had displac'd the favorite lords,
 Pandolfo of the Bardi, Mario Sforza,
 And Jacopo Salviati, the Duke's cousin?
 Holp we not make the imposts too weigh heavier
 In popular estimation by our talk?
 Was thy purse empty, when the city rung
 With rumors of great crimes most like our own,
 Imputed to the Grand Duke's self, with some,
 Dyed deeper with a diabolical craft,

Wrought by the Duchess and a Jewish hag
Confederate in her sorceries, acts to make
Even our flesh'd senses shudder ? [36]

> *Scher.* With disgust.

Pah! I recall 't.   I was asham'd to find
Men, that had brains, so credulous.

> *Masnad.* Why! Thou shouldst

Rather have blush'd to wonder.   Lies as gross
I have read in history, and suppose these too
Will find some godly chronicler one day,
With fools to credit him.   For, mark you! men
Love nothing better than a good round lie
That, blackening others, makes themselves more white
In their own fancies; and a monstrous tale
Has marvelous attraction for some ears
Which shut at simple facts.   Cry thou, Amen!
So fellows like thee and me get their deserts
With royal company in bad renown.
Well now, I say, who fee'd our tongues for this?
Who but the Signor Malocuor?   And where
Got he the ducats?   Not from Francis-Mary;
Nor from Don Pietro.   Seest thou, ha?

> *Scher.* I see:

The Red-Cap 's hawking at his brother's crown.
But wherefore changes Malocuor his game,
Praising the Duchess? —

> *Masnad.* And reviling him?

I know not.   But, thou seest, the tale not now
Is for the common ear: the Cardinal's own

Haply is meant.   Perchance to lash his purpose
To some bold leap.

   Scher. Brave!   That may need our help.

Masnad. But will not get it — not mine — if, as I think,
It vault too high.

   Scher. Thou mean'st?

     Masnad. At the Grand Duchess,
Or the Grand Duke himself.

    Scher. By Bacchus! no!
That were to swallow coals.   'T is desperate-bold
As 't is: our talk will drive the Cardinal wild.

Masnad. Not before us.   But after! ——

    Scher. Then look sharp;
Your steed may throw you, Signor Malocuor!

   Enter, in disguise,
  Cardinal *and* Malocuore.

Masnad. Hush! 't is our men.   Play well now.

    Mal. [*low.*] Have a care,
My gracious lord!   [*Aloud, in an assumed voice.*
   Shall we go higher up?
Or choose our table here?

    Card. [*also assumed voice.*
   Here is as well.

Mal. Have you room, friends?

    Masnad. At your good service.   Sit.

Mal. If we not interrupt your converse. [*Card. and Mal. sit.*
    Masnad. No.

We prate but idly, and of public things.

Mal. [*to a waiter, who has approached them.*

Monte Pulciano. —

         To Masnad.] We are strangers here.

Masnad. From Lucca?

         Mal. Ay. You Florentines detect
Lightly our accent.

         Masnad. 'T is not strongly mark'd.

Mal. Sir, you are complaisant.

     Waiter brings wine and glasses, is paid and retires.[37]

         Please ye to partake
Of our poor beverage. [*filling for all.*

         Masnad. Drink we to the health ——

Scher. Of the Grand Duchess, foremost of all ladies!

     They all rise — CARDINAL *reluctantly;*
who coughs and sets down his glass untasted.

Mal. With all my heart.

         Masnad. Your friend admires not much
Our mistress.

         Mal. Ay, but better loves the Church.

Scher. Perhaps another toast ——

         Card. Nay, that was well:
But I drink rarely.

         Scher. And speak seldom.

         Card. How!

         [*Mal. pushes him secretly.*

Mal. He is taciturn — yet choleric too.   What news?
Is there aught stirring?

         Masnad. You are strange indeed!

Stirring? All Florence is astir.

>   *Mal.* With what?

Masnad. The Cardinal's amours.

>   *Mal.* [*making again a sign to Card.*
>   *to restrain himself.*
>   Cardinal who?

>   *Scher.* His Grace,

The Cardinal de' Medici, our Sovereign's brother.

Mal. [*again touching the Card. who betrays discomposure.*

Sure, they malign him. Who the happy fair?

Scher. Happy? Not much of that! He was rebuff'd.

Masnad. The dame — what think ye, sirs — especially you
Who love the Church? — was his own brother's spouse,
Our lady Duchess!

>   *Card.* [*starting up, and in his natural voice.*
>   That is false!

>   *Masnad.* [*starting up too, and*
>   *half-drawing his dagger.*
>   By Heaven!

Mal. [*affecting to restrain him.*

You have no cause; my comrade's zeal ——

>   *Card.* [*with composure and in his assumed voice.*
>   Your pardon.

Not your report I question'd, but the tale;
Which, for the love I bear our Holy Church,

>   [*crossing himself.*

I say again, is falsehood black as Hell.

Masnad. 'T is well. But give me leave to tell you, brother,
If you come here to battle for the Church

With all who argue her of filthy sin,
You should provide yourself a score of lives.

Card. That is my risk. — But whence had you this story?

Masnad. Whence? Whence you will? 'T is common as
    church-psalms.

Shall I call hither some of yonder groups,
To laugh you into faith? Else, an' you list,
Here is my-fellow had the tale direct.

Scher. Ay, from Bettina. She 's to me, you wot,
Much as your Cardinal would, but could not have,
To him our Duchess. Now Bettina's mistress
Is aunt of Count Ulysses Bentivoglio,
Whose spouse, the Duchess' daughter, Pellegrina,
Taught by her mother, told it unto her.

Mal. It is enough.

        Card. To prove the rumor, not its truth.

Scher. What take you then our Cardinal to be?
A saint in sackcloth? or Saint Dominic?
Body of Bacchus! 't is a gallant prince,
Young, handsome —— Let me see. [*peering in*
                    Card.'s face.
             Why, as I live!
He 's not unlike yourself, though finer far,
And some years younger, and, by right of blood,
Adorer of fair ladies.

        Card. [*rising — to Mal.*
    Let us go.

Mal. [*rising.*] Good morning, gentlemen.

        Masnad. Good morning, both.

Scher. [*to Card., who has turned.*

  And, brother, in your prayers remember me.

        [*Exeunt Card. and Mal.*

 Was 't not well play'd?

     Masnad. God's faith! 't was all put home.

Not Cini's surgery [37] will heal those wounds.

Scher. How he reneg'd! Now, as a soldier true,

 Holdst thou him guilty?

      Masnad. Guilty, by this hilt!

Is Malocuor stark mad, without some base

To build such fabric? At a touch 't would fall

And crush him into atoms.

      Scher. Precious prelate!

This comes of giving princes to the Church.

Masnad. — Without a true vocation. See thou now!

 We both wax godly.

     Scher. Right enough, when rogues

Usurp the purple.

     Masnad. Bravo, my Scherano!

When I am Pope, look thou art made Archbishop.

Scher. I will not covet then my neighbor's wife.

Masnad. Brave! But forget not, Eminence, our Cardinal

 But took his brother's place, young Don Giovanni,

 Whom swart Garzía stabb'd.

     Scher. Whose fault was that?

Masnad. Why Cosmo's. But they are all a cursed race.

Scher. So Isabella cried. And I, Amen!

 Would we were rid of all your serpent brood!

Masnad. Then thou criedst evil. Take their slime away,

The grass would grow too green for thee and me.
Set Florence free again, and sift the laws
The bloody Spaniard model'd for our soil,
Would six score annual murders feed us fat?
Stablish right rule, the first stroke of its wand
Would sweep us clean away, with all our webs,
Which we have spun in palaces.   Where then
The twice two hundred of our valiant corps,
Whose lightning, hurtled by the lion's cub,
Men call the Cardinal Farnese's son,
Pietro Leoncillo da Spoleti,
Frightens the confines with its errant blaze, — [33]
Where shall they forage, then?   And all the bands
High barons and proud princes of the Church
Pay or connive at for their private ends?
Useless, they shrink, and vanish by degrees.
The rights of nature, which our foes call rapine,
And the strong arm are put in sequestration,
Bound by the moral fetters of the weak.
Money must then be earn'd by vulgar toil;
And men of mettle, coop'd like barnyard birds,
No more like falcons winnow the free air
With wings unclipp'd and dip their beaks in blood.
Law helps the coward and makes strong the weak. —
When then, for that his man's-heart durst aspire
To free Italia from a bestial yoke,
They put wise Machiavelli to the rack,[39]
They did good service to us sons of fortune;

For which let us be thankful.   Live the Medici!

> [*Drinks.*

Scher. Amen! if they 're our Providence.   But one,
　His spouse at least, will not be better long
　For thy mock loyalty, see I clearly through
　Our patron's masquerade.

> *Masnad.* Or haply both.

So, Good night, Signor Malocuor!

> *Scher.* How so?

Masnad. Thinkst thou, his height once clomb, your crafty
　Cardinal　　　　　　　·
　Will let the ladder stand to mark his way?
　Push'd down, the steps are broken, or hid, rest sure.
Scher. In cell or coffin then, rot unbewail'd,
　Thou worst as meanest villain of us all!
Masnad. That is wish'd well.   And so I drink, Amen!

> [*Drinks.*

*They pass up the stage
to mingle with the other groups, and*

Scene closes.

SCENE V.

Same as Scene III.

Enter precipitately, the CARDINAL *followed by* MALOCUORE,
both still wearing their disguise.

Card. [*dashing down his hat and throwing off passionately
his coarse mantle.*

Hell's hottest fires on her treacherous soul!
Would I could slay her inch by inch, and make,
For her, a twelvemonth's agony of death!
Mal. [*helping to divest him.*

That were not easy. And your Highness' hopes
Would only be twelve useless months delay'd.
At once, and by a single blow, 't were best.
Card. Do it at once, then!
                    Mal. Has your Grace forgot?
There is another life.
                    Card. What mean'st thou?
                              Mal. Dies
The sorceress on the instant, with her dies
Your great revenge. But live to better hope
Your glorious aspirations and your rights?
              *He pauses a moment, looking intently
on the* CARDINAL, *who motions him to proceed.*

Your royal brother weds again; and then ——

                               [*pauses again.*

Card. Devil!

    Mal. Or saint, even as it suits my lord.

But devil would stand him now in better stead.

Card. Be thou the devil, then. But let thy tongue

    Speak out thy damnable purpose in few words.

    Or, if thou canst, hint what is neither fit

    For thee to utter nor for me to hear. [*Walks away.*

Mal. Has your Grace much remaining of the sum

    The Duchess strove so hard that you might get ?

Card. [*turning quickly.*

    Serpent! thou stingest. —— Twice fifteen thousand
        went, —

    Thou hadst the distribution, and shouldst know,—

    To gain new friends, and to secure the old.

Mal. Would twice five thousand ducats be too much,

    To help your Highness to the throne of Florence

    And your most just revenge ?

                  Card. Take ten times that :

    And ten times more, if needful: what thou wilt.

Mal. Hypothecations on the royal fisc ?

    No; ten suffice. — There is a white confection,

    A tremulous jelly made of sweeten'd milk,

    And scented with the water of the rose.

    Of this the royal pair are strangely fond.

    At the grand banquet, meant to usher in

    That purpos'd chase which never shall take place,

    Eschew this viand. Its taste engenders thirst,

Which might prove fatal.   On the morrow, men
Shall hail your Highness Sovereign Duke in Florence.

[Exit Mal. bowing himself backwards.

Card. And where wilt *thou* be?   Hop'st thou to go free,
Charg'd with that perilous secret?   Could I bind
Thy lips forever, think'st thou I could brook
Thy insolent mien, where even now I read,
As in thy cover'd taunts and ill-tim'd jests,
Abhorrently familiar! swollen presumption,
Bred of a conscious partnership in crime —
Could I bear this? from thee?   Or would I trust
The servant who his loving lord betray'd
To ruin and death?   No, thou vile tool!   To-day
Complete thy function, which the will of fate
Proffers to my ambition and revenge:
To-morrow —   I will break thy edge forever!

*[Exit into the same
cabinet as before (in Scene III.)*

Scene VI.

An Antechamber leading to the G. Duchess's
Apartments in the Pitti.

Signora Malocuore,
passing slowly and thoughtfully through.   She stops
suddenly midway.

Sign. [40] [*to herself.*] Donna Virginia! I were better pleas'd
To want her sweet simplicity.

Enter
from the door facing her, and which is supposed
to lead to the G. Duchess's Apartments,
Donna Virginia.

Aloud.] Is 't so?
Donna Virginia absent from the chase?
How shall her friend and royal sister spare her?
Virg. Better than would I hope my loyal lord,
Who stays behind, being slightly indispos'd.
But what keeps you, Signora, from Caiano?
Sign. A like and yet a different cause.   My lord,
Though loyal I hope, will better do without me;
And I am ailing too.

Virg. That is a jest.

Sign. Then seriously.[41]　I like Caiano much;
　　The Villa Poggio more.　The distance, scarce
　　An hour's easy drive, is soon gone through.
　　And passing-well I love the autumnal chase,
　　When the wind rustling through the scant-leav'd forest
　　Calls blood into the faded cheek, and dote
　　On royal banquets, where the cost and care
　　Are not my portion, but the pleasure is.
　　But, as it happen'd, my well-loving spouse
　　Seem'd in no very loving mood to-day:
　　And so, to avoid the infliction of his spleen,
　　I supervise the change the Duchess order'd
　　In the blue hangings of the Silver'd Chamber
　　(Whence now I think your Highness comes,) more
　　　　pleas'd
　　To glad one person than to worry two.

Virg. Happily said; and, surely, kindly done.
　　Now could I envy you the sweet bright smile
　　That will reward your forethought.

　　　　　　　　Sign. O for that,
　　So chary has the Duchess been to me
　　Of smiles and sweetness, I have long forgotten
　　There was such blessing: and this time, methinks,
　　She will have no will to grant it.

　　　　　　　　Virg. Ah, you point
　　To her strange sadness.　Just before she left,
　　I ask'd what ail'd her.　Kissing me, she answer'd,
　　"Nothing in health"; then, with a pensive smile,

As though it irk'd her to seem so deject,
Added, "There is a weight upon my heart;
A sad foreboding : it will all have gone,
Ere next we meet." So saying, she embrac'd me,
Then, parting, gaz'd a moment in my face
Wistful and sad, and press'd my hand. Her eyes —
Were wet with tears.

        Sign. As yours are now, Madonna.
This is illusion. The dejected spirits,
Pressing upon the heart, allow these phantoms
To cloud the unwary brain.[42] Who has not seen,
In sickness, or when brooding care makes sleep
Desert the wearying pillow, monstrous forms,
Or bodiless heads, misshapen, that still come
Nearer and nearer, spreading on the eye
More large and hideous, and in sequence close,
Rank upon rank, in tapering vista long ;
The last dim phantom lessening to a point,
Lost in the far perspective ? Of such stuff
Were fashion'd these sick bodements. It is said,
The Cardinal and our royal Lady quarrel'd.
This haply has depress'd her lively spirit,
And made your parting mournful. Did your Grace
Remark their greeting ere the train took horse ?
Virg. I thought the Duchess' mien constrain'd and cold.
Yet was it courteous : and the Duke's demeanor,
Gracious and kind as wonted, veil'd it all.
I think none else would note it, but who knew
There had been words between them.

Sign. And himself?

Virg. There was — perhaps I fancied it — at times
A strange abstraction in the Cardinal's looks,
Which, fix'd on vacancy, appear'd to see
Or seek for something.   Once, when in this mood,
The Duke address'd him.   Visibly he started,
And — so I thought — turn'd deadly pale.   But then
He came from his apartment looking pale.

Sign. Doubtless 't was fancy — as your Highness knew
A cause for discomposure.

        Virg. But 't was not
Fancy, I saw him eye the Duchess once
With mortal hatred.   May I be forgiven
If I misjudge my father's blood, or wrong
A Christian prelate! but the look was one
That made my heart stand still.

        Sign. It cannot be.
The Cardinal-Prince reveres — that know I well!
Or, rather, loves his royal brother's spouse,
As truly as — myself, who from the first
Was wedded to her fortunes, — nay, with love
And reverence equal to my honest lord's,
Whose rare devotion none can doubt.

        Virg. Indeed!
Heaven grant it be so!   Heaven itself must grieve
Over these unnatural discords.   Yet I doubt.
The Duchess' heart has had some heavy shock. —
But I must not detain you, dear Signora;
And my lord looks for me. [*going.*

Sign. [*attending her.*] Ah, happy lord!
And happier lady! When you have been wed,
As I have been, for two and twenty years,
Your Prince will be more patient, and yourself,
Believe me, much less anxious.

      Virg. Fie, Signora!
Why, when our hearts are happy in their Spring,
Warn us that Autumn 's coming? But I know
The sere and yellow leaf is not for us,
Whose souls shall know no season in their loves,
Like Francis and Bianca's.

     Sign. O'er whose soul
Come shadows of the Winter even now.

    Exit VIRGINIA *attended by*
  the SIGNORA, — *who presently re-enters.*

Like *them?* Thou simple one! What, should I say
"Heaven grant it be so"! Little couldst thou think
That wish would threaten —— Is it death to both?
I fear me Malocuor has gone too far.
He hates the proud Venetian; the deep wounds
Inflicted by her scorn more sorely rankle
In his dark brooding spirit than mine; the slight
Put on him, when the dead Intendant's friend,
Sennuccio, rose to favor, has given perhaps
Desperate impulsion to the bold designs
Wherein the Cardinal-Prince has long involv'd him.
This childish-hearted lady took no note

Of what I saw, and trembled as I saw,
When Malocuor, by order of the Duke,
Spurr'd on before the cavalcade, to see
That everything was ready. Even now
Perhaps the deed is doing! Help us God!
I would prevent it if I could : but what,
What know I? what dare hint, whose very thought
Is but conjecture? Oh, that heavy thought!
Would, would 't were morrow, and the Duke were
    safe!

Exit, by the door whence VIRGINIA
had entered.

SCENE VII.

A rich Hall in the magnificent Villa del Poggio.
At the top of the scene, a large folding-door, partially open,
gives a view of the Banqueting-Room, brilliantly
illuminated. The tables set out, etc., etc.

There is an uproar — the guests are risen
from their seats, in various attitudes of consternation
and horror. The GRAND DUKE *and* DUCHESS *are seen*
supported in the arms of SENNUCCIO *and others, while*
before them stands the CARDINAL, *gesticu-*
lating and ordering.

Enter
from the Banqueting-Room, through
the open doors, and in precipitation, the
DUKE OF BRACCIANO, *followed as hurriedly by* ABBIOSO, —
both with looks of dismay and horror ; and, less
impetuously, from the side scene, with hat on
and mantle, and spurred, DON PIETRO.

Don P. What is this noise, Orsini ? Thou art pale
And horror-stricken !
    Bracc. 'T is the end of things.
The Duke and Duchess are both poison'd.
       Don P. Poison'd !
How ? and by whom ?
    Bracc. Think whom their death would profit;
Then say by whom ? Let Abbioso speak.

DON PIETRO *stands as if stupefied, looking on them both,*
then, while ABBIOSO *speaks, gazing on the scene*
in the Banqueting-Room.

Abb. [*speaking hurriedly.*
The Duchess press'd the Cardinal to partake

Of a white sweetmeat, which he still refus'd
On plea of health derang'd.   The Duke and she,
Eagerly eating, suddenly were seiz'd
With mortal pangs.   The cry arose, of Poison!
The Cardinal, pointing to a ring he wore,
Declar'd the stone, through Providence, had warn'd
  him,
And charg'd the Duchess loudly with the crime.

Don P. With what design?   How could it profit *her?*
 'T is well for me I sit not next the throne:
 He might have laid this devil's-work to me.

Bracc. He has sent to seize the fortresses already.
 The troops are order'd out.   All in his name.

Don P. These were his speculations for my good!

Facing once more the Banqueting-Room, he moves a step as
 if to go to it, then stops, and, adjusting his mantle:

I 'll not look on this scene.   I cannot aid them.
And righteous Cain must face his God alone.

Bracc. We both were fleeing.   Isabella's death
 Might lend the new Duke pretext for his hate
 Against the Orsini.

    Abb. And my stubborn tongue
Has not sung anthems in his Highness' praise.

Don P. I will ride back.

  Through the doors of the Banqueting-Room,
 attendants are seen carrying out the GRAND DUKE
and BIANCA, *the* CARDINAL *following.   The guests dispersing*
  or gazing on each other in mute horror.

*Don Pietro throws a hurried look on the scene,
and is about to leave hastily by the side where he had entered, —
Bracciano and Abbioso, in like manner, at the
opposite side, — when, Enter through the
folding-door, Archbishop of Pisa,
Bentivoglio, and others.*

What now?   What means that movement?

Archb. His Grace has order'd that the dying pair
Be carried to the Vaulted Room.

     Don. P. The sole
Disfurnish'd and dark chamber in the house!

Benti. And suffers none to follow.

     Abb. God in Heaven!

Bracc. 'T is time we fled.

     Don P. Till better days, Farewell.

    Exeunt, hurriedly,

Don Pietro *at one side,* Bracciano *and* Abbioso *at the other.*

The Archbishop *and the rest, who
group around him, remain; and other guests, both lords
and ladies, are seen coming from the Banqueting-Room, as the scene, closing,
gives place to*

SCENE VIII. AND LAST.

A gloomy, vaulted chamber, with a single arched doorway.
There is no furniture but a large armed-chair. And
the room is almost totally dark.

Enter
through the arch
the CARDINAL; *the* GRAND DUKE
and BIANCA, *supported in the arms of servants;*
SENNUCCIO, *bearing up* BIANCA's *head. Then*
MALOCUORE, *holding a lighted torch.*

Card. Set them down here.

BIANCA *is placed tenderly in the great chair*
by SENNUCCIO. *The* GRAND DUKE *rests on the floor at her*
feet, his head upon her knees.

                           Retire ye. [*Exeunt servants.*
                              To *Mal.*] Let none in.
G. D. A fire is in my entrails. O my God!
   Is there no help? Have pity, Ferdinand, brother!
Senn. I have sent for both your surgeons, dear my lord.
   One must now soon be here.

Card. [*in a voice of thunder.*

　　Who bade thee, dog?

Make fast the door. [*to Mal.*

　　MALOCOURE *pulling his torch through a socket*
　　　projecting from the wall of the chamber,
　　　　　bolts the door.

　　　　　　　They shall not enter here
Till Heaven's act of vengeance is gone through.

Senn. [*leaving the G. Duke.*

　　I will go forth, oppose who may or dare,
And make this treason public. Thou, [*drawing on Mal.*

　　　　　　　　　stand back!

Card. Guard the door, Malocuore! If he strive,
Stab thou the gray-hair'd traitor to the heart!

　SENNUCCIO *and* MALOCUORE — *the latter his back against*
　　　the door — cross swords.

G. D. Forbear, Sennuccio! On thy oath! Sole friend,
Thou canst not stead us: aid would come too late.
O Ferdinand! could not *my* life suffice?
Must thy fangs rend this innocent victim too?

Bian. [*who has hitherto hung over her lord,*
　　　lifting now her head.

　　Die with the spirit of a man, my lord.
Appeal not to that tiger.

　　　　　　Card. Hast thou found
Thy speech at last, vile sorceress? It was thou,
Thou with thy black enchantments and damn'd drugs,

Hast done this deed.   The dose was meant for me.
But thy weak husband took it unforewarn'd;
And thou, to escape the punishment ——

          Bian. Of what?
Knows not the world, that poisoning my lord,
Of will or not, I had done thee precious service?
Thou seek'st to make me guilty, yet thou knowest
I bear within me what might blast thy hopes,
Could I but live so long to give it life.
For this, and thy defeated criminal passion ——
G. D. Water! water! for the love of God!
Is there no drop?

          Bian. And thou seest this, unmov'd!
                              [*to Card.*

And thou, O God, art witness unto all!
G. D. I die, Bianca.   Let thy — arms — thy lips ——
          With an effort, he raises himself on one knee.
          Embracing, she kisses, him.   He falls,
                    dead, across her feet.

Bian. My lord!   My lord! ——
                    I will not wail thee long. —
Sennuccio, hear. —   O agony! this thirst! —
Give — give me breath awhile, kind Heaven! —
                              Sennuccio, —
The laws of God, thou seest, are irreversible, —
And even our indiscretions — soon or late —
Come to the judgment, and are all amerc'd.

Tell — tell my sire, this punishment I bear —
In just requital — of my disregard
Of his parental anguish, my neglect
Of my first duty — when — I fled my home;
And pray him — that he will not — not remember
His child unkindly — for the one great sin —
Of all her life. [*Dies.*

· SENNUCCIO, *who has knelt on one knee reverently
before her, kissing her hand, takes now this hand in both of
his, and bends his head over it — remaining in
this attitude to the end.*

Mal. [*taking his torch from the socket and holding it
over Bianca.*

'T is finish'd. [*Inverts the torch, against the
floor, and extinguishes it.*
Card. [*coldly.*] It is well.
Throw back the door, and let the crowd swarm in.

MALOCUORE *opens wide the door, and a strong
light from within, as from an illuminated corridor,
is poured upon the group, — while
Enter,* ARCHBISHOP OF PISA, BENTIVOGLIO,
and others of the Court.

Behold the consummation of the crime!

Let the Great Duke have burial meet his rank:
The sorceress fling into the public vaults.

> [*Exit, followed by Malocuor.*

*The spectators gather solemnly round
the partially lighted bodies* — SENNUCCIO *still keeping
his position* — BIANCA *lying back in the
chair, the* GRAND DUKE *across her
feet* — *and slowly the*

Curtain falls.

NOTES

NOTES TO BIANCA CAPELLO

1.—P. 206. *A shout, Pietro —*] The remark made in Note (and sub-note) 2, of "The Double Deceit," (vol. IV. p. 255,) applies in this instance. The name, like *Bianca*, is made a trisyllable. But, though it is so far anglicized (with others in the play), let the Actor sound *i* as *e* and *e* as *a*. So with the fictitious and character-name *Sennuccio**: although, by separating the two final vowels, it is made to be of four syllables, give it otherwise the Italian pronunciation, and sound it *Sen-noot'-che-o.*

Bracciano, too, (*Act* III., *Sc.* 3,) though it is less important, has the first *c* sounded as *t*. In Italian, it is but of three syllables (*Brat-chah'-no*); in the text, it is of four.

2.—P. 210. *Then softly bade me rise and speak.*] For the Stage, omit from here to "My thoughts came back," nine lines below.

3.—P. 213. *Desires he feels not. Affluence clips the wings. Of honesty which flies distress—*] For the Stage, substitute, as more directly intelligible :

---

* *Sennino ;* diminutive of *Senno :* applied jocosely, but without disparagement, to a persón who, while yet young, has the gravity, the serious manners, and the prudence of age. We have a corresponding phrase, but comic and somewhat vulgar, and partaking of the grotesque, in the compound *Sobersides.*

> " Emotions that he feels not. Wealth binds down [secures]
>   The honesty that yields to want."

Or :

> " Emotions that he feels not. Wealth keeps home
>   The honesty that flies distress "—

4.—P. 231. — *board.*] For the Stage, read " pallet."

5.—P. 236. *Forget thy art.*] More plainly, for the Stage : " Deal frankly once." Or, read the verse :

> " Forget the courtier. What is said of late ? "

6.—P. 242. *Who has,* etc.] Or, if the Actress prefer it,
> " O hate me not! who have one only grief,
>   The thought that thou art pining unconsol'd "——

7.—P. 253. *Her natural pride —*] See Note 22.

8.—P. 256. *Francis has cloister'd her—*] This he did on the very day of Cosmo's decease, who had most liberally dowered Camilla. With this exception, says Galluzzi, Francesco acted conscientiously in all his father's trusts and legacies. *Istor. del Granduc. di Toscana sotto il Gov. della Casa Medici* (Firenze 1781, in 4to), t. ii. pp. 239, 240. Previously, (p. 176,) he tells us, she attempted to dominate the whole Court, to be the dispenser of favors, and sowed discord between father and son. And (p. 179): the Cardinal Ferdinand curried favor with Camilla, and obtained through her considerable sums of money for his lavish expenditures in Rome.—Whatever therefore the policy of the measure, the new Grand-duke may have felt himself justified in putting this dangerous woman under restraint ; and subsequently, when, as will be seen, he released her on the marriage of her daughter Donna Virginia, her house became the rendezvous of the conspirators who, with the secret impulsion and aid of the Cardinal, rendered Francesco's reign and life at all times more or less unquiet.

9.—P. 257. —*whose near death   Must come of Victor's triumph !*] This, as the exclamation-point denotes, is said ironically by *Malocuor*, who appears to be reciting after what he calls the "psalms." But the historian just quoted, with his prejudice against Bianca, and his steadfast purpose (unknown perhaps to himself, yet obvious enough to his readers) to leave nothing unused that can be presented against her, or against the Grand-duke, whom he seems to hold in equal dislike, gravely recounts as a fact (ii. 299) what I have here made to be predicted as a malignant and extravagant calculation of the event. See *Append. II. y.* 1578.

10.—P. 257. The two princesses Exeunt, *etc.*] The profligate Isabella is described as highly accomplished. It is credible. The Medici were not wanting in talent, whatever their moral deficiencies. To beauty and grace, says the historian of that House, she added letters, poetry, music, and the practice of various languages. *Granducato ;* ii. 268. It is noticeable that he touches very lightly, scarcely indeed perceptibly, the licentiousness of this princess.— See, in Appendix II., p. 378.

11.—P. 259. *But screen'd his strumpet sister in my spite.*] This line is characteristic. But, if preferred for the Stage, it may read:

> " But kept my missives back, to screen his sister."

12.—P. 276. *Master Cappelli —*] " Ciascuno si chiama a Firenze per . . . *ec.*, e s'usa comunemente, se non v' è distinzione di grado e di molta età, dire tu e non voi a un solo, e solo a' cavalieri a' dottori ed a canonici si dà del messere, come a medici del *maestro*, ed a frati del padre." Varchi. *Storia Fior.* III. p. 118, ed. Mil. (8º. 1803.)

13.—P. 279. The Drop falls.] Here the play, being so far complete in itself, may, for the purposes of representation, be made occasionally to terminate, giving thus a shorter drama, although not finishing the tragedy as it is told in history.

Further, though there is a considerable interval of time between all the Acts, the license of the romantic drama being in that respect stretched to the utmost, and though the space of time between the 4th and 5th Acts is greater than that between the 3d and 4th, yet it strikes me as worthy of suggestion, that when the whole of the play is represented it might be well to have some interlude, of music or otherwise, between the falling of the Drop on the death of *Bonaventuri* and the rising of it again on the announcement of *Bianca* as Grand-duchess. Such leaps for the imagination of the spectator are, it is true, no more considered in our English drama, than they are for the reader, who makes them easily everywhere; but it might be an aid to the illusion nevertheless, to adopt the hint I have suggested.

14.—P. 280. — *Have her witch's-arts Enchanted too your Highness ?*] See latter half of Note 22, and in Appendix II. the 4th paragraph under y. 1576.

15.—P. 283. SCENE II.] Or, the first Scene continued, if preferred, with simply the new Entry : " *Enter from opposite sides,* etc."

16.—P. 283. *Met at Firenzuöl the pompous train.*] Or, for the Stage,
Rode forth to meet the ninety in advance :
namely, the ninety Venetian nobles, mentioned in Act IV., Sc. 4, (page 294.) *Firenzuola* is five miles from Florence (*Firenze.*)

The description of the pomp of the Venetian embassy and of its reception, of the solemn espousals of the Grand-duke with Bianca and her coronation as Queen of Cyprus, as given in Scenes 4 and 5 of Act IV., is historical.

17.—P. 285. *Our beast still ramp'd where gleams the lilied crown.*] That is, from the *crest.* This gave way to the *crown,* granted, as the pretentious legend on its circle indicates, by Pope Pius V. to Cosmo. To mollify the people, the centre of the circle bore a large red *lily,* the emblem of the Republic.

Roundle is the general name for a circular *charge.* But in the arms of Medici, the tincture of the roundles being *gules* (red), and their shape convex (like a bun or a button), their specific name is *torteaux* or *torteauxes*. In Italian however these charges are called *palle* (balls)*, which name comes nearer to the *pellets* ("gun-stones") of English heraldry ; but the *pellet* is tinctured *sable*. The reigning branch of the Medici carried *or six torteaux* ("sei palle rosse in campo d' oro")—six red balls in a field of gold. Of the three which are *in chief* (upper third of the shield) the central one after 1465 was blazoned, by concession of the King of France, "in segno di singulare affezione," {Vinc. Borgh. *ut infra cit.*) with three *fleurs-de-lys* of gold, and therefore it was made *azure*.

For the verse in the text may be redd by the Stage : "Our gonfalon bore not the ducal crown."

18.—P. 285. *God's might ! the throne of Clement's bastard son*, etc.] That is of the first Duke (or *Doge*, as was his title of installation,) Alessandro, who, although accounted a natural son of Lorenzo the Younger (Duke of Urbino) by a simple country-girl,† was more than

---

* It is easy to see that this species of charge in the escutcheon would subject the Medici to the malice of their defamers, who said it represented the *pills* of the ancestral profession. This saying at least had humor in it ; but the explanation of their flatterers, who would have it be emblematic of the marks made by the mace of a giant named *Mugello* killed by Averardo under Charlemagne (See Litta : *Fam. Cel. Ital.* (Milano 1825, in fol.) vol. ii.) is simply absurd. In fact these balls are of frequent occurrence in the arms of other Florentine families, as of the *Foraboschi*, the *Cipriani*, the *Squarcialupi*, etc. V. Borghini : *Dell' Arme delle Famigl. Fior.* (Fiorenz. 1585, in 4to, P. ii. p. 57.) Some of the Medici bore seven *palle*, some eight. (*ib.* p. 78.) I think it not unlikely that the design arose from the bosses or studs which are sometimes seen in ancient bucklers. In the escutcheon of 1373, the peculiar crest from which issues the demi-beast, whatever that be, rampant, is strewed with them,—in heraldic phrase, *semé of torteaux*.

† When the Florentine exiles, or their partisans, wrote upon the walls of his lodging at Rome, in allusion to his mother's place of birth, " Viva Alessandro da Collevecchio," he merely laughed, saying, he *was obliged to them for having*

suspected of being a bastard of Pope Clement VII.'s.* (See VARCHI. IV., p. 344.) The mother herself was uncertain which of the two had the better claim to him.—*Granduc.* Introd. xxxii. *V.* App. I. n. 9. c

Cosmo (or *Cosimo*, as the Italians write it), the successor of Alessandro (who left no legitimate children) and the father of Francesco and Don Pietro, was of a collateral branch of the Medici, being fourth in descent from the younger brother of the first Cosmo. Hence the epithet, " unlineal."

As to the origin of this renowned family, Sansovino (*Della Origine e de' Fatti delle Famigl. Illus. d' Italia ;* 4to., 1582 : a mere catalogue) recounts (citing Villani) the absurd fiction which made their descent from rulers in Greece. Galluzzi (*Istor,* ec. supra cit.) says their enemies reproached them with many low conditions : " di aver fatto il Carbonaio in Mugello†, l' Oste e il Biscazziere [*professional gambler*]

---

taught him whence he was, which he did not know before.—VARCHI *Stor.,* ec., V. 198. Galluzzi says she was a housemaid.—*Introd.* p. xxxii.

* Clement VII. (Giulio de' Medici), himself illegitimate, had two illegitimate nephews, one the Alessandro above, the other Ippolito son of Giuliano. It was left to his option by the Emperor Charles V. which of the two should be made the head of their House and prince of the Republic. Ippolito is described by Varchi as adorned with every grace of mind and body : " Era Ippolito Cardinal de' Medici in sul più bel fiore dell' età, non avendo più di ventun' anno," [his competitor was a year younger] ; " era bellissimo e grato d' aspetto, era di felicissimo ingegno, era pieno di tutte le grazie e virtù, era affabile e alla mano con ognuno, era come quegli che ritraeva alla magnificenza e benignità di Leone, e non alla scarsità e parsimonia di Clemente, liberalissimo verso tutti gli uomini eccellenti, o in arme o in lettere, o in qualsivoglia altra dell' arti liberali, cc." (*Stor.* iv. 845 sq.) Yet that true Pontiff, the slave of passion and of predilection and prejudice, and guided in public policy by a love of power without scrupulousness and by the dictates of a supposed self-interest that rendered him incapable of the wisdom of a statesman, preferred to this princely character the profligate and incompetent Alexander. And this choice confirmed the belief of his paternity.

† Fifteen miles from Florence.— There was the villa of Cosmo, the second *Duke*, at the time of his election.

in Firenze, e di avere avuto un Medico, ec." Their adulators derived them from Consuls and Emperors of Rome. Their reasonable origin is from a physician, said (by those who hold a middle course) to have been of Charlemagne. Galluzzi dates however the known rise of the Medici from Averardo (son of Averardo *who was Podestà* [Chief Magistrate, Bailiff (in the old sense) or Mayor] of Lucca, 1230), who accumulated by commerce great riches,* divided in 1319 between his six sons. (*Ist.* I. pp. x, xi.) In the genealogical chart prefixed to Varchi's History, Averardo (surnamed *Bicci* or *Di Bice*) is the base, and from him Giovanni rising is made *Gonfaloniere*, (literally, standard-bearer, as the moderns say *Alfiere*, but used like *Podestà*, to indicate the Chief Magistrate of the city,)† in 1421. The actual reign of the Medici as *Dukes* of Florence (through the subversion of the liberty of their country by Papal intrigues and the power of Austria) dates only from Alessandro just mentioned, the seventh in descent from Averardo, in the year 1532.

For Bianca's blood, Galluzzi says (ii. 84) : " Her father, besides the great authority which he had in the Republic, was connected by relationship with its principal families. He had for his second wife a daughter of the House of Grimani, sister of the Patriarch of Aquileia."

19.—P. 286. —*the Pregadi.*] The Venetian Senate.

20.—P. 287. *Let her, I say, Beware the Cardinal Medici's renown'd fang.*] The entire *Scene* expresses my deliberate opinion as to the

---

* We see thus easily how, as Varchi observes (I. 8), partly by their prudence and liberality, partly through the imprudence and avarice of others, but not without long trials and contests, among which must be counted their banishment from Florence three times in ninety-four years, the House of Medici attained in fact, but not as yet in name, and in the face of perpetual enmities, and with the drawback of undying and dangerous hatred, the mastery of the Republic.

† " E nel vero la signoria col gonfaloniere, e massimamente senza l' appello, era magistrato tirannico, e *per mezzo di lei*, oltra mille altri scandoli e sollevamenti, *si fece Cosimo poco meno che padrone assoluto* di Firenze." VARCHI. IV. 342.

history of the Grand-duchess Bianca. Taken with Appendix I., it will
supersede with those who care not for authorities, and scarcely trouble
themselves at all with notes in a work of this nature, any exposition
derived from the carelessness, the want of insight into character, or
the criminal misrepresentation of historians. The more studious
reader will find every satisfaction in Appendix II. — The *Biographie
Universelle* indicates a Life of *Bianca* in these words : " Siebenkees a
écrit une vie de B. C. d' après les sources originales, Gotha 1739, in
8° . . . traduite en anglais par Ludger." This translation is on the
Catalogue of the N. Y. Society Library, but has disappeared in some
manner from its shelves, for after repeated inquiries I have failed to
obtain any knowledge of its existence.

21.—P. 288. *The sorrow that*, etc.] For the Stage, omit these two
verses.

22.—P. 289. *Titian, had he liv'd,   Had pointed to the air of native
pride   That dignifies thy beauty, and had said*, etc.] Noble saw two
likenesses of her at Strawberry Hill, one a miniature, the other a portrait ; " the former [taken] when Bianca was at the height of her
charms, the other not long before her death. * * * Her countenance,"
he adds, " discovers that native pride which made her scorn to be
anything less than wife even to a sovereign." *Mem. Illus. House of
Medici** (Lond. 8°. 1797,) p. 287 *sq.* Although his argument, that, if she
had yielded before marriage, the Duke " would have been content
with her favors without marrying her," (p. 278,) I do not consider
tenable,† yet the quality of mind he ascribes to our heroine, if he did

---

* An inaccurate and superficial work, which, although I have made use of it for
the purposes of the drama, I cite only for the interesting item of the pictures.

† And in fact there is the example of Cosmo, who married Camilla Martelli after
she had borne him Donna Virginia. A better confirmation of our heroine's chastity would be found perhaps in the fact of her private marriage with the Grand-
duke. This ceremony was performed by the Duke's confessor two months after
the death of Joanna (1578), according to Galluzzi, who adds: *the guardianship*

not mistake the pictured expression, is such as does not accord with low profligacy, much less with the despicable traits which Galluzzi imputes to her, who indeed thereby contradicts his own description. "Assai potenti," he has said, speaking of Bianca when Francesco was yet but Prince, "erano le attrative di questa giovine, poichè oltre i meriti della bellezza aveva ancora ottenuto dalla natura un ingegno tale che somministrava tutte le arti per rendersi l' arbitra del suo amante. *Le grazie, la vivacità congiunta con una certa facondia,*" ec. (pp. 87, 88, t. c.) This fascination the public were taught to consider the result of magic arts and of philters ; and the eulogist of the Cardinal Grand-duke has not hesitated gravely to record the scandal. See in *Appendix II.* "y. 1576," 4th paragraph.

Titian, who (as said in *Act* I. *Sc.* 4.,) actually painted Bianca, (See Append. III.) died three years before the point of time in the text.

23.—P. 290. *Joy for the offspring, hope of which I nurse*—] From this line to the close of the passage, the Stage will substitute :

> For my throne's heritage, thou this day shalt be
> Dower'd by thy country with those honors which
> The world will value. Thy true crown is here.

24.—P. 290. *When Your Highness' brother*—] Omit from here to "But for this cause,"— seventh line below.

of the three princesses took away suspicion from her living in the Palace. Had Bianca yielded her favors already, there had been no need of a private marriage, and if her amour with the Duke were notorious, there could have been, in the first place, no occasion for avoiding suspicion, and secondly, if attempted by such an artifice it would not have been successful. Not to say, that a known mistress of the Grand-duke would not have been appointed guardian to his female children, although, as in the case of Mad. de Genlis, a *liaison* simply suspected would offer no impediment. But all argument falls to the ground if it be fact that Don Antonio' de' Medici, whether really her son or only imposed upon the Grand-duke as such (as Galluzzi would have it), was publicly recognized as illegitimate. See *Appendix II.* y. 1576 ; also *ib.* note 24, p. 408.

25.—P. 291. *Twice happy,* etc.] Omit here five lines.

26.—P. 296. The Ambassadors —] Omit from here to "About this hour," (ninth line below.)

27.—P. 299. *My father,* etc.] Omit to " But I should shame to own."

28.—P. 299. *And her too —*] Omit to "This coronation over,"—seven verses.

29.—P. 299. *She cannot live,* etc.] The most difficult point for me to get over in the biased statements of the hostile historians is Bianca's expressions to the Cardinal at the close of the y. 1580 (in a letter) : " Io vivo più a lei che a me, poichè vivo in lei, per il che senza lei non posso vivere, ec."—(*Granduc.* ii. 344.) See, besides the *Cardinal's* own doubts in the succeeding lines, what turn *Bianca* is made to give to them in *Act* V. *Sc.* I. They are however too extravagant, I will not say to be genuine, (for I have known at least one spiritual and vivacious woman of high breeding and of proud temper, and who possessed that very fluency of language which Galluzzi ascribes to Bianca, to indulge in quite as extravagant terms of affection in writing to a stranger to her blood, neither husband nor lover, and with even less motive)*—but too extravagant to seem genuine ; and the malice that did not hesitate to blacken her in other respects would find no compunction against such a counterfeit. But supposing them to be truly of Bianca's writing, and that they are not to be interpreted by any vivacity of disposition and vanity of eloquence, what follows ?   That there was more than a legitimate attachment between the Cardinal and his brother's wife. And this is to concede the whole point in discussion, and to justify, even historically, the part I have, equally with the romancer (or romancers.) assigned to the Cardinal. V. Append. I.

---

* One thing is worth observing : such persons cannot be sincere. If Bianca did write that letter, she was wanting in candor.

30.—P. 300. *No, it were better*, etc.] Omit to "As yet,"—eleventh line below ; then omit the words " To rectify this wrong."

31.—P. 309. *From taint by such a traitor—traitor, ay !*] Which may read, at the option of the Theatre :

> From taint by such a traitor.
>> *Card.* Traitor!
>>> *Bian.* Ay !

32.—P. 310. *Death !* '*I should sink to this !*] Or, avoiding the ellipsis : "Death ! Am I come to this !"

33.—P. 320. *She might have had*, etc.] This was his mistress, a handsome woman, whom he had brought back with him from Madrid in 1584. The Prince in his profligacy seemed to expect that she would be admitted at Court, and was displeased when Bianca, as was natural and proper, refused to receive her. V. *Granduc.* II. 357.

34.—P. 322. *The Pope gives dispensation —*] See *Appendix II.* at y. 1585.

Immediately before the verse (in *Act* III. *Sc.* 4.),

> " When I throw off this purple which I hate,"

occurred in the first MS. the following three verses. They were superfluous, therefore weak. I introduce them here simply to illustrate the text above, and, historically, the Cardinal's ambitious and intriguing character, which was in fact the character of a true churchman where ambitious,—profligately so.

> The Pope is my creation, hence my creature.
> For he sees not, weak man, that not of love,
> But for my ends, I help'd to heave him up.

35.—P. 326. *Wrought by the Duchess and a Jewish hag   Confederate in her sorceries*, etc.] See Appendix II., y. 1576.

36.—P. 328. *Waiter brings wine and glasses, is paid and retires.*}

But to keep up the life and variety of the picture in the background, he moves about in the discharge of his functions, carrying flasks etc. to the different tables. — The Stage requires hints of this kind, but I am sorry to think is not likely to observe them.

37.—P. 331. *Not Cini's surgery* —] Cini was the Cardinal's physician.

38.—P. 332. *Whose lightning, hurtled by the lion's cub,* etc.] Or, for the Stage :

> Whose lightning, hurl'd by Peter Leoncil,
> Whom men call Cardinal Farnese's son,
> Frightens the confines with its devious blaze.

"Lion's cub" is an allusion to the name *Lioncillo* (leoncello.)

This miscreant was actually at the head of the large number of men named in the text. The historian tells us, that brigandage and assassination had come to be considered knightly service. As now-a-days in Italy the Church has been, from political motives or from indifference to the public welfare, the great supporter of such wretches, so in those times it was the Church-feudatories chiefly that had them in service. See *Append.* II. y. 1580, ¶ 2, — also y. 1575, ¶ 2. As men above the vulgar herd joined these blood-bands, the language at least attributed to the assassins in the text is not greatly beyond their degree, whatever may be thought of their sentiments.

39.—P. 332. *They put wise Machiavelli to the rack* —] This was nearly a century before. Machiavelli died in 1527, sixty years before the time of the Scene. But the condition of things was not much changed from that of his troubled day, and his was a name not easily to be forgotten, any more than that of "Antichrist" (Clement VII.)

40.—P. 337. Sign.] For the Stage, commence : "Donna Virginia absent *etc.?*"

41.—P. 338. *Then seriously.*] Omit to "my well-loving spouse," and read the passage :

Then seriously, thus. My loving spouse
Seem'd *etc.*

After which, make the last two lines of the part :

In the blue hangings of the Silver'd Room, more pleas'd
To glad *etc.*

43.—P. 339. *Who has not seen* —] Omit to "It is said," ninth line below, reading the verse :

To cloud the unwary brain. 'Tis freely said.

Then omit, from "Did your Grace," thirty-one lines, reading thus, from the commencement of the alteration :

And made your parting mournful.

Virg. Yet I doubt
The Duchess' heart *etc.*

Or in fine, omit, in the performance, the entire Scene, which was written merely to interpose time between the revelation of Malacuor's design and its perpetration. But our English Stage (as I have elsewhere had occasion to remark) sets time and space at defiance ; and the accustomed audience rarely protests against any violation of probability that saves them from fatigue.

ADDITION TO NOTE 18.

The influence of a family of wealth will depend greatly upon its numbers and its ramifications. Galluzzi, as an evidence of the potency of the Medici, records this fact, that even after the pestilence of 1348, there were no less than fifty males of that House surviving. *Introd.* xi. Without this numerical preponderance, it may be questioned whether, notwithstanding their riches and their talents, their ambition could have made head against the determined opposition of their rivals and of the better lovers of their country.

Of the Capelli, Bern. Segni, who wrote under Francesco, particularizes the ambassador Carlo, mentioned in the text (*Act.* I. *Sc.* IV.), who, he tells us, raised in Florence a monument to his horse, which was standing in his, the historian's day. *Storie Fior.* vol. i. *ed.* Milan, (1805, in 8°) p. 225. We may suppose the Cardinal Grand-duke, in his anxiety to remove every object that might recall the memory of Bianca (*Append.* II. prope fin.), ordered this monument, whatever it was, to be destroyed. Another Capello (Vincent) is mentioned by the same historian as being General of the Venetians. *Ib.* ii. 151.

APPENDICES

I.

The following observations, intended at the time as the sole appendix to the play, were written six years after the completion of the latter; when I had forgotten that I had so fully illustrated in my text every particular that bears upon the story, as to render any comment or explanation needless. Still, as a brief analysis of the historic question involved, they may not be uninteresting to the general reader.

The footnotes are of the date of the transcription.

For many of the incidents, and even for the groundwork or suggestive type of some of the characters in *Bianca Capello*, I am largely indebted to the romance of the same name by A. G. Meissner (*Leipz.* in 16to, 1784), who probably obtained his particulars from the collection of Celio Malespini of Verona, *Part.* II. *Nov.* 84, which I have not seen, but find particularized by Galluzzi as conspicuous among several written on Bianca's fortunes.(1)

(1) *Granducato*, ii. p. 85. The historian speaks of *Mondragone* and his wife as intermediary, in the romance, between the Grand-duke and Bianca, but, with his usual inconsiderate or malevolent bias, only to cast a slur upon the latter by remarking that the Duke had found no need of go-betweens. Francesco might have, and, with still more likelihood, would have found the need, in his position, even were Bianca the "vile seducer" that Galluzzi and his copyists make her.

The character of Bianca will always perhaps be a subject of historical doubt. The weight of authority is against her. She was probably weaker than I have made her (2); but I do not believe she was depraved or grossly criminal. The historian of the Grand-duchy of Tuscany has spared no pains to render her atrocious. His large work,

But that is not the point. *Mondragone* is introduced by that very name, and with his wife, in that very function, by Meissner. He is the *Malecuore* of the Tragedy.

In Roscoe's *Italian Novelists,* vol. III. (Lond. in 8°. 1836), some specimens are given of Celio, but not the story of Bianca. Celio Malespini, who held, we are told, the post of Secretary to Francesco, is supposed to have begun writing his numerous little novels soon after 1575. Roscoe translates after the edition in 4to. *Venezia* 1609. "In many instances," he says (*Introd.* ibi,) "the mention of persons and of particular times and places, is introduced. It is thus he alludes to Bianca Cappello, afterwards consort of Francesco de' Medici, grand duke of Tuscany, whose nuptials were celebrated in 1579, and are very minutely described by the novelist." — It will depend upon the time when his novel was written and the place where published whether the whole story is told by Celio or not. If the above-mentioned edition was the first, we may well suppose it, for the Cardinal Grand-duke died in that year, and the volume it will be seen bears the imprint of Venice. — Meissner would seem to refer to some unedited memoir, some private scandalous chronicle, as the chief source of his materials. " Jenes berufne Manuskript von der geheimen Geschichte des Hauses Medizes, welches Orrery nutzte, und worauf Sansovino, nebst noch manchem anderm baute, mag allerdings für den wahren Historiker und Biographen nicht zulänglich sicher seyn; für den Halb-Roman hat es eine treffliche Eigenschaft, — Interesse." *Vorerinn.* Was this done to conceal his obligations to the Italian romancer?

(2) See subnote on p. 360 sq. Bonaventuri was killed in 1570. The Duchess Joanna died in 1578. In all that interval, a widow, besieged by the passionate assiduities of a royal lover, and surrounded by courtly examples both of unchastity and of the indifference with which it was regarded, in an age of very general profligacy, she would have been indeed a Penelope (as *Isabella* calls her in mockery,) — no, more — if she had not yielded. But there are two sides to the story of Penelope as well as of Bianca, and some ancient writers have made the wife of Ulysses the common mistress of all her suitors. Cs. App. II. note 5.

written expressly to glorify the duchy and its petty sovereigns,(3) enters into details which waken more than incredulity, and few thoughtful persons can rise from his discolored and distorted portraiture of the fair Venetian and his carefully toned miniature of the Cardinal Ferdinand, without a conviction that the pictures in their general effect might change places.

The Cardinal, a false brother and a bad man(4), in a family where murder and incest were familiar crimes, had cast a longing eye on the grand-ducal crown, which the physical infirmity of his brother's spouse made it more than probable would one day be his own. When Bianca, by no other means that I can see or suppose, than the magic of her beauty and her manners, ascended the throne as the legitimate successor of Joanna, all his schemes seemed to be blown to the winds.

(3) And written under the patronage and by the command, as he himself expresses it, of the then reigning monarch, a younger son of the House of Austria, whose lofty name he puts upon the very title-page, withholding reverently his own. The favor of this prince (Peter-Leopold, afterwards Emperor of Austria,) would certainly not be forfeited by an endeavor to blacken the character of the Archduchess' rival.

And here I may as well state, in preparation for the whole of the Appendix following, that Galluzzi claims to have drawn his material exclusively from the Medicean Archives, . . *"tutte estratte fedelmente dall' Archivio Mediceo."* In the same brief advertisement, however, he alludes to the existence of popular fallacies as to certain events, and tells us he enters into minuteness of detail therein, for the very purpose of correcting these errors of belief and of tradition, — of course by the *Archives.* Now, are the Archives infallible? Are they, in fact, entire? or in their entirety, veritable? Would the Cardinal have been likely to leave anything that would tend to inculpate him in the matter of Bianca and the Grand-duke, or not to give prominence as well as permanence to inventions which would account morally for his detestation of the former, and palliate, with most men, the atrocity of his unchristian and unprincely efforts to blacken for ever her memory? He had the power to tamper with the Archives, and he was not a man to leave it unused. Consult. in Appendix II., Note 12, also 19.

(4) See below, in Note 15, what Sismondi says of him.

And when finally, as Grand-duchess, she was about to become a mother, he resolved to rid himself by one blow of both obstacles to his ambition. Bianca's great weakness, as well as doubtless one of her principal attractions, seems to have been a benevolent amiability. She did her best at all times to reconcile her lord with the Cardinal, whose profligate intrigues and importunate avarice had alienated his ducal brother. And she succeeded only too well. The Cardinal is invited to a banquet. He refuses to partake of the blancmange which was his inviter's favorite dish, and when both Bianca and the Grand-duke, after eating freely of it, are seized at the very table with pangs that denoted poisoning, he prevented all assistance from being rendered to either, had them shut up indeed in a disfurnished and gloomy chamber of the villa, and took measures even before their death to secure possession of the fortresses and put down by armed force any attempts that should be made to prevent his becoming master of the city.(5) Proclaiming loudly that the Duke and Duchess had attempted to poison him and by mistake had swallowed their own bane, he retracted this absurd invention by declaring there was no poison in the case at all, that the Duke and Duchess had both died of a surfeit.(6) As this story was more absurd, if possible, than the other, since the deaths were nearly simultaneous, and the preceding symptoms had indicated some sudden and violent action upon the vitals, he had the bodies opened. Now at that day science had not advanced so far as to make the detection of the secret administration of poisons, especially if of a vegetable origin, in all cases possible. Indeed even at the present time, it is known, and we have authority for the assertion, that there are venene substances whose operation cannot be traced after death.(7) And this must be particularly the case, to ocular in-

---

(5) There was no hesitancy on his part. The commander of the citadel at Leghorn showing some unwillingness to acknowledge his authority, the Cardinal had him hung. See Appendix II., Note 24.

(6) See Appendix II., y. 1587, second paragraph.

(7) I have mislaid a newspaper quotation from a lecture by our townsman Prof.

spection, where the poison has been slow in its effects, because, in the first place, of its probable elimination from the system, (8) and, secondly, of the liability to confound its indications with those of natural disease. Now, if the account which Galluzzi gives of the *tertian fever* with its *vehement thirst*(9) which seized the Duke and Duchess so sin-

Doremus, bearing directly upon this point. But it will be sufficient to cite the following, in respect to metallic poisons, which can be traced : —

. . . "It is known, that three or four grains of arsenic, a quantity *insufficient to produce any striking local changes*, will destroy a person under all the usual symptoms of poisoning by this substance. The same may be said of corrosive sublimate : — three or four grains of this poison *would suffice to kill an adult; and yet*, from this small quantity, *the local changes would be barely perceptible.*" TAYLOR, *On Poisons in relat. to Med. Jur.* &c. (Phil. ed. 8°. 1848) p. 27. And again : " That death should ever take place in poisoning, without any physical changes being produced on the body, is not more wonderful than that it should occur under attacks of tetanus or hydrophobia, in which diseases, as is well known, no post-mortem appearances are met with sufficient to account for their rapidly fatal course." (*Ib.*)

But this is still more complete :

. . . "To take arsenic as an example, — *if the dose has been small, and the person has survived the effects for a certain period, it is not likely that the poison will be detected* in the soft organs of the body. *The deceased may have survived long enough for the whole of the poison to be expelled.* According to Briand, *after ten, twelve, or fifteen days, not a particle of arsenic* or tartarized antimony *will be discovered* in the bodies of animals poisoned by either of these substances. (*Ib.* p. 80.) See further on same page.

The subject is resumed in Append. II., Note 22.

(8) As I have shown in Note 7, Briand gives *ten, twelve*, and *fifteen days* for the complete disappearance of the poison. Orfila himself (*Traité de Toxicol.* 5e éd. Paris, in 8°.; t. 1. p. 427) assigns *from twelve to fifteen.* The Grand-duke survived *eleven* and Bianca *ten days*, — according to the *Archives.*

(9) See, in Appendix II., p. 1587, and footnote. — The Cardinal Ippolito de' Medici was affected similarly, and died after four days' illness; that is, according to Varchi; but six, as I compute it; for he was attacked on the 5th of August and expired on the 10th, (1585.) The moment after he had eaten the broth in which

gularly, and so conveniently for the Cardinal, within two days of each other, and terminated, with an interval of a single day, in the death

the poison was conveyed, the Cardinal began to suffer. He grew rapidly worse, " and went on wasting little by little and having *continually a very slight and slow fever.*" (*Stor. Fior.* v. 181, 182.)   He was poisoned, as some supposed, by his cousin Duke Alexander(a), as others, by Pope Paul III.(b)   That most fear-

(a) The most probable hypothesis. And if what Segni appears inclined to believe, although he cites the story merely as a rumor of the day, be true, viz., that Ippolito had previously tried to blow up the Duke with gunpowder (vol. ii. p. 85), the latter might, if the rumor were current before the death of Ippolito, have satisfied his own conscience by the supposition of its truth, if afterward, he might himself have originated it as an offset to his own atrocity. One scarcely knows what to hold to, in so contradictory accounts; but such a crime, besides that it is plausible to attribute the attempt to the known political enemies of Alessandro, who were many of them zealous but not over-scrupulous friends of liberty, one of whom finally effected his assassination, such a crime is inconsistent with the character of the young Cardinal, who, though passionately ambitious, and openly resentful of the injustice done him in the elevation of his junior, Alexander, had nothing in his impetuous, candid, and generous character which allows us to impute to him the design of a coward and a murderer. Unfit to be a churchman, partial, almost ostentatiously, to arms and to the chase (see *Appendix* III.), he led the life of a gay but not dissipated prince, and died, according to Segni himself, with unaffected piety and with the modest charity of a Christian—as a Christian should be. This local historian tells us, very differently from Varchi, that the ill-fated young man expired in *thirteen hours* after the attack, and that two of his friends died subsequently; for, according to Segni, instead of the Cardinal's being indisposed and in bed when the poisoned broth was brought to him, he and his friends were *supping together gaily at Itri*. — Such is history; Varchi, writing under Cosmo, and Segni under his successor; yet, in so tragical an incident, varying both as to the inception and the termination of the affair! It is, that, in such a case, Rumor, never perhaps single-voiced, has more than the usual number of tongues. The latter writer continues : The friends of the Duke ascribed the murder to Pope Paul, "come quegli che, desideroso de' gran benefici posseduti da lui per dare al Card. Farnese, l' avesse in questo modo fatto morire." Some indeed ascribed the event to the pestilential air (as Bianca and Francesco's death was attributed to intermittent fever.) Segni considers it the truest and most certain report, which lays it at the door of Duke Alexander. (*Ib.* 82, sq.)

(b) *Alessandro da Farnese, Cardinal d' Ostia*, — who succeeded Clement VII. in that chair whose existence still remains, but will probably not much longer, the opprobrium of human sense and of manhood, and should make a Christian blush to throw imposture in the teeth of Mohammedans, — the so-called seat of St. Peter, who never put a round in it. According to Varchi (an historian of rare ingenuousness) Paul III. was a finished dissembler, concealing his real vices by outward decorum and sanctity. (*Ib.* 89.) It is likely; it belonged to his profession and his place. He died, this man who could be suspected in his old age of causing a cowardly assassination, to swell by misappropriation, not to say robbery, the state and splendor of his reprobate bastard son* and of his grandchildren (see again Varchi *in loc. cit.* 131, 5. The detail, after his faulty but interesting manner, is curious. Also, from p. 250 to end of the vol.) — he died, this Vicegerent of Christ, with the words : *If my family had not ruled me, I should be stainless.* Everybody remembers what Hildebrand's last words were, what Cardinal Wolsey's, what perhaps those of a dozen gallows-birds, as well as princes of the Church, have been. When a man has lied and dissembled all his life, he will not be likely to want a good name after death, if an additional falsehood can buy it for him. The vulgar superstition

* It is useful to my vindication of the character of Bianca, to note here another striking historial discrepancy. This scapegrace, who, according to Galluzzi, *had all the vices of Duke Valentine* [Caesar Borgia] *without his talents* (Intr. liv.), and of whom Varchi tells in detail that revolting personal outrage which ended in the death of the gentle Bishop of Fano (S. F. *ap. finem*), is described by Segni (an intelligent as well as honest writer) as not without learning and well able to behave himself (*ib.* 15*.—v. iii. p. 14.) Again, on the other hand, his father, Paul III., who, Eli-like, encouraged his profligacy by his criminal indifference or impolitic leniency, was, according to the first-named author, *a man of rare talents and of extraordinary sagacity!* (*Ib.* liii.) I wish to enforce on the reader's sense these continual discrepancies in judgment and in fact-record, and must be pardoned for a little irrelevancy.

of both, be correct(10), the former was eleven days suffering, and the latter ten, and the difficulty of detection would be very greatly increased. Besides, these investigators, if they were such (for there is no mention of anything more than the opening of the bodies and a

ful, because least evitable, mode of assassination, which in the beginning of the century had flourished under the auspices and with the coöperation of the Holy See, was still horribly familiar to the great. Francesco himself was suspected of practising it, and Cosmo was, as mentioned in the text, accounted "a subtle poison-mixer." (See Appendix II. *ad init.*) Varchi has several stories of the kind, as *e. g.*, besides that of the Cardinal Ippolito, the remarkable one of the beautiful Luisa Strozzi, wife of Luigi Capponi, poisoned by her own relatives on mere suspicion of the likelihood of her falling a victim to the libertinism of Duke Alessandro (v. 104–106), but according to Segni by the Duke himself, because she had refused to yield to his desires(e). *Storie Fior. l.* 7°. (vol. II. p. 65, sq. ed. Mil. 1805, in 8°.)

(10) But I have argued that the record of the Medicean Archives cannot in the story of Bianca be accepted as correct and is not likely to be even truthful. *Note* (3): also various places in *Append. II.* It is said that in the Introduction of the work cited in Append. II. Note 4, Miss Strickland, on the authority of Evelyn, accuses Burnet of destroying historical autographs. Yet the Bishop of Sarum was both a good man and a virtuous prelate. The Cardinal Grand-duke was neither, even in the eyes of Sismondi, and he hated Bianca with a hatred which he took no pains to conceal. Append. II. *pr. finem.*

which believes that in the death-hour nothing can be uttered but the truth is a convenient one, nor will either Paul III. be the last vicious personage, nor Elizabeth Surratt the last convict, whose final declaration will be accepted by a partial historian, or be availed of by a cunning barrister, as evidence of innocence.

(e) Yet Segni, whose honesty as a writer is unquestioned, claims for such a monster, who he tells us (ii p 50) corrupted even the sacred virgins and committed in the very sanctuary (like the diabolical Pope John XII., or the corsair-pope, the 23rd of that pontifical name) "assai vergogne nefande", both abilities and good dispositions, and attributes (*this* unphilosophically, if not absurdly) his immeasurable licentiousness to evil counsels. It had been more rational to ascribe it to the gift of his mother, aided by that profligate in purple the Cardinal Giulio — or by the Cardinal's coachman. But in conclusion he admits, that he was "universally hated ", because, notwithstanding his even-handed justice, high courage, and resolute will, "he had withal acquired the name of cruel, of voluptuous and impious, to such a degree that he had become an object of disgust to everybody." (lib. 6°. *prope init.*) All of which furnishes one of many instances of the difficulty which attends the search for truth in history.

I may add, as being of interest and not ungerman to my text, what Segni has to say of Alexander's illegitimacy. It appears that a third party, as I have just hinted, might have put in a claim for priority with the two Medici. . . "Alessandro de' Medici, il quale era figlio naturale di Lorenzo, nato d' una schiava chiamata Anna, la quale avendo avuto ancora che fare con Giulio Priore di Capua e poi Papa Clemente, ed *ancora con un vetturale*, che tenevano in casa quando erano ribelli, era incerto di chi fosse figliuolo." (t. I. *ed. cit.* p. 165.)

simple inspection of the viscera,) would understand it was the Cardinal's pleasure they should not find anything to confirm suspicion, and it would have been a miracle of independence and moral courage had they dared under the circumstances to disappoint him.(11) Here the infamy of this vile churchman does not end. Giving orders for the sumptuous burial of his brother, he had Bianca thrown upon the common heap of bodies of the abandoned poor and vicious. This might have been done to confirm in men's minds the opinion he had diligently disseminated of her utter worthlessness and of his disgust and hatred of an adventuress and "sorceress" who had dishonored temporarily his family. But there was something more than this in his conduct ; it evinced a rage that was savagely vindictive ; the rage of a bad man who had been more than disappointed, who was conscious that he had betrayed himself and hated the involuntary possessor of his degrading secret. In short I believe, that, as I have painted him, and the romancers before me, the Cardinal had offered love to his brother's wife (it was quite in the mode of the family) and to his dismay been rejected. The indications of this doubly criminal passion can not have escaped historians. The Capello family, one of the richest and most distinguished noble houses in Venice, was as good as the Medici in its origin, and the Venetian Republic in its desire to exalt Bianca (which it would not have shown — despite the insinuation of Botta(12) — were her life infamous) had made her Queen of

(11) In the case of the Cardinal Ippolito, the body after death became discolored, and, on opening it, the omentum (caul) was found corroded. But his household were interested in finding the traces of poison. Those who performed the like operation on Francesco and Bianca were interested in not finding such evidence, and the examination on their part was probably one for form, as on the part of the Cardinal Duke it was a challenge to the suspicion of his enemies. See Appendix II. Note 22.

(12) Who, as an historian, should have had knowledge enough of humanity to understand what was going on everywhere around him. A change of fortune for the better obliterates at once, or at least veils over for the time being, all previous

Cyprus. Thus put on a par with the Grand-duke, what plea could the Cardinal have found for making that immeasurable distinction between them after their common death ?(13) In the rage of his hatred, this prince of the Christian Church furnished one of the very best facts in evidence of a criminal passion whose repulse had outraged his extravagant pride and wounded past cure a selflove which was the most vital part of his spirit.

Like Philip II. of Spain, and, I may add, Henry VIII. of England, the Grand-duke Ferdinand of Tuscany is represented with smooth face and fair and effeminate features. They were the mask of a character which had the revengeful malice, the remorseless cruelty, the treacherous cunning and hypocrisy, and the immeasurable ambition of a bad and masculine woman.(14)

And yet this man made a wise, a politic, and even, it is said, just sovereign.(15) The case is not singular either in Europe or in the

disadvantages, and when Botta sneers at the eagerness with which both the Capello family and the Venetian Republic made haste to acknowledge and to glorify the adventuress as Grand-duchess whom as a fugitive they had proscribed and proclaimed for punishment, he forgets one of the commonest of the traits of the human character. Would he not himself have found splendor in the risen sun if its rays fell on his stand-place, or would he have got out of its warmth in winter? The dogs are wiser, and the moth, though it rushes to its own destruction, has a better instinct. I affirm that Bianca's family acted in both instances precisely as every other family would have acted, and were in neither position mean or unreasonable.'

(13) If it be said, because he held her to be worthless, the "pessima Bianca" he afterwards declared her (r. Append. II. *ap. fin.*), then his brother should have shared the same fate, and their common father before them. Where was Isabella buried?

(14) All of which traits happen to have been the moral features, ugly to deformity, of the Medici in general.

(15) Sismondi says, and well, of Ferdinand: "He had as much talent for government as one can have without virtue, and as much pride as one can preserve without nobleness of soul." *Rép. It.* (Paris, 1840, in 8°.) *t.* x. p. 227. We have seen (p.

East. The Mogul Emperor, Aurungzebe, attained the throne on which
he sat so nobly, by the murder of more than one brother.

August 16, 1861.

II.

Being extracts from memoranda taken during the preparation for
Acts III., IV., and V., with additions and comments subsequently
made.

Cosmo bore the reputation of being a subtle maker of poisons ;
Y. 1574. and it is certain he endeavored to destroy Strozzi by them.
But Strozzi did the same for him. GALLUZ. *Granduc.* ii. 185.
The historian's language is positive : "E *certo* che egli tentó di usarne
contro lo Strozzi." Yet observe the high character which he gives to
Cosmo, after this charge and the assertion that his criminal laws,
founded on the Spanish maxims then prevalent in all Italy, *were ab-*
solutely destitute of every sentiment of humanity, and "egli venerava le
istruzioni e i consigli dei suoi congiunti Vice Rè Don Pietro di
Toledo(1) e Duca d' Alva, che furono i due più sanguinari Ministri
che abbino conculcato l' umanità " (*ib.*) ; and then see to what amounts
the like charge against Francesco. Sismondi, who says that Cosmo

373, subnote *c*) that *even-handed justice* is assigned to that infamous profligate,
Duke Alexander. Here are the very words of Segni, and in detail : "le quali [*sc.* le
faccende pubbliche] . . . egli amministrava da sè stesso con grand' animo e con
molta risoluzione, ed avrebbe soddisfatto in gran parte alla giustizia, perchè la
faceva al piccolo come al grande, ed udiva volentieri le povere genti, se i piaceri
giovenili noll' avessono distratto pur troppo da questi consigli, *ec.*" Stor. Fior. *lib.*
6°. t. ii. p. 19.

(1) This D. Pietro di Toledo, Viceroy of Naples, confessed in 1559 to a Secretary
of Duke Cosmo's, that, after his possession of the government, there perished in
the single city of Naples by the hands of justice *eighteen thousand persons.*
Granduc. *Introd.* p. 2.

had established a manufactory of poisons in his palace under the pretence of making chemical experiments, (the passage is quoted under y. 1578,) is more consistent, although we shall see that in his summing-up of the character of Francesco, he contradicts not only Galluzzi, but certain facts which do not depend upon the allegations of historians. And Botta, we shall find, does just the same. See note 20.

A year after the death of Cosmo. — The conspiracy against 1575. Cosmo, and for which Pandolfo Pucci had atoned with his life in 1560, was renewed against his successor, and by the son of this very Pucci, Orazio, whom the Grand-duke by numerous benefits had endeavored in vain to make forget his father's merited execution. [Here again Galluzzi gives a trait that does not agree with his picture of Francesco. See under 1578.] The Cardinal at Rome learning of the plot informed Francesco of it [which Galluzzi considers generous, although, as the conspiracy was directed in the name of the ancient liberty against the whole reigning family, he was to have been one of the victims,] and advised the arrest of Pucci. About twenty youths in all were complicated, and the confiscations amounted to 30,000 ducats. This severity and the fiscal exactions irritated the people and rendered hostile all the connections of the young nobles. *Granduc.* ii. 248.

Masnade [bands of predatory soldiers, brigands or assassins according to circumstances, and serving as instruments both of rapine and revenge] increased fearfully; the nobles having them in pay for their feuds and vengeance. *Ib.* 265. — Sismondi writes in relation to the extent of brigandage after 1563 (the year of Bianca's arrival in Florence) : Alfonso Piccolomini, Duke of Monte Marciano, and Marco Sciarra, in Romagna, the Abbruzzi, and the Campagna of Rome, commanded several thousands of men. *Répub. Ital.* t. 10, p. 218 sq.

The administration of the criminal laws frightened the innocent 1576. as much as the guilty, and flattered the powerful with hopes of easily eluding them. "Quindi è che le risse, le prepotenze e gli assassinamenti crebbero a dismisura." In eighteen months from the death of Cosmo, there were counted in Florence alone one hundred and eighty cases of deaths and wounds by assault. *Granduc.* ii. 265.

Don Pietro de' Medici profligate and depraved. His beautiful wife Eleonora di Toledo imitated him. Her brother refused to listen to his complaints, and prevented their reaching Don Garzia her father. The Spanish chivalry put the husband up to avenge his dishonor, and he murdered her by night, July 11, with repeated blows of his poniard, at Caffagiolo, an ancient villa of the Medici (*ib.* 267.) Her death attributed to disease of the heart.

Isabella, both beautiful and accomplished. Favored the amours of her brother with Bianca. Duke, her husband, especially jealous of his own kinsman Troilo Orsini; strangles her with a cord at his villa of Correto on the morning of the 16th July. Court informed that she fell dead in the arms of her attendants while washing her head (*ib.* 269.) — Botta tells us that Troilo himself killed with his own hand the Grand-duke's page, between whom and this licentious princess there was a mutual passion. The picture given by this last modern historian, of the two royal ladies, D. Pietro and, united with the godly group, Duke Cosmo, is done with that relish with which he seems to paint extreme depravity in high places, sparing no feature, and heightening without mercy the ugliness of all. Let me make a copy of the original, as certain touches will not bear transferring to an English panel. "*Eleonora* .. " giovane graziosa e di maravigliosa bellezza. Corsero romori, e ne fu anche fatto fede dalle cronache contemporanee, che Cosimo, invaghito di tanta bellezza, con scellerato amore si fosse con esso lei mescolato, per modo che gravida di sè alle nozze del figliuolo la mandasse. D. Pietro poi oltraggiava i due sessi, l' altro abbandonando e del proprio abusando.(2) Infame tresche erano queste, nè anco

(2) Cosmo, who affected a regard for morality and for religion, or better had a politic respect for both, enacted laws of great severity against this revolting vice and against the sin of blasphemy. (It is Segni who classes them thus together in

celate : il pubblico le sapeva, s' aggiungeva lo scandalo al misfatto. Pietro frequentava i bei giovani ; Eleonora prestò l' orrecchio a chi la vagheggiava." *Stor. d' Ital.* Libr. 14°. (Milano, in 12°, 1843, t. iii. p. 166.) "Delizia della Corte e quasi fiore di Firenze per gioventù, bellezza, grazia, ornamento di poesia, perizia di musica, moltiplicità di favelle era donna Isabella de' Medici, figliuola del Duca Cosimo. Ma tali sorti di fiori nella Medicea Corte si contaminavano e si lasciavano contaminare." [The reader will please recall what I observed of Bianca, surrounded by and inhaling such an atmosphere of moral corruption. But in the instance of Isabella the "flower" shriveled and blackened by no outward influence of the elements ; it had destruction at its core. The egg of the caterpillar was deposited before the germ had begun to develop itself on the parent plant. It was the pernicious blood of the Medici in Cosmo, and haply, on the mother's side, of the Toledo.(3) Observe what follows.] "Portò la fama che Cosimo

the same sentence.) But the law fell into disuse from the indifference of the magistrates, — perhaps from their knowledge to what degree this unmentionable bestiality prevailed among the highest order. Pandolfo Pucci was one of those who thus sinned against nature, and did it without any particular concealment ("*sfacciatamente.*") It seems he knew what to calculate upon. Through the influence of his brother Ruberto, lately made Cardinal by Paul III., he was pardoned. But Giov. Bandini, for the same classical atrocity, was kept in a dungeon at the bottom of a tower for nineteen years, — rather, as Segni thinks and well, for his abusive words of the Duchess Madama Leonora than for the crime. *Stor. Fior.* ed. cit. ii. 272.

(3) Cosmo, who, according to honest Segni, was censurable for the same subservience to the Emperor(a) that Galluzzi accuses Francesco of towards the King

(a) "Non faceva altro che intratenersi per amico e per buon suddito (per parlar meglio) dell' Imperadore." (ii. 255.) The language, in its sense, not tene, is forcible. — So also in the matter of his nuptials, this pattern Cosmo, — who, by the by, Segni, who must have been aware of the niceties and morality recounted in an after age by Botta, tells us "nel viver suo era molto onesto," (ib. 270,) — celebrated them with great magnificence, although a famine was prevailing at the time, occasioned chiefly by his own avarice, — "cagionata dal temporale, e molto più dall' aver l' anno innanzi il Duca dato la tratta a' grani, de' quali cavò scudi 50,000, e seccò tutti i granai del dominio." (ib. 215, sq.) Thus in both these instances, of a degrading policy and an extravagance of pomp which mocked the necessities of his people, and insulted their sufferings, the great Cosmo set the example which his son and successor is reproached for having followed. That this was so does not excuse the latter, but it makes the censure of the historians in his precisely parallel case if not malevolent, yet altogether partial. And it is for this reason that I have cited these instances of selfish and ignoble error

stesso troppo più l' amasse che a padre si conveniva." (*Ib.* 167.)
Who has not heard the story of the artist, who from his scaffolding
beheld —— The Cardinal's words of soliloquy in Act IV. Sc. 4 are
gloss enough in English.

For thirteen years the Duke had been enamored of Bianca, with a
passion growing every day more ardent. Nothing too good for her :
palaces, delightful gardens, *etc.*, *etc.* — his very brothers paying her
court — sole dispenser of favors. A Jewish woman said to assist her
in incantations and the composition of philters to increase the Duke's
passion. But let me quote, as I wish to examine this point in full.
After indulging in the expression "orgogliosa impudenza della Cappello" (*haughty impudence of the Capello*,) — to which on the succeeding page he adds *black perfidy* ("nera perfidia,") Galluzzi proceeds in this fashion : "La Bianca, cui troppo premeva sempre più
accenderlo e mantenerlo costante, non risparmiava veruno di quelli
artifizi che son comuni alle *femmine del suo carattere,* senza omettere
l' uso dei filtri, dei prestigi, e di tutto ciò che la credulità donnesca(4)
ha saputo imaginare d' inganni in tal genere ; una donna Giudea era
la fedele ministra di questi incantesimi, e il pubblico che imaginava i

of Spain, espoused at his suggestion, instead of the Archduchess he aspired to,
Leonora di Toledo, sister of that very Viceroy of Naples whose atrocious inhumanity is cited in note (1). She brought him a son or a daughter every year.
As D. Pietro married the daughter of D. Garzia, who was brother to this lady, it
follows that in the person of his wife he poniarded also his cousin-german.

(4) The E. of Bothwell had certainly nothing *womanish* in his composition,
though much that was devilish, yet we find him on his death-bed making a confession of having used "witchcraft" (*prestigi*) and "sweet-water" (*filtri*) to excite
the Queen's affections. See Miss Strickland's *Letters of Mary Q. of Scots,* etc.
Vol. III. I have been unable to procure a copy, and cite from a newspaper re-
view of 1843. Mary was the contemporary of Bianca. The *credulity* we might
say was that of the age, did we not know what is going on in our own skeptical
century, and in our matter-of-fact country, not to speak of France, where, succeeding to the spiritualism of Home, a common soldier of Jewish origin performs the
miracles on sick and lame and blind attributed to Christ.

più stravaganti mezzi per eseguirli *concepiva sempre più del orrore per il di lei perverso carattere.*" (*Ib.* 271.) Now let us hear what Botta says: "Bianca Capello, nata al mondo *per mostrare la potenza degli attrativi femminili* [observe throughout the parts I have italicized], e la laidezza di un uomo a cui era da Dio comandato non solo di governare, [I cannot see that Heaven had anything to do with it ; the government of the Medici was, as Botta himself has shown, an absolute usurpation founded in perfidy and corruption, and the family that administered it, from Alessandro down, were mostly worthless as princes and despicable or detestable as men,] ma di edificare un popolo atto ad ogni gentil creanza, [Varchi, who knew them better, being of them, in the reign of Cosmo, has ascribed to the Florentines no such aptitude,] *fuggiva* nel 1563, ec. *Bella e spiritosa e di grazie moltiformi dotata* (imperciocchè *o che scherzasse, o sopra sè stesse, o il leggiadro volto con sembianza di mestizia annuvolasse, sempre risplendeva in lei un cotal lume di avvenenza lusinghiera, di vaghezza ghiotta, che l' uom rapiva*) *aveva, ec.*" (*ubi cit.* p. 169.) Yet after this description of a beauty and grace that must have been all but irresistible and that he himself affirms *transported everybody*, — a description which, if we may judge by one trait, the "*vaghezza ghiotta*" (*charms that kindled appetite*), easily discernible in her portraits, (*v.* App. III.), is a faithful, though a lovely picture, — he pretends to say she had recourse to philters and to incantations to increase the passion of a man not yet forty ! However, of that presently. — The historian, with his usually sarcastic and often terrible pen, tells us that their loves were shamelessly open. "Non sentivano vergogna nell' amore : in fronte del popolo con modi scoperti il Principe il confessava, impudicizia ed impudenza regnavano.(5) Cosimo l'ammoniva" ——— a precious mon-

---

(5) I ask again, if their loves were so impudently shameless, how came it that, after the death of Joanna, Bianca was admitted to the palace under the plea of guardianship for the young princesses, and why the secret marriage ? These facts cannot be reconciled, as before observed (p. 360,) with open impudicity.(a)—But

(a) In that place, it is true, I expressed more than a doubt of my heroine's chastity in her widowhood. It seemed to me at the time incredible, that even the Cardinal in his "declaratory act" should have falsified

itor, even were there no Camilla! (*v.* Botta's own words on p. 378),
——"la principessa sposa piangeva"—— that is but supposition, a
fancy family-picture, though painted with an eye to nature(6), ——"e

suppose they can; suppose the Prince did indeed unveil his pas-ion to the
public gaze; when have princes done otherwise, in every land, and to our very
day? In moral, or at least morality-boasting, England, the children of law-
less royal love, whether gotten on a duchess or an actre-s, are ennobled, and the
bend sinister or *baton coupé* of the Earl or Duke stands not in the way of lawful
marshaling by pale or quarter with the proudest escutcheons. But in Italy! and
at that time! when half the petty thrones were file 1 by bastards, and where,
not forty years before, the child of three fathers, begotten on a wanton household-
drudge, was the first acknowledged sovereign of the "Illustrissima Casa"!
Galimatias!   .

(6) Not because the princess-spouse bewept his infidelity, for she knew that
offence was common with all princes, but because she felt it a reproach to her
own ill-favored visage, its pallor, and her dwarfish form. The whole picture, in-
cluding the monitions of the saintly Cosmo, is drawn from models of the imagination, and is what the reader has been familiar with in the nursery:

"In vain his father's kind advice,
In vain his mother's care," *etc.*

I have no idea of apologizing for incontinence, much less adultery; but I do maintain
that had Francesco been guilty of nothing worse than seeking solace with the
widow Bonaventuri, he would be judged at least as leniently as his contemporary
and posthumous son-in-law, that darling of all true hearts, the great Henry IV. of
France, who, but for his Minister, would have committed the same folly as Francesco (if in Francesco it was a folly to marry Bianca), and who, had he not had
that Minister, but a false and aspiring brother to shape for men his reputation,
might have come down to us in more questionable form, his vices all exaggerated,
and his frank, generous and valiant heart shrunken under their swollen heap to a
pitiful littleness. As it was, it is observable that the most mischievous aspersion
of his character came from the pen of his blood-relation the Princess of Conti.(a)

the date as well as other particulars of D. Antonio's birth. But when I c nsi ler what appears to have been
done in the account of the Duke and Bianca's illness, I see no good reason w' y, in the v ry face of the peo le,
that arch-maligner should not misrepresent the print of time in one case as well as in the other. See (24);
also subnote to (C).

(a) The handsome and talented Louisa-Margaret of Lorraine (gran laughter of that magnanimous and
valiant captain, Francis of Lorraine, Duke of Guise) in her *Histoire des Amours du grand Alcandre*, which

gli dava esempio d' ogni virtu"——what were they? She could not but of chastity, or she were as foul as her sister-in-law, who was neither pallid, nor diminutive, nor ill-favored, to render chastity easy, —— " ma nulla giovava, perchè la Bianca, col suo volto, *non so se mi debba dire angelico o diabolico.* era più forte del padre, della moglie, e di quanto il mondo pensasse o dicesse." (*ib.* 170, sq.) All of which is merely rhetorical. And now for the absurd story of the philters, and told thus absurdly : " *Oltre le grazie della persona——And what were these physical attractions, besides which, etc. ? Beautiful and spiritual and endowed with manifold graces* (these are his own words, above quoted,) — *since, whether she was mirthful or grave, or clouded her elegant and charming visage with a semblance of sadness, there always shone out in her such a light of seductive attractions, of appetible beauty,*

And who does not know what that very Minister, that virtuous Sully, whose friendship as well as administration honored both reciprocally, who does not know what he has told of the effect of Henry's amours, leading him, as they do every man, the honest and the good not excepted, into subterfuge and even falsehood? Unhappily for Francis-Mary, he had not what the historian of the Medicean duchy assigns him, *every quality that is desirable in a sovereign.* Had he had, and been *gracious and benevolent to his subjects,* he might have said at least what Henry said, who said most things wittily and well : " I am myself the best assurance for my people. My predecessor feared you and loved you not ; but I love you, and I have no fear of you." And in that case History would have looked, though sorrowfully, yet gently on his vices of habit and temperament, overshadowed as they were by those of Henry, both an inveterate gamester and, to the very last, incorrigible — I cannot say libertine ; it is not a word that suits a man like him, who probably found women lewd, not made them so ; but — to his latest day intemperate woman-lover.

bears the same satirical relation to the Court of Henry IV. as Bussi's *Histoire amoureuse* to the not less licentious one of Louis XIV. She too in her widowhood made, like Bianca, what the French call a *marriage of conscience* with one of her lovers, the famous Marshal Bassompierre : a fact worth noticing as tending to confirm by similitude of instance what, notwithstanding the brand of illegitimacy put upon Don Antonio, was perhaps the true state of things between the G. Duke and Bianca. Bianca was too scrupulous, or too proud, or too artful, whichever you will, to submit to his embraces except after a secret ceremony which satisfied the conscience. Unless it was performed from a moral and religious motive, or to cover her good name, I cannot see what was the use of such a rite. The public espousals could not in decency take place two months after the death of Joanna, but the secret nuptials did.

as ravished the beholder —— "Oltre le grazie della persona, usava
Bianca, per fomentare la passione del Granduca, i filtri, i prestigi ed il
ministerio di una Giudea, cui il mondo credeva esperta d' incantesimi,
ed era veramente d' inganni. La fattuchiera [*sorceress*] era *Bianca*,
non la Giudea." (*ib.* 171.) Thus, either from Galluzzi (for he uses
the same expressions), or directly from those Cardinalized archives
which awakened no suspicion with the former, we have Botta repeat-
ing with emphasis this puerile story, without at all being conscious
that in ascribing to Bianca such marvelous beauty and such entranc-
ing manners, he makes it nearly impossible, whatever her self-delusion
as to the actuality of sorcery, that she could have resorted to its fallacious assistance. What would be the object? If she already held the
Duke a slave to the double enchantment of her person and her mind,
— and Galluzzi tells us that his passion was continually increasing, —
where was the need of anything beyond ("oltre")? And *philters!*
for whom? The Duke on the day of his death was but forty-seven
years of age, or forty-nine, computing after Segni(7); and Botta is

(7) Who tells us Francesco was nine years old when sent to meet at Genoa the
Emperor's son Don Philip (afterwards Philip II. of Spain). And this was in the
year 1547. — *St. Fior.* t. ii. p. 879.

It has not escaped me, that the historians may mean that Bianca plied these arts
to keep the Duke from inconstancy. Indeed Galluzzi says as much (*sup.* 380), and
Muratori tells us, after a contemporary, that in the popular rumor which ascribed
the poisoning to Bianca, she was thought to have been urged by jealousy, being " a
woman of proud spirit." See *infra* 27. The Duke was then no longer under her
influence. Where then was his infatuation, or what was become of Bianca's
power? If they still existed, then she had no need of drugs and magic charms;
if they did not, and he became her slave to the degree which we shall shortly see
asserted, then his chains were forged by magic, and the eyes of the *angelic
visage* "rained influence " by the drugs!

In fact, nothing can be more contradictory than the accounts of both historians.
Galluzzi, besides his prejudice, is blinded by the Cardinal Grand-duke's Archives;
Botta is guided by that satiric spirit and prejudgment which see evil rather than
good and find a delight in making the picture more effective by its shadows, although

writing of a period eleven years earlier (1576). He was consequently at that time but thirty-six or at most but thirty-eight years old ; and if Bianca's sorcery was so notorious as to fill the city with horror, the Duke must have known of it. Are we to suppose then, that in the full vigor of his best manhood he suffered such practices ? If he had occasion for them, then his passion could not have gone on increasing ; for love the least sensual, as the most of it is wholly so, diminishes under such circumstances, if it does not become at once extinct. As for Bianca herself, we are told it was in 1563 that she fled from Venice. Supposing she was then eighteen,—though I would rather believe she was two or even three years younger, for women at eighteen are not so easily led astray by a first passion as when its stimulus is still a new and almost uncontrollable sensation, — supposing her to be eighteen at that period, she was then in 1576 but thirty-one. Where then, I repeat, was the use of sorcery and love-potions to urge a man deeply enamored, himself in the flower of his manhood, to greater passion for a woman who could not have lost a beauty that was at any time reputed marvelous, and who is said to have had such ravishing grace of manner and so seductive sweetness of look, that, whatever the mood she might be in, or might assume, she transported every heart ? But, not to carry mere argument too far on a point which so little deserves it, let us adduce the force of a parallel example. About a century and a half before this time, Valentina of Milan, Duchess of Orleans, a woman like Bianca beautiful and intellectual, was said to owe her influence over her brother-in-law, the unhappy Charles VI., to sorcery. She was even obliged to forsake the Court for some time to escape the insults of the populace, who probably were stimulated by the King's uncles and their wives, as in the case of Bianca they

at the expense too often of real nature and the observation of historic truth. It is to be observed, that it was after all the villany ascribed to her by both these writers, that they chronicle the secret marriage and the subsequent grand espousals with the coronation, both of which acts are the strongest evidence that the Grand-duke's passion had not abated.

were by the artifices of the Duke's brother. Calumny did not stop here, and to want of chastity in favor of the insane king added even the report of her poisoning him for the benefit of her husband !(8) But we are in the 19th century, three hundred years since Bianca lived and loved, and was adored—although we should hardly suppose it from the number of fortune-tellers who under various styles advertise the black art in the journals, — we are in an era of very general instruction and greatly increased freedom from superstition, yet what comes to us, even now while I write, from the land where the beautiful Venetian lived and was adored and finally suffered ? The spread of cholera is attributed to the malignity of evil-disposed persons, and an unfortunate woman in Naples who professed to be of the trade of Bianca's Jewess is actually cut into pieces as having been instrumental in its propagation. See then the people of Florence wondering at the extent of Bianca's influence, precisely as in that earlier age the people of Paris did at the elegant Visconti's, and in their blind amazement prompted to an easy explanation after their own mode of thinking by the Cardinal's agents, and you have the story.(9) The Jewess may have been a sorceress like her ancient compatriot, but was probably some female-nostrum vender, or woman's-doctor, possessed of (or so

(8) It was the handsome, dissipated, and ambitious Louis of France, her husband, whose actual dabbling with the fallacious art gave a color of truth-likeness to these scandals. Martin calls him "adepte temeraire des arts *damnables* de la magie." *Hist. de France.* (Paris, in 8°, 1844) t. vi. p. 263. See too *ib.* p. 269. And Henry IV. of England, in the last of his despatches, did not hesitate to accuse him, not her, of causing the malady of Charles VI. by *sorceries et diableries.* *Id. ib.* 301.

(9) If the people were filled with horror at Bianca's supposed practices, what protected her from their fury any more than Valentina? The fanaticism of a mob is the hideous growth of no peculiar age or country. The deformed and bloodthirsty giant was the same in the 16th as in the 14th century, and is the same in the 19th that he was in the 14th. Lola Montes was hooted and pelted in Munich, and so was her royal lover, who was neither *stupid* nor *cruel*, nor a *Medici ;* yet nobody ascribed his infatuation to anything supernatural.

claiming) secrets of embellishment and rejuvenation, a priestess of the thaumaturgy of the toilet ; but the stories set afloat are like, both in themselves and in their origin, those circulated, more than a hundred and fifty years before, against the fair and intellectual grandmother of Louis XII.(10) In fine, if Bianca was the victim of the self-delusion ascribed to her, her practices under it were to increase or secure the affections of her husband, of infidelity to whom there is not breathed against her even a suspicion. It is rather remarkable that while unwilling to ascribe the Grand-duke's excessive passion for Bianca to anything but her nefarious arts (how many would be glad to know them !) there is no thought of attacking Camilla Martelli for a like infatuation on the part of Cosmo, — Cosmo, the strong-minded,

(10) In Bianca's day, the belief in magic was still prevalent even among the educated. Not to cite again the credulity of Bothwell (who was however little more than a rude soldier), that popinjay of a king, yet gallant cavalier, half woman, half man, Henry III. of France, ashamed of his fantastical grief for Mary of Clèves, Princess of Condé, ascribed its excesses to enchantment. This was about the very period now in question, while, twenty-two years earlier, books on astronomy and geometry had actually been condemned in England as treatises of magic, notwithstanding the advances made there as elsewhere in both those sciences.

In the intervening age between Valentina and Bianca, or about a century before the latter's empoisonment, we find the usurper Richard laying his withered arm to the witchcraft of unhappy Shore. And less than a score of years after the latter, or in the first decade of the 17th century, Mary Stuart's son, James I. of England, a man something more than educated, was a good believer in witches; while in France Eleonora Galigai, the foster-sister and favorite of Mary of Medici (Francesco's daughter), was put to death, although in reality for her insolent presumption and the venal abuse of her influence, yet on the charge of practising sorcery.(a) And this was about the time when Galileo stood up in the Inquisition, before the slaves of ignorance and the children of superstition, to defend by subterfuge, or by fables which he believed not, the conceptions of his God-inspired mind.

(a) It is a coincidence that the chief point in the accusation against her was that she consorted with a Jewish doctor, familiar with the art.

politic, and resolute,—who was so mastered by his love that even his physicians could not keep him from that enchantress. (GALL. ii. 176.)

We now come to the "*nera perfidia.*" The Duke was anxious to have male children, and rather than not have any was contented they should be illegitimate. Bianca set to work to gratify him ; but her body being rendered unfruitful by sickness and dissipation ("disordini") she contrived this scheme. Three women of the vilest class (GALL.) or of vulgar standing (BOTTA), about to be confined, were engaged to part with their offspring. One of them only (providentially —in two respects) brought forth a male. This was carried, in a lute, to the bedchamber where lay the Duchess affecting, like our Mrs. Cunningham, a mother's throes. (The reader has heard of a musical instrument before as a vehicle of supposititious children to royal houses.) As the Duke was perpetually with Bianca we are told, up to the last moment. when on some pretext she sent him off, we are left to wonder by what subtilty of contrivance and by what good fortune she could deceive him as to her situation. I need not explain my meaning. Every man will comprehend it, without being read in gestation. Thus much however. A woman may feign pregnancy to strangers, but not to her husband. The "outward and visible signs" are such, that unless he were deprived of his eyes or had his arms amputated, the imposition would be impossible. Besides, the Duke in his ecstacy of expectation would have been the last man not to satisfy himself, in the innocent way that all curious expectant fathers do. I dare say he did a hundred times. (*Mensibus graviditatis jam firme exactis, superimposita prægnantis abdomini manu, motiuncula, quasi fœtûs tantillum subsultantis, sensibilis creberrime fiet.*) But let us suppose a miracle, and that the Duke could through six months be kept away from any contact with the woman he adored. Was the Cardinal too deceived ? We shall see presently how he acted upon the Duke's death. Botta however finds nothing wonderful in the transaction ; for, according to him, Bianca had the effrontery to tell the Duke himself of these false pretensions and that the little Antonio was but the son of a common man and woman of the country ! And the Duke. —*it was all one,* says that historian, *for the stupid and cruel Medici* (. . fu tuttuno per lo stupido e crudele Medici,") — was perfectly satisfied! He might well add, in this belief, "Se Francesco fosse più vile, o Bianca più furba, io nol saprei." (*v. cit.* p. 172). Now this *stupid Medici* (the epithet of *cruel* was out of place in the present matter) is pronounced by Galluzzi, in very positive language, to have been *the most accomplished as well as talented monarch of his time !*(11)   Let me make then

(11) *Cs. infra* (20.) — It will there be also found, that Sismondi, like Botta, deprives him of all talent as well as virtue. Where does the truth lie? What becomes of his known patronage of the arts? of science? of letters? Speaking of his taste and magnificence in the adornment of Florence, Galluzzi says : " Il gusto particolare de erigere nuove fabbriche e riparare e ingrandire le vecchie si distinse nel G. Duca Francesco superiormente alle altre sue inclinazioni." ii. 473 . . . . *Consequently,* he continues, *the fine arts flourished with no less splendor than in the reign of Cosmo, and elegance and good taste spread themselves every day more and more among private citizens.* ib. 474. In the text I have alluded to the famous Benvenuto Cellini. Galluzzi particularizes, in architecture, *Ammanato* and *Buontalenti,* in painting *Allori* and *Poccetti* (he might have mentioned others), and *Giovanni Bologna* in sculpture. The Grand-duke's disposition for these arts he chronicles as "singolare." 475. . . "Egli stesso, *come intelligentissimo delle medesime,* sovente ne ragionava con gli artefici e con i gentiluomini della sua Corte *ad oggetto d' inspirare nel pubblico il gusto di favorirle e l' inclinazione di professarle.*" (*ib.*) To him was owing the increase of the reputation and consequent growth of the Florentine Academy, out of which arose by separation, as in some organic creatures the offspring from the parent, in 1582 the *Crusca.* " Allo spirito nazionale ormai indirizzato da Cosimo alla letteratura e alli studi si aggiungeva L' INCLINAZIONE PARTICOLARE DEL G. DUCA FRANCESCO PER LE LETTERE E PER I DOTTI. *Like his father, he loved the domestic and familiar conversation of the most esteemed* [among the learned—"i dotti "], *and took pleasure in maintaining with the absent a confidential correspondence ; and therefore he failed not to honor, succor, and protect them in their occasions.*" . . . 477 *sq. The Grand-duke was versed in Natural History, and among its branches applied himself with especial diligence to Mineralogy and to Metallurgy.* 478. So with Botany. — He appreciated and favored writers of history. The two Universities of Tuscany flourished under him despite

this remark. A man may be wise, and learned, and have even knowledge of the world at large and of the female sex in particular, and
yet become the slave of passion. But, "in vain," as we are told,
"the net is spread in the sight of any bird"; and he would have
needed to be more than stupid, an idiot, a human beast, to give sanction to a trick which, apart from its disgusting wickedness, left still
the grand desire of his heart unsatisfied; for Francis wanted not an
adopted child, the product, although male, of unknown parents, but
a son of his own, and born to him by the woman he loved. And I
may say it would have been *impossible*, had Bianca revealed the truth,
that he would have sought to buy for this vulgar bantling a principality in Naples. Yet that he did this we are told by Botta, and Galluzzi
goes still further. Philip of Spain had thoughts of conferring Siena
on the strumpets-brood. Philip of Spain was not a fool, if history can
be tortured into satire to make Francesco one. What then could have
perverted his judgment, or seduced his not too easy faith (at least in
matters not religious)? Was there then any doubt as to the illegitimacy of Don Antonio? May he not have been born after the secret
marriage of the Duke, and the Archives have been made to tell another
story? The Cardinal's generosity was, to say the least, suspicious.
See (24). It was in allusion to this rumor of Philip's intention that
there occurred at first, in the scene between the Cardinal and Don
Pietro (*Act V. Sc. III.*), this passage:

> More, thou art wrong'd in the present: our sire's wealth
> Must make the nest warm for the cuckoo's brood.

the Inquisition, and, what deserves commendation, he himself *conferred, from his
own knowledge of persons and of the requirements of science, the professor-
ships*. When asked in 1581 by a monk (*Frate*) for the Chair of Philosophy in
Siena, he wrote back with his own hand that he *did not want monks in such
lectures* (" Frati in tal lezione.") ii. *ad fin*.

How with such evidence before him, and by himself recorded, Galluzzi could so
far forget his own portraiture of this enlightened Prince as to libel his entire
reign, can be explained only by a want of that philosophy which with benevolence
is the joint parent of charity.

How stands this Jezebel's bastard son Antonio?
Held by the people second to the throne,
With sixty thousand ducats annual income,
Fiefs, palaces, villas. Art thou touc'd? Why so;
'Twas well reminded. Hear then this. From Spain
I learn King Philip will bestow Siena
On this same brat, who flaunts with borrow'd right
Our boasted name.

    Don P. *That is not true.*

             Card. *Ask else*
Thy friend Dorara. Wilt thou not awake?

I thought the Cardinal's language would be ascribed, as I meant it, to his evil disposition and unprincipled designs. It was the hand of an unscrupulous enemy painting the object of his hatred with the darkest colors furnished by malevolence to his imagination. The passage however had to be sacrificed, because the words of Bianca in the final Scene,

     " I bear within me what might blast thy hopes,
     Could I but live so long to give it life,"

would have given verity to the imputation that this D. Antonio was born before her marriage with the Duke. But with these facts, taken from Galluzzi himself, of the extraordinary honor in which this boy was held, and of the wealth that was heaped on him, and which it will be seen the Cardinal Grand-duke did not take away, and of the principality designed for him by Philip, is it possible to suppose, that, let alone a positive illegitimacy, any such abominable transaction had taken place as that wherewith, through the malignancy and policy of Bianca's arch-enemy, the records have furnished Galluzzi and the inadequately perspicacious historians who with credulity or carelessness have adopted his views?(12)

(12) And it is not impossible that history, whose record is as often made up of falsehoods as of truths, if not oftener, has lent undesignedly its dangerous distortion, to what was already counterfeit, by copying without consideration the studied scandals of the times. What has our war of the Rebellion taught us? If, two

But let us follow the amazing story further. Bianca, who had confessed her shameless duplicity and to the great content of the stupid
Duke, yet wants to get rid of her accomplices in a secret action that
was no longer secret and whose results were satisfactory on all sides,
but the Cardinal's. So she has two of them secretly put to death and
their assistants removed by exile. But the chief person, a Bolognese
governess, is retained. By and by, she wishes to get rid of her also.
So she sends her back to Bologna; and, on the way, soldiers from
Florence set upon her, and she is mortally wounded. Her statement,
taken juridically, was to the effect that *she recognized the assassins
as Florentine soldiers and cut-throats of Bianca !*(13) This from the
lips of a dismissed servant—a woman too ! and a woman utterly unprincipled by her own confession, if, as she pretended, she had been
employed by Bianca to superintend the execution of her frauds. And
the precious document (observe !) is sent, not to Francis, but to the
Cardinal Ferdinand at Rome ! How it got into the Archives and remained there, was best known doubtless to the personage in whose
behoof it was concocted, — that is, if it was more than the revengeful
malice of an unworthy servant, sent away in disgrace. Certainly, it
was a roundabout way for Bianca to take with this one woman, Bianca
the " artful " as well as " spiritual," when she had so noiselessly rid
herself of all the rest.(14)   In what court of the United States, or of

hundred years hence, some historian should have had nothing to copy from but
the atrocious calumnies of Jefferson Davis and his so-called Ministers, and should
have found confirmation of the same in the congenial malice of most of the news-
papers of Great Britain and of France, what would be the record of the Union
Government ?

(13) . . " di aver conosciuto che il suo feritore *con altri compagni* erano soldati Fiorentini e sicarj della Bianca." GALL. ii. 273. — For what other purpose
did her lady use them? The Governess did not say. She must have been herself the supervisor of more iniquities than child-coinage, to be familiar with the
faces of the assassin-servants. And that simpleton Bianca. not to employ new
ones !

(14) It is not to be at all supposed that a woman of the Governess's position, if

Great Britain, is it, that such testimony would be taken as proof suffi-cient of the guilt of the suspected party, and the latter too unheard *
Yet it is precisely this ex-parte evidence that comes down to us as his-

any other, would travel from Florence to Bologna, a journey then of several days, alone, much less at a time when the whole confines were swarming as we have seen with freebooters. Even if without companions, she must have had a *rettu-rale*, or a guide and attendant if riding a mule.(a) At all events she could not have been alone; for we are told she caused herself to be carried to Bologna, being doubtless so far on her way thither as to be in the very midst of the masnadieri. What became then of her companion, escort, driver, or companions? Supposing that her murder was intended, it is evident that when one man could do the job effectually it would hardly have been committed to more than two (for that there were several is implied in the very words of the narrative). Yet they left her merely wounded! She had power still to travel, and strength when she arrived to make her deposition! This was bungling work. The truth of the story may be conjectured to be this: — The party of which the governess made one (travelers in those days, as now, or lately, in Italy, if they had no party, waited for their oppor-tunity to join one, but rarely if ever journeyed by themselves) were attacked by one of those bands of brigand-soldiers of which we have spoken as among the pests of Francesco's inefficient reign. Shots were fired to stop the party, or because of their resistance, as they probably traveled armed, and one of them — *archibu-sata*(b) — struck the woman. This was a fine opportunity for revenge on her part,

(a) It was about this time that coaches began to be of anything like frequent use in traveling; but even then they were reserved for persons of rank, and the introduction of them was looked upon with displeasure by sovereign princes, some of these forbidding their general employment by edict. When Segni speaks of a "retturale" (*vetturino*) in the story of the origin of Duke Alexander, the man's employers were princes. Henry of Navarre, when King of France, had but one carriage, and was obliged to do without, as he said on one occasion, when the Queen was using it.

(b) The arquebuse,* the first form of the musket, was a most uncertain, as clumsy and unwieldly weapon. Those that Philip II., of Spain, introduced into his army, required a forked rest to steady them; and it is reasonable to suppose that these huge matchblocks, carrying a very heavy ball, were the kind adopted by Francesco. This adds to the absurdity of the idea of sending out assassins so armed. Poor Bianca! they will not allow thee even sense in thy diablery! Fancy a band of these arquebusiers making ready to shoot a governess, who of course stands still to accommodate them, while, perched on eminences in the various long distances of the future, three historians are gravely taking notes!— We see too, that with such a weapon the probability is increased of the woman's having been wounded by accident, or by divergence of the ball.

* Webster, in his derivation of this word, is in the clouds, where he gropes too often for a composite ety-mon. It does not signify a hook-gun, nor for that matter a gun at all in the sense in which we use that word. The "arquebuse" was the direct successor of the crossbow or arbalist (*balestro*), and therefore popularly, inevitably I might say, took the name of *hollow* or *tube bow*. "Archibuso: cioè arco busio, ovvero bucato. Arco, perchè succede alle balestre, e a' verretoni, e agli archi degli antichi." *Abat.* SALVINI. Not. nel *Tratt.* 7°. della Ling. Tosc. del Buommattei. ed. Mil. 1807. I. 208.

tory, unsustained even on its own side by one solitary proof of actual guilt. And for this, alas, we read in life-dictionaries, some of them of great repute, of the *artful and cruel* Bianca! —. Herein she is more unfortunate than her unhappy contemporary Mary Stuart, whose imputed complicity in the assassination of her husband has more than one rebutting evidence coexistent with the charge itself. (15)

even if she were not put up to her villanous aspersion by an agent of the Cardinal's, who appears to have had emissaries and secret servants everywhere.

(15) What Hallam has said of a corresponding character of the 14th century, is worth observing. "The name of Joan of Naples has suffered by the lax repetition of calumnies. * * * The charge of dissolute manners, so frequently made, is not warranted by any specific proof or contemporary testimony." *State of Europe*, etc. v. i. p. 467 (N. Y. in 8°. 1863.)

Between Joanna and Mary Stuart there is considerable resemblance, both in individual traits of person and of character and in certain conspicuous points of their histories. Each was suspected of conniving at the murder of her husband, and each confirmed the suspicion with most minds (but, I think, illogically,) by marrying the principal assassin.(a) And between all three of the personages before us, the contemporaries Mary and Bianca and their quasi-prototype of two centuries before, there is the common point of a calumniated character. Yet Joanna whom Hallam thus partially exculpates was probably the most condemnable of all three. Does not everybody know of his own experience private instances of detraction, and of misapplied accusation of crime or misconduct whereof the really guilty party escapes all censure? History is but a repetition on a large scale and before the world of what transpires in the narrow and obscure circle of familiar intercourse.

(a) This is not the place to argue such a point, but, writing for the future, I take up space to assert that a woman, who had been privy to the murder of her husband, would not, — except she were of the very lowest order of humanity and of the most degrading associations, — have consented, of free will, to marry his assassin.

Shakespeare, in a grotesquely unnatural scene, makes *Lady Anne* to be won by *Gloster* even while the usurper confesses to have killed her husband. This is natural enough in the result of his wooing, as commented on in his soliloquy, and only unnatural because of the exaggeration in brevity of time, and that lack of every consideration of propriety of language, manner, and sentiment which is a frequently occurring fault of that great poet. It is natural, I say, so far as the influence of such a suit on the mind of a vain, ambitious and weak woman; but then Anne of Warwick had not been privy nor consenting to the murder of Edward. A case absolutely to the point; for the widow of Prince Edward did marry his chief murderer. And the tyrant would have also had the Princess Elizabeth his niece, had the latter consented; for her mother was willing to betroth her to the butcher of her own three sons and of her husband. Yet none would be so mad as even to suspect Anne or the Queen Dowager of complicity in any of these assassinations.

Remember, all these foul accusations are made, not against a vulgar,
ignorant, and low-minded woman, but one who by the united testimony of her worst defamers was, like Mary herself, gifted with
intellect as well as beauty, and was moreover of a lofty spirit,
although what to one writer is simply lofty becomes, in the vituperation of another, haughtiness and insolent presumption. Add to this,
that Francis, whether "cruel" or not, was still a Medici, that he had
suffered, if not sanctioned, the assassination of his own sister and of
his brother's wife for their debauchery, and would hardly have en-
dured, above all he a man not indifferent but passionately enamored,
therefore liable to jealousy, and one who, according to Galluzzi, *never*
forgave, any departure from chastity by Bianca. As I have said, there
is no suspicion breathed against her except what may be gathered
from a vague and uncertain epithet or phrase.(16) Had there been
cause, a single example, the historians would not have failed to

(16) All of Galluzzi's terms and epithets show what a view he had taken of
Bianca's character; and Sismondi follows him without distrust ("l'artificense et
débauchée"); while Botta, according to his manner, with intensity of accumula-
tive sarcasm, treats us to this extraordinary satirical climax, on the occasion of
Bianca's coronation: "Addì dodici d' ottobre la scappata di Venezia, la doppia
adultera d' un marito legittimo e di una moglie legittima(a), la stipendiatrice di
un' Ebrea ribalda, l' ucciditrice di tre donne chiamate da lei a finto parto(b) fu
portata trionfalmente con la corona in testa." *t. c.* 174. One would think that
where Eleonora and Isabella lent examples of royal dissoluteness, where Don
Pietro sinned against nature, and Francesco (as said) retailed the poisons of his
father's private shop, Bianca might have been reserved for the middle tints of the
picture, nor made to bear its broadest sunlight and intensest shadow; but the

(a) One instance is not proved. For the other, nine hundred and ninety-nine women out of a thousand
would in the same circumstances have done as I suppose the widow of Bonaventuri may have done, and the
thousandth would have thought she was doing no harm in committing adultery with the eyes. This, in any
age and any country. And Botta, if he knew mankind as he ought to have known, must have been aware
of this, call it weakness, or depravity, (and it is both). Why then launch into such special vituperation
against this one calumniated head? Christ would have turned round on her accusers and written in the
sand.

(b) I need not repeat, where was the use of slaying them, if Bianca did not hesitate to reveal the plot?
Botta here, in his love of verbal painting and epigrammatic force, forgets probability, if not ignores his own
assertions.

quote it, and we may rest assured that in her relations as Grand-duchess she did nothing to lessen the devotion of her lord, a devotion which taking the archival record of his death as veritable (which I do not) was evidenced, even in the belief of his enemies, by his latest breath. *Cons.* y. 1587.

One word more. The account of Bianca's foisting a spurious off-spring on the Grand-duke is renewed, in the form of a suspicion, on every recurrence of her pregnancy. The historians endeavor to jus-tify their aspersion by her supposed sterility, a supposition which ap-pears to rest on no reasonable foundation. Bianca, to have the grace that is ascribed to her by her calumniators, must have been perfectly well-made, and was therefore fitted by nature for reproduction. She had born a daughter (Pellegrina) to her first husband. What ground was there for supposing that married to the Duke, a member of a pro-lific family, and who had had children by the feeble, stunted and pallid Joanna, she should suddenly lose fecundity? *v.* under yy. 1586, 1587. Galluzzi, we have seen, says she had become sterile through the use of medicines and by dissipation ; and Botta repeats, with an addition, — " Per medecine, per disordini, per corrutela." These assertions must be, at the strongest, conjectural ; but what do they mean ? There is, I repeat, no one charge, no suggestion even of incontinence on her part, not a word said of intemperance : and merely high-living would not produce sterility, nor would obesity, unless it were natural and not the result (if it ever be) of intemperate living. Are such vague charges to be admitted without one syllable of proof? and of all the contemporary writers, edited and unedited, is there none to back these attestations with a single instance ? Let them then be dis-missed as the malice of her arch-enemy and the inconsiderate abuse of those who are not her friends. To prove Bianca sterile there was a powerful motive ; to assert that she was so is not to prove it. This

spirit of the dead Cardinal hovered over the name he had made infamous and sought to obliterate, and added his immortal hatred to the sarcasm of a pen cruel at times as the poison, the halter, or the knife, of the writer's hated Medici.

talk of sterility caused in a married woman of thirty by her dissipation may do for the 16th century, but will not for this.(17) If Bianca, after producing Pellegrina, really was incapable of bearing more children, it was the defect of her organization and had nothing to do with her course of life. But the probability is, that that vile poisoner, the second son of the poisoner Cosmo, was only at his father's practices. What were the colic spasms which took off, once before, his brother's hope of issue by Bianca? It may have been even that the premature delivery of Joanna (see y. 1573) was some of his doing.(18) He knew not then that his brother would wed Bianca ; and it is certain that his rage at that disappointment of his hopes was greater than was decent. See, as before, yy. 1586, 7. These terms "disordini," "coruttela," "medicine," were, I little doubt, invented by the Cardinal or his partisans to substantiate the accusation of the plot, and to justify the assertion that her various pregnancies were simulated.

Finally, the Duke, who, according to Botta, knew that this was a supposititious child, recommends him, according to Galluzzi, to the care of the Cardinal, and the Cardinal Grand-duke, as I have twice implied and as will be seen presently, takes care of him, and suffers him to enjoy the name he thought too good to be defiled by a child of the Senator Capello! In fact, the whole thing is an absurd jumble. I believe the facts are just as I have given them in the play. If that be romance, never did romance in my opinion come so near to history, as surely in this episode of the House of Medici never did history borrow so much from romance.

Joanna died the 11th of April, 1573, — "attraversatosi il feto *già* 1578 *morto* nell' utero," —not having strength to sustain the remedies of art. (*Granduc.* ii. 299.) This was nearly two years *after* the deaths of Isabella and Eleonora. Noble, whom for obvious reasons I have followed in the text, says she died April 6, 1578, in premature

(17) Witness the present Queen of Spain.

(18) I am speaking with due reflection, when I say I do not believe the Cardinal was in anywise too good to have abused his intimacy for that purpose.

labor, shocked by the murder of Isabella and Eleonora, who were both strangled on the same day. Galluzzi would have it that the honors paid to Vittorio (Bianca's brother) on coming to Florence contributed to Joanna's death. (19)

.. "Era [Joanna] di piccola statura, di faccia pallida, e di aspetto non vago." (*ib.* p. 299.) The Cardinal a great favorite of Joanna's. [We may suppose him therefore fomenting the dissatisfaction of the people, who, we are told, libeled the Duke while they praised the Duchess.] This period was the epoch of the fiercest discord between the brothers, "non più velata dalla dissimulazione ma ratificata al pubblico da molte apparenti dimostrazioni." (*ib.* 300.)

Antonio e Piero Capponi and Bernardo Girolami, the most distinguished of the rebels who had acted with Pucci and Ridolfi, fled to France, where they openly defamed Francesco. And the Cardinal maintained constant relations with that country. (*ib.*) Here too Galluzzi shows a spirit of animosity to Francesco ; for he says that the desire of vengeance, "passione predominante nelli spiriti deboli," [a false assumption and contradicted by his own example, not to say of the Cardinal, yet of Cosmo, whose mind was anything but a weak one] animated him to put an end to the chief conspirators there. [Yet he had endeavored to disarm Orazio Pucci by numerous benefits, and it was the Cardinal who suggested the arrest of this hereditary rebel.] Curzio Picchena da Colle was Secretary of the Embassy, a young and enterprising man. He was provided with poison, etc. Forty thousand ducats promised for each death, *besides expenses !* (*ib.* 301.) This too Sismondi, who adds: "Il lui [le G.-d. à Picchena] fit passer des poisons subtils, dont Cosme 1er *avait établi dans son palais une manufacture,*

---

(19) We are reminded of the avowal or boast, — "all extracted faithfully from the Medicean Archives." The singleness of his sources of information tends to render Galluzzi's volumes unreliable as a history.

It will be elsewhere seen, that a modern writer has found in the same Archives evidence sufficient to overthrow *all*, and absolutely, the opinions previously formed as to the character of that abominable woman, Caterina de' Medici! They must be, as he says, *a precious deposit of historical documents !*

qu'il prétendait être un atelier de chimie pour les expériences "; and so on, after Galluzzi. *Répub. Ital. t. 10. p. 226 sq.* — Girolami died, and the rest [mark this !] lay the murder on the Duke ; of whose criminality Galluzzi adduces no one proof. They, the conspirators, dispersed themselves in France and England ; but the cut-throats of the Grand-duke followed them and "in course of time gave him all the satisfaction he desired."(21) A Florentine assassin, broken on the

(20) We have seen how Botta speaks of Francis, — *the stupid and cruel Medici.* Sismondi's summing-up of his character is as follows: "François, tout aussi perfide, tout aussi cruel, que son père, mais bien plus dissolu(a), bien plus vaniteux,

(a) Than Cosmo! who was said, on more than suspicion, to have debauched both his own daughter and the betrothed of his son. Where are the victims of Francesco's lust ? We hear of none but Bianca, who is reproached with having made him hers ! And for her his passion, which in 1576 had already lasted thirteen years, showed no abatement. This in itself is inconsistent with the charge of dissoluteness, which supposes indulgence in various amours, and cannot apply to one attachment, whether sanctioned by the Church or not.

In note (11) I quoted largely from a special chapter of Galluzzi's showing that in the particulars that made Cosmo's reign illustrious Francesco's was not less splendid than his.* We are told there, besides, that the former spent whole days in the galleries of his art-collections. With such a record, he could not have been dissolute were he married to half a dozen Biancas and enamored of them all. In dissoluteness man gives up his brain. The abuse of those life-energies which God designed, as with other animals, but for the reproduction of the kind, is incompatible with continued study and such application to the interest of the arts and of learning as we have seen ascribed, with compulsory truth, to the G. Duke Francis.

In every drawing of an historical character, consideration should be had to the manners of the time. We shall presently see what were the morality and decency of the Court of Catharine of Medici. The Bassompierre incidentally mentioned in a previous passage, who bridges over for us in this relation the end of the 16th and the beginning of the 17th century, is an evidence that the profligacy of persons of rank in the era I am busy with was not evanescent either in its grossness or its excessive turpitude. That favorite of Henry IV., and ornament of the Court of Louis XIII., confessed to a ruffianly complicity in the most brutal of all outrages; an act for which he came nearly being stoned, as he deserved to be fully, by the people of the place of the occurrence.† This was in 1604, seventeen years after the death of Francesco, who is handled by historians as if he were the only sinner, where in his position there was scarcely any other class. So with his alleged cruelty : it was the characteristic of the age. Henry III. of France, a prince who, though debauched by the devilish artifices of a bad mother — a Medici, was not without virtues, got rid of two dangerous enemies, the Duke and the Cardinal of Guise, by assassination. This was in 1588. In 1589, he was himself murdered.‡ In 1584, William of Orange underwent the same fate in the Netherlands. Not thirty years before (1555-6) occurred in England the burning of the heretic bishops and other reforming clergy, while Scotland was defiled in 1547 by the murder of Cardinal Beaton, of Rizzio in 1566 and of Darnley in 1567. In 1520 took place the massacre of the

* I am not claiming for it beneficence, nor wisdom. The money bestowed in collecting, at extravagant prices, treasures of ancient art in statuary and in medals alone, should have been rather devoted to his people's solid advantages. But neither was Cosmo in the least degree beneficent ; and compared with his reign who bears the either of *Great*, in what is Francis' less honorably conspicuous, even by Galluzzi's own acknowledgment ? The strong animal blood of the Medici was as productive of vices and of crimes (taking the record at the worst) in one as in the other.

† Happily, the villany designed was not consummated, although the outrage was. See his own Memoirs, ap. Pet.tot, t. XIX. (Paris 1822) p. 323. As he was rewarded for his vile complaisance by an honor that gratified his vanity as a courtier, we may suppose that his compunction — (" ce que je fis a grand regret, et ces pauvres filles pleuraient " —) was stifled by one of the meanest of motives.

‡ To the great joy of his Catholic subjects, and of the Pope, Sixtus V., who " feared not to sanction in cold blood, in full consistory, the regicide . . and elevating the name of James Clement above those of Judith and Eleazar Maccabeus, compared the miraculous event to the Incarnation and the Resurrection of the Lord "! MARTIN (after De Thou): *Hist. de France*, ed. c., t. xi. p. 210, note.

wheel, confessed to having been sent expressly into France by the G. D. to murder Troilo Orsini [one would have thought the D. of Bracciano had been the more likely instigator] for six thousand ducats, and after-

bien plus irascible que lui [how does this accord with his dissimulation, as Galluzzi states it?], *n'avait aucun des talents par lesques Cosme 1ᵉʳ avait fondé sa grandeur* [it was something more than *talents* Cosimo employed]. Aussi fut il, plus encore que lui, l'objet de la haine des peuples, et cette haine n'était mêlée d'aucun *sentiment de respect pour son habileté.*" *R. It.* t. 10. p. 225. Galluzzi, inconsistent with himself, writes in positive contradiction to all the chief points in ' ' repulsive picture. After saying he was the greatest dissembler of all princes, ... able with his inferiors, and with his equals haughty to the degree of wishing their humiliation, he declares on the other hand, his laws show him to have been a Prince *just and impartial, an enemy of corruption,* "*amorevole con i suddetti*" [reconcile this to the "inexorable, etc." above, for I can not], *e fornito di tutte quelle qualità che si desiderano in un Regnante.*" If he was *furnished with all those qualities which are desirable in a sovereign,* what are we to

nobles in Sweden. The atrocities of that pious hypocrite and sanguinary egotist, that superlative compound of all that is vile in the priesthood and odious in kings, Philip II. of Spain, who could not die without a fourteen-times-repeated sacrament, the atrocities perpetrated or sanctioned by him everywhere where his power extended, from the privacy of his palace to the utmost reach of his wide dominion (1556-1598), are familiar to the history-class of every school. And in 1572 took place the Massacre of St. Bartholomew, when the groans of thousands of butchered heretics made music to the ears of Satan, and echoed so delightful to the fancy of Gregory XIII., that, not content with celebrating the glorious event by cannon-firing, illuminations and a solemn procession to the churches of a God of Peace, he had a medal struck, in which the Destroying Angel on one side was balanced by his own bust on the other.* Everywhere blood, blood; and blood shed tyrannically, barbarously, basely. But centuries make no difference in the record of human crime. Two hundred and ninety years after the infernal blood-bath of St. Bartholomew, a traitorous part of the low Irish in this city enacted in a narrower shambles, on inoffensive blacks, the God-defying butchery which the papistical zealots perpetrated on Coligni and his coreligionists, — crushing out their brains with stones and suspending their quivering bodies to lampposts, and, with a savageness of fury that cannot be called vindictive rage, beating to death, dragging through the kennels, and hanging up his muddy, half-eviscerated and scarcely-recognizable remains, their own countryman who in his military office was man and citizen enough to adhere to his duty, — and this from no religious antipathy, but from a latent envy, mingled strangely with barbarous contempt, and roused to violence by partisan hatred of the great government that protected them and enabled them to obtain from a corrupt and semi-foreign municipality, disloyal like themselves, their absurd privileges. Two years later, after acts of atrocious inhumanity committed in cold blood by the despairing Rebels, and wanton piracies, and robbery, and schemes of disgusting villany for the conflagration of great cities and the introduction into them of the desolation of pestilence, occurred by the hand of a political fanatic the death of President Lincoln, even such a murder as those of Henry III. and IV. of France and William of Orange. Were I to write one word as the Finis of the universal history of mankind from fabulous Adam down, — a word that should express the lesson to be gathered for man's hope of moral betterment, — it would be —— DESPAIR.

* The Holy Father, who saw the necessity of reforming the Calendar for the sake of the Church, had no idea of a reformation in the Church itself. So, in addition to other signs of approbation, the aged apostle of peace and good-will unto men caused a picture to be made of the massacre and exhibited in the Vatican " en lieu très-apparent et honorable ", where, according to M. Martin, it stimulates devotion still. *B.* 597 sq.

ward retained for other murders. He said moreover that the Ambassador and Secretary had frequent interviews with him for the purpose. [All this, remember, on the assertion of a hired assassin. But it is certainly an extraordinary indication of the state of the times in which such an accusation could be made against an ambassador.] The Secretary (Picchena) in consequence was arrested. Out of friendship however for the Medici he was released, but banished perpetually. *Granduc.* ii. 325, sq. See remonstrances of the Queen of France on this murder of Trollus, etc. *ib.* p. 336. (21)

think of those aspersions upon his rule, and upon his character both as a man and a prince, which are read not only in Sismondi as above and furnish material for the gloomy etchings of Botta, but are scattered throughout his history by Galluzzi himself? "*I suoi talenti e le sue cognizioni erano certamente superiori a quelle di qualunque Principe dei suoi tempi, ec. ec.*" *Granduc.* ii. 423. It is impossible to get over the positiveness of this declaration, which moreover is maintained by an enumeration of the accomplishments for which the historian claims this superiority of Francis-Mary in talent and in knowledge to all the Princes of his time. Those who are curious in the matter will find on consulting his second volume, *Cap. X.*, such a record of Francesco's devotion to the fine arts, to the embellishment and renown of Florence through them, his encouragement of learned men, his own acquirements in the sciences, as will not only make them marvel at Galluzzi's prejudice, but pronounce the assertion of Sismondi, that the people's hatred of Francesco was qualified by no sentiment of respect for his abilities, a monstrous misrepresentation. *v. supra* (11).

(21) This was the Queen-Mother, Catharine of Medici, whom I have alluded to as lending her aid to the worst and most indecent debaucheries that ruined what was good in Henry III.(a) A detestable woman, the chief promoter if not instigator of the Massacre of St. Bartholomew(b), whose horrors she contemplated with

(a) In all her policy, Catharine made great use of handsome women and amorous intrigue, having always about her a swarm of *brilliant and facile beauties* (the phrase is M. Martin's), who went familiarly by the factious name of her *flying squadron* — "l'escadron volant de la Reine." MART. *Hist.* X 75.

(b) Charles was full of hesitation, and even of horror as the hour approached; but Catharine stood by his side, his evil monitor, and when argument failed roused the devil of his nature by impeaching his manhood. *Id.* (after D'Aubigné), *ib.* 370. Alberi however, a life-writer presently to be cited, maintains not only that neither of them desired or provoked the massacre, but that both used their utmost power to moderate its excesses! *Vit.* ut inf. p. 105.

Bianca, while the Grand-duke treated the Cardinal harshly,
1580 acted with great suavity and an appearance of affection and
submissiveness. — The Cardinal wanting money, and Francesco refusing an anticipation of his revenue, Bianca procured the

perfect indifference.(c) Daughter of Lorenzo, Duke of Urbino, and niece of
Giulio, Clement VII., even her merits, like her vices, were those of her family.
That she should remonstrate against the poisoning of Troilus could have been
only because, under the circumstances, it insulted her supremacy(d), not from
scruples of conscience ; for her hand, the Medici hand, was recognized in the sudden deaths of Jane of Navarre and Mary of Clèves, and some suspected even that
she poisoned her own son Charles IX.(e)

(c) She did something more, and the historian cites it as an evidence of the depravation of morals in her
Court : " On vit les filles d'honneur de la reine mère, et Catherine elle-même, examiner, avec des remarques
obscènes, les corps dépouillés des gentilshommes huguenots de leur connaissance." ib. 550. The example
is one rather of the horrible callousness to which the common cruelty of the age had brought even the gentler
and timid sex. As for the feminine remarks, they too are rather an illustration of the coarseness of the
time than of its licentiousness : it was depravity simply naked and shameless ; for, save in the closeness and
the adornment of its drapery, the carnal-spirit, or beast-man, is much the same in all ages.

But that ingenuous and pleasant chronicler, Pierre de l'Estoile, in his curious but valuable medley, Journal
de Henri III. (Mem. pour servir &c., in Petitot's Collection, t. 45, p. 78,) tells us something more startling than
even this indecent cruelty. Catharine, it seems, was not at all behind certain of her noble subjects, who
availed themselves of the pretext, often false, of heresy, to put to death their own relations, in order to get
possession of their property, — what might be called a natural concomitant and consequent of such commo-
tions, wherein right and wrong are often, both by accident and by design, confounded. " En ce tems [just
after the St. Bartholomew] la bonne dame Catherine, en faveur de son mignon de Rets, qui vouloit avoir la
terre de Versailles, fit étrangler aux prisons Lomenie, Secretaire du Roy, auquel ladite terre appartenoit, et
fit mourir encore quelques autres pour recompenser ses serviteurs de confiscations."

(d) She so avowed indeed to the G. Duke's Secretary . . . " perche il G. D. non tien conto di me, anzi con
tanto displacer mio e del Re ci ha fatto ammazzare sugli occhi Troilo Orsini ed altri, che non ci par ben fatto,
essendo questo Regno libero, e che ognuno si può stare." loc. cit.

It is curious to note how the powerful animal character of the Medici is traceable even in the females. As
a rule, children take more after their mothers than their fathers, but both in Catharine and in Mary of Medici
we have the traits, not of the mother's blood but of the father's, while Charles IX. of France may be thought
to have derived his evil dispositions from his mother, as undoubtedly they were encouraged, intensified, and
brought into frightful action by that unprincipled and pitiless woman.

(e) L'Estoile has preserved for us a rather indifferent epigram of the time on Catharine, which compares.
her to Jezebel. It concludes thus :

" Enfin le jugement est tel :
Par une vengeance divine,
Les chiens mangerent Jezabel ;
La charogne de Catherine
Sera differente en ce point,
Car les chiens n'en voudront point." Coll. cit. t. 47. p. 80.

These who would see how an Italian in Florence, having at heart the honor of its once ruling family, and
writing, in this century as did Galluzzi in the last, under the auspices of a Grand-duke of the Austrian House,
and moreover an ardent Roman Catholic, has sought to explain away all the facts which have been brought
to bear against both Catharine of Medici and Charles IX., may consult Eugenio Albèri, in Vita di Caterina
de' Medici ; Firenze, in 4to. 1838. The writer says in his Preface : " Mi son trovato condotto a rovesciare
tutte le opinioni finora ricevute intorno a lei, ec." (an extensive undertaking) ; and paying special honor to

favor for the Cardinal, who thereupon came to Florence to show reconciliation. *ib.* 333.

The bands of predatory soldiers, who were protected secretly by the Church-feudatories, — nay, sometimes openly assisted them, so that, says the writer, " la depravazione facea apprendere l' assassinamento come un esercizio cavalleresco," — added to the troubles. The most famous of these wretches was Pietro Leoncillo da Spoleti, supposed son of the Cardinal Farnese, who with a band of four hundred miscreants in various squads infested the frontiers. *ib.* 340.

1583
1584 The Cardinal dissembling "affects confidence and friendship with the Grand-duchess." *ib.* 382.

One of the Grand-duke's favorites at this time was the Auditor of the Treasury, Carlo Antonio del Pozzo, universally hated for his severity in office, but of rare learning and acute intellect and aptitude for emergencies, which compelled esteem. This office he held in 1572 —— Promoted in 1582 to the Archbishopric of Pisa —— Conducted himself always with rectitude and disinterestedness, and, showing gratitude to the Cardinal to whose favor he owed his first steps in goodfortune, he used his influence with both to maintain their brotherly unity. Such a man could not always please *the corrupt and weak*

the *Archivio Mediceo* . . " quel prezioso deposito di storici documenti " — wherein, he says, " con esito corrispondente alla aspettazione, mi e venuto fatto di rinvenire gravissime ed irrefragabili testimonianze in favore del nuovo criterio ch' io già mi era formato di Caterina de' Medici," he proceeds to assert that the crimes imputed to her will be found *all* to resolve themselves into the injustice of the two factions she endeavored to conciliate, but which were emulous in her vilification.

Having myself endeavored to redeem the character of *Bianca Capello* from the calumniation of personal enemies, I could not but look with interest upon this effort in a similar, yet in point of facts contrary, direction. He has massed together a variety of interesting documents both as to the two chief personages of his *Essay*, as he modestly calls it, and to characters with them historically connected intimately or remotely ; but he fails to overthrow, and indeed avoids attacking any one of those facts which are adduced, not by partisan or Protestant writers, but by contemporaries and plain chroniclers who not only present internal evidence of probity, but are universally admitted to be reliable. Catharine of the Medici must, for all the industry and patriotism of her countryman, remain a Medici, — dissolute, dissembling, intriguing, inordinately as selfishly ambitious, false of tongue and frigid in heart, cruel, unscrupulous, remorseless ; her very merits, as I have elsewhere intimated, the merits of her father's family where best, — talented, adroit, resolute, audacious, magnificent in the use of wealth, whose resources she but valued for the purposes of her policy and the real or supposed lustre of her iniquitous administration. A bad mother, and wicked among the wickedest of queens, she ruined body and soul two monarchs, both her sons, and has left for herself a renown indelible as that of the Massacre with which it is associated, and, since undivided, even more infamous.

Francis. — Abbioso, having now returned from Venice, because of
the rupture with that Republic, professed himself openly the enemy
of the Cardinal, to whose hostility he attributed his difficulty in getting
the Coadjutorship of the Bishopric of Pistoia at Rome, "per esser
guercio e difforme." But the new Archbishop of Pisa knew how to
preserve the esteem of all parties. Affecting [note in this sentence
the contradiction to what is said above of his constant rectitude and
disinterestedness] to make the Duke and Bianca " gli arbitri di tutte le
parti graziose del suo ministro, e mostrandosi esemplare e zelante, si
acquistava opinione di santità e si preparava la strada al Papato."—
The Cardinal dissembling, but ill-satisfied with this position of affairs ;
——and Francesco, showing openly disregard of his dissatisfaction,
augmented the boldness of his ministers and more exasperated his
brother. (ib. 388–390.)

1585   Cardinal Ferdinand causes the election of the Cardinal Peretti
as Sixtus V., and becomes thus omnipotent with the new Pontiff.

At the marriage of Donna Virginia with Don Cesare d'Este [sub-
1586   sequently Duke of Modena], appeared her mother, the beautiful
Camilla Martelli, after a confinement of twelve years. The Cardinal and D. Pietro courted her continually and induced the chief
people of the city to honor her, in order to disgrace the Grand-duke.
p. 404. *The rumored pregnancy of the Grand-duchess induced the two
to return to Florence to watch events.* — Grand-duke shuts up again
Camilla, moved especially thereto by the secret visits of his brothers
to her. p. 405. *The brothers correspond on the reputed pregnancy of the
Grand-duchess — profess to each other suspicions that she is going to
impose a supposititious child upon the G. D., to shut them out of the succession. p 406.* D. Pietro appears throughout the dupe of the Cardinal.

1587   The Cardinal, appearing to be reconciled, sent a gentleman, his
confederate, to Florence, to announce his presence in Sep-
tember. The historian says : " Facilitó maggiormente questo ac-

comodamento l'essersi ormai assicurato [Francesco] della vanità delle
sue speranze, poichè la gravidanza della Granduchessa si era già
disciolta *con una colica e non senza grave pericolo della sua vita* [ob-
serve this !] di modo che il caso di aver prole era ormai disperato."
ib. 419. If the pregnancy was assumed, why was the deceit ended ?
I should rather have suspected that the *colic*, which *put seriously
in peril her life*, was the result of poison administered through the
impulsion of one whose interest was involved in the *vanity of the
Duke's hopes.* ·

The Cardinal arrives October 1 —— Received with every mark of
affection and cordiality —— Went immediately with his brother and
the Grand-duchess to Villa del Poggio at Caiano — where it was customary to resort for the chase every autumn —— *Grand-duchess exerts
herself to make a sincere union between the two brothers* —— On the 8th
October, Grand-duke attacked with fever, which the physicians pronounced to be tertian —— Two days after, the Grand-duchess with the
same. — Besides the Court-physicians, Baldini and Cappelli, the Cardinal's physician, Giulio Cini, rendered his assistance. They kept the
malady concealed at first, but nevertheless confused rumors got abroad.
It was reported to the Pope, the Grand-duke had made himself sick
with eating mushrooms. But on the 10th October, it was written, *he
had a continual fever and excessive thirst.* (*ib.* 423.) On the ninth
day, the fever increased, and death ensued, October 19th. "Volle
sempre medicarsi a suo modo con cibi e bevande gelate [the desire
for *food* would be caused by the gnawing pain in his stomach, and for
the *iced drinks*, why not ?], e siccome nel corso della malattia dimos-
trò *una sete ardentissima*, fu creduto che morisse arso dai cibi e bevande
calide delle quali faceva uso assai smoderato."(22) When he knew

(22) I suppose this case of Bianca and the Grand-duke, as well as that of the
Cardinal Ippolito, to be one of poisoning by arsenic (*see* Taylor as before
cited, chap. xxiii. p. 252 sqq). According to that English toxicologist. arsenic,
though it irritates and inflames. has no chemical or corrosive action on the viscera,
although on p. 255 one doubtful instance is recorded of a seriously corrosive ac-

the malady was mortal, he called his brother, demanded pardon for the past, communicated to him the countersigns of the fortresses, recommended his spouse, Don Antonio, his ministers, and all who were

tion, the effects corresponding to that in the visceral membrane of the Cardinal. But Orfila, a much higher authority, ascribes a destructive action to irritant poisons: *Œuv. cit.* T. I. p. 75; also 421. He considers it incontestably proved, "que les plaques gangréneuses des téguments *peuvent également appartenir à tous les poisons qui agissent avec une très-grande activité.*" *ib.* 676. This is the language, not only of experience, but of common sense. Yet while he cites (p. 76 t. i.) a case in point from Hoffman (cf. *ib.* ii. 896), he quotes on p. 421 the observation of Brodie, that spots of congested blood are often taken for eschars, and instances from the same eminent English surgeon (in *Philos. Trans.* for 1812) a case where a woman dying on the fourth day, "à l'ouverture du cadavre on trouva la membrane muqueuse de l'estomac et des intestins ulcéré dans une très-grande étendue" (484 sq.). He gives moreover (with which I will conclude my ample, but I hope not uninteresting, accumulation of instances) the case from Etmüller of a young girl poisoned by arsenious acid, "*neither whose stomach nor entrails offered any trace of inflammation or of gangrene; nevertheless arsenic was found in that viscus.*" i. p. 420. Comp. ii. 895.

See *ib.* in vol. ii. p. 904 sqq., for a consideration of maladies which may be confounded with acute poisoning. The passage affords nothing to abate suspicion in the case of the Duke and Bianca, and, whether the account of their ten and eleven days' suffering be correct, or the popular one of almost immediate dissolution, there can be no doubt that the ill-fated pair were poisoned(a). while there is every probability that it was effected by arsenious acid.(b) Galluzzi says, "Nella sezione del suo cadavere [del G. D. *sc.*] la sede principal del male apparve nel fegato" (*ut supra*, 424): *on the dissection of the Duke's body, the principal seat of the malady appeared to be in the liver.* Now, it is precisely the *liver* which, according to Taylor, is attacked by arsenic. And further I may add, that when

(a) Sismondi himself did not doubt it: . . . "empoisonné [François], ainsi que sa femme, dans un repas de réconciliation, *etc.*" x. p. 227, — citing, besides Galluzzi, *Anguillesi, Notizia del Poggia a Caiano*, p. 117; a work I have not been able to procure. Botta rejects with easy contempt the popular traditions, but does not commit himself to any opinion of his own.

(b) The mineral poisons, and the mechanical poison (so to call it) of comminuted glass, were probably the only ones in criminal use in the 16th century. In the first decade of the 17th, we observe Shakspeare writing,

. . . "the thought whereof
Doth, like a poisonous mineral, gnaw my inwards."

dear to him.(23)   The Cardinal, *comforting him, sent to take possession of the fortresses, ordered the assembling of the troops*, etc. 421. (24)

they bled him (twice!) his surgeons took the best means to give effect to the poison.(c)

(23) Was this the stupid and cruel Medici, of Botta? the perfidious, merciless, dissolute and vainglorious son of Cosmo, of Sismondi? the dissembling, inexorable and arrogant Prince, of Galluzzi?   A man, I well know, may be of a loving disposition and tender almost to effeminacy, yet have that contradictory quality in him, that, when roused by anger or perturbed by bodily fear, he will be in the former case ferocious. and in the latter remorselessly, no, unhesitatingly cruel. But while this absolute fact, not hypothesis, goes to confirm the unfavorable side of Francesco's character as displayed (after the manner of his day) toward his inveterate and dreaded political enemies, yet it will not explain his devotion to his friends.   A man who in his dying hour has forethought for all who are dear to him, particularizing each one, who, with that magnanimity which belongs to delicate and noble souls alone, exaggerating in his own eyes his own errors and losing sight entirely of the grosser offences of others toward him, could ask forgiveness of the brother who had persistently maligned, intrigued against, as well as hated him, and insulted the woman he passionately loved, such a man was more truly Christian than those who, forgetful of charity, emblazon but his errors and magnify his crimes.

In thus speaking, it will be seen I assume the record copied by Galluzzi to be correct.   But my belief, I beg leave to reiterate, is positively to the contrary.   I do not credit one word of this death-bed scene.

(24) . . "il quale *non tardì a farsi riconoscere per padrone;* perciocchà, avendo mostrato il Castellano di Livorno *alquanto di renitenza* a consegnare quella Fortezza ad un gentiluomo da lui inviato colà con contrassegno, *il fece impiccare.*"   MURATORI, *ubi cit.*   The haste of the Cardinal, it will be observed, is not more remarked by Muratori than by Galluzzi.   It is a precious passage that, "The Cardinal. *comforting him,* sent, &c."

Now, if the Cardinal was beloved of the people (*Galluzzi*), and if Francis died

---

(c) "In case of arsenical poisoning, the liver . . . is generally more strongly impregnated with arsenic than the other soft organs.   The proportion of absorbed arsenic found in it is, according to M. Flandin, *nine tenths of the whole quantity carried into the circulation.*   Where arsenic is not found in the contents of the stomach, and death has taken place within the usual period, it may commonly be detected *in the liver.*" Taylor, p. 29.   Orfila, on the contrary, who frequently condemns the opinions of Flandin, scarcely mentions the liver, if at all, among the viscera attacked.   Further, he prescribes bleeding (*after vomiting*): i. 73.

Bishop Abbioso, Bianca's daughter Pellegrina, and Ulysses Bentivoglio her son-in-law, were charged with the care of Bianca. She
died on the 20th of October. (25)

to the undissembled joy and with the universal hatred of his subjects (*Sismondi*),
why did the former make such haste to seize the fortresses? to seize them even
before the breath was out of his brother's body? Of whom was he afraid?
Was not the throne yet firmly settled? Or was there any doubt of the
illegitimacy of Don Antonio, whom he had made by a most atrocious plot to be,
and still makes the world believe to have been, foisted on the Grand-duke, while
a modern historian, to cap the climax of absurdity, declares him to have been, *the
stupid Medici*, perfectly satisfied when the Grand-duchess with a sublime effrontery avowed the treasonous imposition? Again, if the Cardinal was persuaded by
his documents, received from the judicial examination of the Bolognese Governess,
and which he took care to have preserved in the Medicean Archives, that Don
Antonio was but a sprout from the soil of the people, having no claim to any consideration other than that of an innocent victim of the venality of his mother, why
did he continue the Grand-duke's benefactions to him, so immeasurably beyond
his occasions even were he noble?[a] It is obvious that there must have been
doubt and uneasiness in the popular mind, or where was the need to publish that
act declaratory of the nativity of D. Antonio? And by the by, assuming the
account above to be correct, that on his death-bed the Grand-duke recommended
this very youth to his brother's care, how came Botta by the story that the Grand-
duke knew all about his origin? Seldom does history offer us such trumpery as is
comprised in the account of the rise and fall of the Grand-duchess Bianca But
the Cardinal was able to make history for himself, and I verily believe he did it.

(25) In the second month of this same year, Mary of Scotland was murdered in
another way. The coincidence is worth noting. Both nearly of an age, but
Mary a little the older[b]; both handsome, and with a fascination of manner that
enhanced the beauty from which chiefly it was derived; both amiable, yet not

[a] "A Don Antonio de Medici conservò il trattamento e le onorificenze assegnateli da Francesco."
Grandus. li. 422.

The idea that he should have done this out *of regard, not only to his brother's memory, but to the innocent
boy whose more than bastardy he was proclaiming in his very face, is preposterous.* D. Antonio was probably as legitimate as Elizabeth of England, who too was the product of a secret marriage, and, moreover, by
an act of bigamy.

[b] Bianca fled from Venice in 1563. If she was then eighteen, she was forty-two years old when poisoned.
Mary, born Dec. 8, 1542, on February 18, 1587, when she was beheaded, was but a little over forty-four.

Taking this account to be accurate, we have these remarkable facts, that two persons, husband and wife, were seized with intermittent fever within two days of each other, and that, in despite of the resources of art, — for we are not told that the Duke prescribed for Bianca "a suo modo", — died within a day of each other, conveniently to make the Cardinal sovereign. It were easier to believe the murderer himself, who said (as imputed to him), that Bianca, having tried to get rid of him, had the remarkable stupidity to poison the very dish her husband was sure to eat of, and of which she herself was known to be fond, and that unable, without exciting suspicion, to prevent the Duke's indulging his appetite, herself, in her desperation and dis-

without pride and spirit; both intellectual, and one accomplished; the lives of both romantic, but one (Mary) knowing little else than misfortune, the other fortunate until her death; both calumniated, but Bianca having added to her imputed crimes the sin of witchcraft, the latter charge being reversed in Mary's case, for it was her husband who confessed he tried its futile practices upon her, while Bianca employed it, according to the Archives, on her husband, and (wonderful to relate!) with her husband's perfect knowledge. And (may I add without presumption), as in the case of *Mary Stuart*(a), so some future tragic poet may reverse the picture of *Bianca Capello*, and paint her, not such as the Grand-duke loved her, but as the Cardinal hated. The change would be still easier than with Mary, and the tragedy would be more effective. But the poet would pervert. not history, but that truth which lies often hidden in the midst of history and is only to be found by those who independently seek it out for themselves.

(a) I understand that Mr. Swinburne, in his drama of *Chastelard*, has adopted, and with earnestness, the popular view against her. It would be difficult perhaps for an Englishman to do otherwise. Were I to write a tragedy on a theme which has been consecrated by the pen of Alfieri and of Schiller, I should, and with conviction, take the other side.

The greatest source of Mary's misfortunes, and of her partial guilt, or at least of errors that partook of guilt and are arraigned as such, was her light, pliant, and thus inconstant temper. If she pardoned Bothwell, it should be remembered that she forgave too the insolent, the treasonable murder of Rizzio, although in the passion of the moment she had declared she would avenge it. In fact, she was unfitted to be a queen by those very feminine qualities which would have made her loved, honored and admired in private life, precisely as Elizabeth, by the very opposite, more than respectable as a sovereign, would have been detestable as a simple matron.

The greatest real blot upon the character of the Queen of Scots is probably that which is suggested by the name of the drama above-mentioned. The vanity of Châtelard had not carried him so far in his presumption had he not misread the encouragement in Mary's eyes. And she suffered him to be sacrificed to save her reputation. In this too she was purely feminine, women who are very women feeling no more regret for those who perish by their coquetry than for the moth which singes its wings in the candle they dress by.

18

appointment, had the courage to perform a kind of internal hari-
·kari!

As the Duke's body was ordered to be opened, it was carried on the
evening of that day to Florence with private honors, met at the gate
by the clergy of San Lorenzo, the German guard and a number of his
courtiers, and taken to the Church. For Bianca, Serguidi [Vittorio's
successor in the Cabinet] was ordered to keep the body untouched
till evening, and then to have it opened in the presence of the daughter, her husband, and the physicians. [The torchlight would not facil-
itate an inspection which otherwise was not intended to be more than
formal. What passed in the minds of the daughter and husband, if
not of the physicians, may be conjectured.] It was carried in the
same way as the Duke's to Florence on the 21st, then buried in the
vaults of S. Lorenzo, *in such a way as not to leave any memory of her:*
" non volle il Cardinal Granduca che si ammettesse fra i sepolcri dei
Medici, ma lo fece seppellire nei sotterranei di S. Lorenzo in modo tale
che al pubblico non restasse di lei veruna memoria." *ib.* 420. Was
either Isabella or Eleonora buried in the public vaults? Yet both
were notoriously guilty of many adulteries, for which finally they died,
and one of them besides was said to have committed incest with her
own father, and the other to have gone to her virgin nuptial-bed already pregnant by her father-in-law. Bianca did not *lend an ear to
every one who ogled her*, nor indulged in mean amours with her husband's pages. Yet History passes lightly over those godly actions of
the princesses, or touches them with a pencil which has no caricature
or a pen which writes no syllable of reproach, while for Bianca there
is no abusive name too foul. Historian vies with historian to redouble
epithets of contumely and to charge the picture of her imputed mis-
demeanors with the exaggerated traits of sarcasm. Why is this?
Because, like Mary of Scots, she had personal enemies,(26) and the

---

(26) As the Cardinal, her lord's brother, was her adversary, at whose instigation
and by whose machinations, aided often by the money he had solicited and obtained (O the meanness! and O the perfidy!) through her aid, came all the evil

archives of her husband's family have passed through fingers which
had the power to subtract and multiply at will.

Implacable in his vindictive hate, the quarterings of Bianca's arms
were removed by order of the Cardinal Grand-duke, and for them substituted those of Joanna. He could not bear to hear her even called
Grand-duchess. "Egli, irritato di tanti artifici ed intrighi di quella
donna, *non potè contenersi più lungamente nella simulazione.* Ordinò
pertanto estinguersi ogni memoria che esistesse al pubblico della sua
persona, e che si togliessero dai luoghi pubblici le di lei armi inquar-
tate con quelle de Medici con sostituirvi quelle di Giovanna d' Austria.
In progresso nel doversi far menzione di lei, *non potè soffrire che li
si attribuisse il titolo di Granduchessa,* ed egli stesso in un atto de-
claratorio dei natali di D. Antonio volle che si denominasse replicata-
mente *la pessima Bianca.*" 425, 6.

The historian goes on then to relate what he calls the *imaginary* accounts. Bianca wanted to poison the Cardinal by a tart. The Cardinal had a ring which changed color, and warned him. He would not
partake of the tart. Francis, not aware of the danger, ate of it, and

that accompanied her latter days and survived her in an infamous renown, so it
was the natural brother of Queen Mary (Earl of Murray) who was the secret instigator and promoter of all the schemes of her Protestant enemies. Muratori,
ad ann. 1587, records the tragical result in this manner : — "L'anno fu poi questo,
in cui Elisabetta, Regina Eretica d' Inghilterra, con eterna sua infamia, condannò
alla morte Maria, Regina Cattolica di Scozia, non suddita sua, dopo la prigionia di
moltissimi anni. *Fu ella e prima e dipoi oppressa da infinite calunnie de'
suoi nemici,* per tentar pure di giustificar l' atto barbaro e tirannico d' Elisabetta,
riprovata da chiunque portava il titolo di Principe(a)." *Annal. d' Italia* (in
4to, Napoli, 1773), t. x. p. 462. Exception being made to his undissembled prejudice against the *heresiarch* Elizabeth, his remarks are just, and would apply,
mutatis mutandis, to Bianca.

(a) This is an error. It was approved, as an act of policy, (as if policy could ever sanction crime, or lend
more than the shadow of palliation to usurped power and to injustice !) by two or three, among whose
names, if my memory does not deceive me, was the honorable and ever to be honored one of Henry of
Navarre.

Bianca, fearful of the consequence, partook. *ib.* "Imaginary," so far
as this statement goes. But whence came the narrative which reverses
all this, and which Noble gives, and I have adopted in the play? (27)
This account says, that there was served at the repast *blancmange*, of
which the Duke was extremely fond. Ferdinand would not eat of it,
pretending illness and disordered stomach. The poisoned pair were
removed, in convulsions, to the only gloomy apartment in the whole
villa. After their death, and then only, the Cardinal threw open the
doors. He pretended Bianca wished to poison him, but, seeing her
husband eat of the envenomed sweetmeat, *etc.* (as above.) Here, it
will be perceived, there is nothing in the detail that partakes of the
marvelous or appeals to popular superstition. And it is perhaps for
that reason, which adds to .ts probability, that Galluzzi avoided men-
tioning it, for it certainly was as worthy of record, even if based on
vulgar fallacy, as its fellow-tradition. But in fact, this story has a
particularity as well as plainness and naturalness of description which
will not allow us, when considering all the circumstances preceding
and following, and the ambitious and rancorous character of the Cardinal, — a dissembler even by the acknowledgment of his eulogist,
forever plotting, and as unscrupulous as untiring in his schemes of personal aggrandizement, — will not allow us, I say, to ascribe it wholly
to the ordinary invention and exaggeration of popular rumor;
although, were it otherwise, the story, accepted by writers of that

(27) In Muratori we are tol l, the Grand-duke died of an affection ("infermità")
supposed not to be dangerous, and Bianca *fifteen hours after*. According to a
cont. mporary, many believed that Bianca, "donna di altero spirito," poisoned
the Grand-duke out of jealousy, and then herself; others, that the Cardinal poisoned both. *Annal. d' It.* t. c. p. 461.

It is plain enough, that the supposition of empoisonment, whether a murder or
both murder and self-murder, was widely prevalent, if not the universal belief in
Florence. The circumstances of the twofold death, and of the malady preceding
it, were then such as to excite this belief or suspicion. Consequently, if we set
aside the nearly simultaneous attack and its results, they could not have been
such as detailed in the Archives.

and subsequent times, is sufficient for the purpose of the dramatist who believes, as I do, that he does not pervert the truth and give, to the great names of history, characters, whether for good or evil, that are undeserved.

III.

Portraits of Bianca, etc.

Having alluded in the text to a picture of *Bianca* by Titian, I have thought it would interest the reader to be told of certain portraits, both of her and of the *Grand Duke*, still extant in Italy.

At the time the tragedy was written, I did not know that the immortal colorist had really given to the world a likeness of its heroine. I merely supposed so probable a fact to aid the *costume*, — that is, to invest the scene with those adventitious circumstances which lend it reality, and make a picture of Venetian life, for example, seem truly such by local *accidents*, which recall from time to time the place and era to the spectator's mind. But it appears that there is actually such a painting extant, and that it is, as I pretended, " One of the best from old Vecelli's hand." *v. infra, p.* 416, *sqq.*

In Count Litta's costly work (*Fam. Cel. Ital.*, Milano 1825, in fol.), in Vol. II., is a bust-portrait of Bianca after Bronzino (Gallery of Florence). It is in colors. The face is very full, with the golden-tinged fair hair which Titian and Giorgione loved and understood so well to paint, very regular, long and delicately-arched eyebrows, full and expanded forehead(1), eyes large and blue, and lively in expression,

---

(1) Too much so for beauty. This is partly owing to the manner of dressing the hair, which is reverted on all sides, but partly may arise from the bad judgment of the painter in exaggerating its surface, — as many English artists do, absurdly and untruthfully, the size of the eyes.

nose not delicate though regular, (there seems to be a defect in the drawing, or in the copy, which has thrown it a little to one side), and rather too large in the nostrils, lips curved and in proportion, but not handsome, and with an expression not agreeable ; the contour of the face more round than oval, — indeed of a faulty oval. There is nothing of the pride which Noble saw, or thought he saw, in the pictures at Strawberry Hill, nor yet of dignity, but rather of good humor and a slight degree of mischievousness and jocoseness. You see from the complexion and from the fulness and *morbidesse* of the flesh, that she must have been a voluptuous-looking blonde, one of that kind of women whose flesh is very white and delicate in the skin, but not firm, with eyes of a true blue, red lips, and faultless teeth, who more than any others have power both to waken passion and to keep it lively in the amorous.

It is probable that this polychrome is a bad miniature of an unfaithful picture ; for, as I have implied, there are faults in it which will indicate, to any one moderately familiar with the art, that the portrait was not true to nature, and that its faults have been exaggerated by the copyist-designer. It is true, the picture is of the Grand-duchess, not of the blooming maid whom Bonaventuri, with a fortune that makes his name seem almost the adaptation of fiction, snatched from her native soil to transplant where at a future day she should become the adornment of a royal garden, but even thus regarded, over expanded and partly faded, there is something *clumsy*, so to say, about the face, which cannot be Bianca. I am the more disposed to believe this from the fact that in Litta's plates the engraving after Titian of the Cardinal Ippolito in Hungarian costume differs strikingly in the expression as well as in the eyes from the copy of the same work in the collection known as the Pitti Gallery.(2) Here we have the eyes

(2) *Tableaux*, etc. *de la Gall. de Florence et du Palais Pitti :* in fol. Paris 1814. *T.* III. *Tab.* 12. — This and all the works consulted in the Appendix will be found in that Library which the far-reaching judgment and the munificence of Mr. Astor ordained to be something more than an ornament of our city.

placed at a normal distance apart; but in the former they are so close together as to add very unpleasantly to the sharpness of the face in general, which is handsome but rather effeminate.(3)

(3) As the Cardinal is mentioned with some particularity in both the preceding Appendices, and is an interesting character in himself, especially to those who consider what might have been the fortunes of Tuscany, had he, instead of his cousin, been chosen to grace the unlawful title of Duke, with Cosmo thus shut ou' perhaps forever from the opportunity of an election, a description of his picture will not be amiss, although it bears but a remote connection with the text, and in an illustrative point of view is valuable solely from the light it throws upon the Romish rank of Cardinal conferred upon the younger sons of princes or the bastards of men of power, without regard to character or qualifications or age, as a provision and a probable steppingstone to the Papacy. In this same casual light we are to consider the ecclesiastical function of the Cardinal Ferdinand, who, equally unqualified, though in another way, took it up as if it were but the mantle of a dead man, when his brother, D. Giovanni, on whom it was originally bestowed, came to his untimely end.

The Cardinal Ippolito is represented with both mace and sword, and on the ugly hat or *toque*, red like the rest of the habit, is a variegated plume, the principal feather of which is green. We are told that this portrait was taken at Bologna in 1530, when Titian went thither to paint Charles V. Ippolito was then in his twentieth year, an age when foppery is pardonable in a handsome man, nor is to be repressed though you wed him to the Church. Titian at the time was in all the splendor of his power, and Vasari ranks this among the best of his portraits. The nose is delicate and rather sharp, the mouth well-formed, but, contrasted with the nose, sensuous. The expression of the eyes, as of the character of the face, is that of a generous, amiable, gentlemanly fellow, but who was not wanting in irascibility. There is no appearance of that pride which Varchi says he had in excess, neither in the style of his head nor its carriage, nor yet in the attitude, which, by the by, is without dignity, if not awkward, the habit moreover being to the last degree ungraceful.

There is another picture of Ippolito done by Pantormo. He is here in armor, and a legend tells us he was then in his eighteenth year. He looks eight and twenty, even in the beard, which may be called an impossibility in so mere a youth. It is a fine face, manly, very regular, very handsome. One hand rests on

On the same folio with *Bianca* is a portrait of the *Grand Duke* Francis, after Rubens, with an air decidedly distinguished, the face good and regular, if not handsome. You would take the subject, if in the ordinary costume of our own day, to be a man of consequence and of high fashion, and somewhat of a free liver. It resembles much the picture of Cosmo by Bronzino, in the Pitti, not merely in feature but in the style of the head. In this latter picture, by the by, the expression of Cosmo is not what one would have anticipated from his character, but is positively good, as well as amiable, and highly intellectual.

Another bust-portrait of Francis, by Bronzino, is in the Pitti Gallery. The head large and intellectual, with great breadth and height of forehead; eyes somewhat stern; lips well-formed and full, and perhaps sensual; nose, good; the face oval.

In the same Gallery again (I speak of course of the engraved collection) is a portrait which is only supposed to be that of Bianca Capello. This also is by Bronzino. There is the same want of oval in the face as mars the one given by Count Litta; the forehead is very high, but not so broad, nor are the eyebrows so long. The nose is heavy, but regular, the mouth well-formed. The style of the face corresponds to what I have ascribed to the other. In the explanation of the Plate (29th of the Gallery : *T.iii.*), we are told: "Nous avons un autre portrait de Blanche par le *Titien*, qui est très-différent de celui-ci, et la gravure, due au burin de F. Clerici, en a été publiée par A. Locatelli, éditeur de *l'Iconographie Italienne des hommes et des femmes illustres.* (4)

his helmet, the other on his favorite dog. This is the picture that best reminds me of Varchi's repeated eulogies; but, considering Titian's mastery in portraiture, this, which differs widely from his, may be supposed to be no true likeness.

(4) After my death, when my countrymen may condescend to read these dramas, I hope that some one interested in their publication will procure this work of Locatelli's, and, if the picture be as fine as represented, which may be supposed, being by Titian and of a woman, cause a careful copy to be taken for the play. I should do this now myself, and make the copy with my own hand, but my limited means

Le Titien l'a représentée dans toute sa beauté ; beauté que Botta hésite à appeler angélique ou diabolique. Tout indique que ce portrait fut fait par le Titien encore jeune, car on sait qu' à ses débuts il soignait extrêmement ses ouvrages. Il n'avait pas encore acquis cette habileté, cette franchise de pinceau, qui ne suffraient pas de retouche, comme on le remarque dans ses dernières productions.(5)

"Ce que nous disons vient à l'appui de l'opinion de ceux qui pensent que c'est là la Blanche Cappello de Bronzino, quoique les deux portraits n'aient presque pas de ressemblance entre eux.(6) Titien

are exhausted in the manufacture of these volumes, for which I have difficulty in finding. not readers merely, but even a publisher.

(5) This is a positive error, and a very curious one. Titian was born in 1477, and died, as the writer himself says, in 1576, being then in his hundredth year. Bianca, we have seen, left Venice in 1563 ; consequently, when Titian was eighty-six years old. If painted two years before her flight, when we may suppose her to have been at most sixteen, he was then eighty-four.

The error is enhanced by what the writer says of the *retouching*, although the passage is obscure in its construction and contradictory. Titian, or I am deceived, never gave up entirely, notwithstanding his temporary change of manner. that frequent manipulation which in itself alone would distinguish his handling from that of Rubens even were not the results and the general effect so different in the two chief colorists. This punctiliousness, this going over and over again, to bring the part up or down to the tone required, and to educe that harmony which is so undefinable and yet so sensible, was in fact a part of his method, and not merely the derived habit of his school, whose master was Bellini.(a)

(6) This difference in portraits is another, though a minor one of the perplexities of history. We scarcely find two pictures of any eminent person done by different hands, that are precisely alike. Sometimes the divergence is so great that no trace of resemblance can be found between them. The likenesses of Bianca Capello, if we include even that by Titian. do not probably differ from one another so much as the two of Mary Stuart given by Albèri in his Life of Catharine

(a) It was while this play was going through the press, that news came of the destruction by fire of Titian's masterpiece, the *Peter Martyr*, a work which even Haydon, when denying ideality to the Venetian school of color, expressly excepted. It is an event that I wish, for my own satisfaction, to thus chronicle, though with a feeling of pain that will have been shared by all the artist-world.

mourut en 1576, et la Duchesse en 1587. Le portrait qu'il nous en a
donné indique une jeune fille de moins de vingt ans, et c'est une œuvre
d'une perfection exquise. Bronzino, au contraire, nous présente cette
femme célèbre déja sur le retour. * * * Dans le tableau de Vecel-
lio, la coiffure et le vétement sont de Venise, tandis que les accessoires
dans le portrait de Bronzino ont un caractère florentin, ce quelque
chose d'espagnol qui au XVI° siècle se répandait dans toute
l'Italie."(7)

It is easy to see, even from this evidently defective portrait of
Bianca on the wane, that she must have been, in the high day of her
attractions, as I judged by the picture in Litta's plates, one of those
blóndes, whose flesh is rather soft than firm, but exquisitely fine of
surface, and in which the red and white, red of the brightest and
white of the purest, are so commingled, without the skin's appearing

of Medici. The one from the Orleans Gallery is fat, voluptuous, heavy in the
nose, bad in the mouth; and we should have to look long to find out a point of
similarity between the picture of Catharine herself (when Regent), as given from
the Florentine Gallery, and the very attractive one, as Queen, which precedes the
title and is after Allori.

The portrait of a beautiful woman will be more or less beautiful. according to
the circumstances, with herself and with the painter, under which it was taken.
That, which at one time and with a certain pencil comes out embellished, is at
another time and by another hand di-figured. The sun himself, or his apprentices,
distort, and everybody knows how photographs may libel. It must be accepted
that when History is single-voiced in attesting to the charms of any noted personage, and the effects ascribed to them corroborate the testimony, that picture, which,
with all allowance made for the anticipation of the imagination, so certain to prepare for us disappointment, is positively ugly, or without attractiveness, has been
itself a failure, not the subject of it over-drawn.

(7) He need not have confined it to Italy. It was the court-fashion of the time.
We see the high and ample ruff in the portraits of Mary of Scots and of Elizabeth
of England. In the one of the former that is particularized in the previous note,
it is of the most preposterous description and as it were a caricature of the fashion
in the supposed *Bianca* of Bronzino.

mottled, that it is difficult to say where one begins and the other ends. The fairness as well as fulness of the flesh is especially conspicuous in the neck, in the hinder part of which, and behind the ears, the white grows captivating. Eyes of the deepest blue, large, tender or lively, according to the will or the emotions of the owner ; light, but very long lashes ; brows regularly arched, very distinct, and of a rather deeper brown than the hair, which latter sparkles in the sunshine like threads of gold, is so fine as to be taken up by the lightest air, yet so thick as to show deep shadows ; nose regular, but too fleshy to be delicate ; a mouth well formed, — of a red, deep rather than bright, and dry, — the lips full and voluptuous without being sensual ; the chin round and fleshy, and, with the lobes of the ears, looking as if tempting to be pinched or pressed. Add to this, the charm of harmony and softness yet brightness of colors, those *manifold attractions* which all the writers speak of and Botta seems to grow enamored of, and which come not only of beauty but of mind, and of the heart, which latter lends the Christian grace of gentleness and winning amiability, and we have before us that Venetian, who the Cardinal taught Florence to believe was subtle and perfidious, and whom Botta, without questioning the suspicious Archives, or following Galluzzi implicitly, knew not whether to pronounce *angelical* or *of the devil*.

END OF THE FIRST VOLUME.